night

General

*Under Pressure: The Writer in Society: Eastern Europe
and the USA*
*The Savage God: a Study of Suicide*
*Life after Marriage: Scenes from Divorce*
*The Biggest Game in Town*
*Offshore: A North Sea Journey*
*Feeding the Rat: Profile of a Climber*
*Rain Forest* (with paintings by Charles Blackman)

Fiction

*Hers*
*Hunt*
*Day of Atonement*

Criticism

*The Shaping Spirit*
*The School of Donne*
*Beyond All This Fiddle: Essays 1955–1967*
*Samuel Beckett*

Poetry

*Lost*
*Penguin Modern Poets, No. 18*
*Apparition* (with paintings by Charles Blackman)
*Autumn to Autumn and Selected Poems 1953–76*

Anthologies

*The New Poetry*
*The Faber Book of Modern European Poetry*

# A. ALVAREZ

# night

*Night Life,*

*Night Language,*

*Sleep, and*

*Dreams*

W.W. Norton & Company   New York  London

Since this page cannot legibly accommodate all the copyright notices,
pages 289–290 constitute an extension of the copyright page.

Copyright © 1995 by A. Alvarez
Portions of "The Dark at the Top of the Stairs" and "The Sleep Laboratory"
appeared previously in *The New Yorker.*
All rights reserved.
Printed in the United States of America by W. W. Norton & Company

Manufacturing by The Haddon Craftsmen, Inc.

Library of Congress Cataloging-in-Publication Data
Alvarez, A. (Alfred), 1929—
Night : an exploration of night life, night language, sleep and dreams / A. Alvarez.
p.       cm.
Originally published: London : J. Cape, 1994.
Includes index.
1. Dreams. 2. Dream interpretation. 3. Sleep—Psychological aspects.
4. Sleep—Physiological aspects. I. Title.
BF1078.A54     1995     154.6—dc20      94—35989

ISBN 0-393-03724-X

W. W. Norton & Company, Inc., 500 Fifth Avenue, New York, N.Y. 10110
W. W. Norton & Company Ltd., 10 Coptic Street, London WC1A 1PU

1  2  3  4  5  6  7  8  9  0

*To Alfred and Irene Brendel*

I have been one acquainted with the night.
I have walked out in rain – and back in rain.
I have outwalked the furthest city light.

I have looked down the saddest city lane.
I have passed by the watchman on his beat.
And dropped my eyes, unwilling to explain.

I have stood still and stopped the sound of feet
When far away an interrupted cry
Came over houses from another street,

But not to call me back or say goodbye;
And further still at an unearthly height,
One luminary clock against the sky
Proclaimed the time was neither wrong nor right.
I have been one acquainted with the night.

'Acquainted with the Night', Robert Frost

# CONTENTS

# ILLUSTRATIONS

# PREFACE

This is a book about the many faces of night: the night around us and the night within, the literal and the metaphorical, the dark of the moon and the dark night of the soul. It is about the world we inhabit after the sun goes down and the artificial lights come on, and the world we inhabit when we sleep. It is about sleep research and the physiology of dreaming, the interpretation of dreams and the different ways in which dreams reappear in our waking lives and creative work. It is also about the people who guard night for us and make night life possible. It is a book about how we illuminate night, negotiate it, inhabit it and, finally, ignore it.

When movie makers fake a night scene by shooting it through heavy filters, they call the process 'day for night'. We now take for granted that we can do the same by using electric light, that the working world moves seamlessly from daytime to night-time, and all it takes to change from a day person to a night person is a minor adjustment to the body's internal clock. Yet the inventions that have made this possible are little more than a century old and there is still something not quite right – maybe not even quite sane – about a working life led at night.

There is something else not quite right about night life, something shadowy in every sense. However efficiently artificial light annihilates the difference between night and day, it never wholly eliminates the primitive suspicion that night people are up to no good. They work under the cover of darkness because what they do cannot bear the scrutiny of day. By night, the police are alert in a different way and to different signs than by day. They are less concerned with the big picture than with details. They search the shadows looking for whatever seems out of place or out of key, and when they see a person on the move in the small hours, their first reaction is, 'Why is he here? What's he up to?' They assume, at best, that no one is around at night without a special purpose – usually one that he or she would prefer not to flaunt by day.

Even Las Vegas is not immune to this suspicion of presumptive guilt, although it is a city of light in a strictly literal sense – of neon signs and relentlessly bright interiors – where everything is done to eliminate the distinction between night and day: no windows, no clocks and, after midnight, regular infusions of pure oxygen pumped through the air conditioning to perk up the gamblers when they begin to wilt. The casino owners willingly pay fortunes in electricity bills in order to ensure that nothing will deflect their customers from the serious business of losing money. But the secondary purpose is to eliminate the sinister aspects of night and to relieve the players of their innate guilt for being at the tables when they should be in bed. No matter how brilliantly we illuminate the night, the moral problem of darkness won't go away.

My personal stake in the subject is threefold. When I was a child, I was unreasonably frightened of the dark, a peculiarity I now find astonishing. Then, in middle age, I became seriously addicted to the pleasures of sleep. The Victorians had a proverb about sleep: 'Six hours for a man, seven for a woman, eight for a fool.' By their standards, I was very foolish indeed. But as well as a passion for sleep, I have a passion for poker, and poker games tend to go on and on – even in clubs where no one is pleading for 'just one more round for the losers'. As a result, I regularly find myself up and about when most good citizens are tucked up in bed, and in the small hours big cities change character in unexpected ways. So I began with the intention of investigating these three mysteries: fear of the dark, and the very different mysteries of human sleep and sleeping cities.

Researching a book on a topic as wide-ranging as night is like pulling out a conjuror's handkerchief: one thing leads to another in an unending, outlandish chain. The apparently simple process of closing your eyes and falling asleep leads to the far from simple subject of sleep research, which in turn leads to brain research, which is ultimately connected with the problem of consciousness. Consciousness leads to the problem of the unconscious, to dreams and their interpretation and to psychoanalysis. And the language of dreams led me back to my first love, literature.

That long journey forms the central core of the book. On either side of it, I have tried to talk about night and how we live in it: What happens when the sun goes down? How does darkness feel? How do we illuminate it? How do we make it safe?

A great many people have helped me. I am grateful to Sharon Borrow and her colleagues in the sleep laboratory at Atkinson Morley's Hospital; to the officers of the 9th and 10th precincts of the New York Police Department, particularly Captain Vincent Rosiello, Lieutenants Kevin Gilmartin, Michael Sneed and Michael Herer, Officers Luis Cabrera,

Michael Grullon and Dean McManus; and to the officers at Brixton and Kentish Town stations of the Metropolitan Police, especially Police Constables John Cruttingden, Howard Potter, Mick Cooper and Michael Blakeley. An elderly man with a limp and a notebook, and with a tape-recorder concealed about his person, is not the kind of companion cops are looking for when they go out on night patrol. Nevertheless, their kindness and good humour never faltered and I had a marvellous time.

Various people have read and commented on various parts of this book at various times. I am particularly grateful to Tony and Cindy Holden, Priscilla Roth, Morton Schatzman, Mary Sue Moore and Luke Alvarez, to Tina Brown and Pat Crow at *The New Yorker*, to my editor at Norton, Starling Lawrence, to Frances Coady, Pascal Cariss and Dan Franklin at Cape, to my long-suffering agent, Gillon Aitken, and to Michael Feldman, who made me think. But I am grateful, above all, to my wife Anne, who not only put up with me during the four long years it took me to research and write the book, but also read it, reread it and then read it again, patiently, sympathetically and with an unfailingly beady eye.

# INTRODUCTION:
# LET THERE BE LIGHT

*October, 1802. Hartley at Mr Clarkson's sent for a Candle – the Seems made him miserable – what do you mean, my Love! – The Seems – the Seems – what seems to be & is not – men & faces & I do not [know] what, ugly, & sometimes pretty & then turn ugly, & they seem when my eyes are open, & worse when they are shut – & the Candle cures the SEEMS.*

Coleridge, *Notebooks*

*Light hath no tongue but is all eye.*

John Donne, 'Break of Day'

In the last hundred years we have lost touch with night. Maybe the foetus in the womb knows it, but even the womb's night is intermittently lit by the ruddy glow that penetrates the mother's body when she takes off her clothes. True darkness – the kind you get underground or in a sealed room or in the artificial blackness of a sensory deprivation experiment – is a different order of experience and for twentieth-century man, who can eliminate it with the flick of a switch, it is mostly a source of pure terror:

You don't try to scare people in broad daylight. You wait. Because the darkness squeezes you inside yourself, you get cut off from the outside world, the imagination takes over. That's basic psychology. I'd pulled enough night guard to know how the fear factor gets multiplied as you sit there hour after hour, nobody to talk to, nothing to do but stare into the big black hole at the center of your own sorry soul. The hours go by and you lose your gyroscope; your mind starts to roam. You think about dark closets, murderers, madmen under the bed, all those childhood fears. Gremlins and trolls and giants. You try to block it out but you can't. You see ghosts . . . Ghosts wiping out a whole Marine platoon in twenty seconds flat. Ghosts rising from the dead. Ghosts behind you and in front of you and inside you. After a while, as the night deepens, you feel a funny buzzing in your ears. Tiny sounds get heightened and distorted. The crickets talk in code; the night takes on a weird electronic tingle. You hold your

3

breath. You coil up and tighten your muscles and listen, knuckles hard, the pulse ticking in your head. You hear the spooks laughing. No shit, *laughing*. You jerk up, you freeze, you squint at the dark. Nothing, though. You put your weapon on full automatic. You crouch lower and count your grenades and make sure the pins are bent for quick throwing and take a deep breath and listen and try not to freak. And then later, after enough time passes, things start to get bad.

Vietnam, as Tom O'Brien described it in *The Things They Carried*, was a time warp, a return to the Stone Age and to Stone Age terrors, where the horror of the war was intensified by the field of battle itself, by its utter remoteness from the modern world and the conveniences we take for granted.

Darkness of that kind, night compounded by cloud-cover and impenetrable rainforest canopy, is hard to find. Further north, even out in the wilds and a long way from anywhere, the dark of night is never absolute. I discovered this for myself the hard way a long time ago in the mountains. For two nights, although in different years, I was forced to bivouac on the same peak in the Italian Dolomites. The first bivouac, on a large ledge just below the summit, was a comfortable affair. There was no moon, but the air was warm and the sky was full of stars. It was the kind of clear, peaceful night the Welsh mystic poet Henry Vaughan called God's 'dark tent', 'calm and unhaunted'; and, because the earth turns and the stars move, he also called it:

> God's silent, searching flight;
> When my lord's head is full of dew, and all
> His locks are wet with the clear drops of night.

The stars as dewdrops in God's hair is a strange and beautiful image, but that night on the Cima Grande di Lavaredo it seemed utterly appropriate. The summer starlight was hushed and mild and comforting, and also surprisingly bright. My companion and I slept well, lulled by the sound of goat bells from the valley far below.

The second bivouac was an altogether sterner occasion. It was on a tiny ledge in the middle of the great overhanging north face, and both of us were soaked to the skin, without food or extra clothing. There was a full moon that night, but before it rose the night was doubly black with storm clouds – it was a snow storm that had slowed us down and forced us to bivouac – and we were too preoccupied with the practical business of sorting our gear and making ourselves safe on the little ledge to register the darkness as anything but an inconvenience. Then the sky slowly cleared and the moon came up, picking out the distant peaks in cold blue light, turning the valley into a lake of darkness. We would have been better without it. The brighter it shone, the more remote and isolated it made us feel. It was like an inquisitor's spotlight, an unwinking reminder of our rashness and fragility. By the time the moon finally went down, we were so involved in the simple business of not freezing to death – blowing on our fingers, pummelling each other to keep the circulation going – that we scarcely noticed the dark. It was like our hunger, just another trial to be endured and nothing like as searching as the cold.

I learned a lot of things that night, mostly about myself. But in retrospect, I also learned about the gift of fire. Both of us smoked and I remember, even more vividly than the cold, the warmth and comfort we created every time we lit up. Those little pools of light in our cupped hands helped keep us going.

They were our lifeline, our link to daylight, and they made me understand why human survival, as well as civilisation, begins with fire.

Nobody knows for certain when man first produced fire mechanically. The archaeologists believe there were fire-makers in China 350,000 years ago, in Europe by 250,000 BC, in Africa and West Asia 50,000–100,000 years ago. According to William T. O'Dea, who wrote the most authoritative book on the subject, fire-making by using sparks from flint and pyrites on tinder probably came before the other ancient method of rubbing hardwood against softwood (the hardwood powders the softwood to make tinder and the friction between the two creates heat), because the latter 'implies a rather more advanced stage of tool manipulation'.[1] What is not in doubt is that, until about one hundred years ago, the only source of artificial light was fire: millennia of fire, scraps of flame in the darkness of prehistory, fragile, easily extinguished, infinitely comforting. For ancient man, whose night was full of terrors, God's first triumph was always a triumph over darkness:

> And the earth was without form, and void; and darkness was upon the face of the deep. And the spirit of God moved upon the face of the waters.
> And God said, Let there be light: and there was light.
> And God saw the light, that it was good: and God divided the light from the darkness.
> And God called the light Day, and the darkness he called Night. And the evening and the morning were the first day.

Before the Creation, there was only primordial chaos – formless, empty and dark. When God, with His first command, created light, He was also creating Himself, for light brought order from chaos, knowledge from confusion and ignorance. The conquest of darkness was an act of self-definition as well as a proof of His supreme omnipotence.

'Let there be light' was an appropriately bodiless command for the strange and revolutionary Hebrew conception of an abstract single Creator. The Greeks saw their gods in more vivid, concrete terms and endowed them with all the domestic vices: they were quarrelsome, lustful, jealous and petty-minded, just like any bickering human family. Even so, the ancient Greeks reasoned in much the same way as the ancient Hebrews: godhead equals light equals order; chaos equals darkness equals fear:

> By the sixth and fifth centuries BC the faculty of vision and the attributes of knowledge had run together in the Greek word *theorein*, meaning both 'to see' and 'to know'. Knowledge was henceforth a register of vision. Ignorance therefore becomes a lack of knowledge predicated on objects not being visible, so darkness equals ignorance. In turn, the dark becomes a source of fear as if a knowledge of visible objects were the only defence against terror and anxiety.[2]

What you see is what you know, and what can be heard or felt or smelled but not seen is terrifying because it is formless. There are only two ways to make night tolerable: by lighting it artificially and by sleep which shuts down the senses.

This belief in light as the ultimate good was repeated, over and over again, in myth and in sun-worship. The greatest gods in the Sumerian and Egyptian pantheons were the sun-gods, Shamash and Ra; the Aztecs worshipped the sun and the Brahmins had a god of fire, the seven-armed Agni. Even the

Jews, who abjured graven images, celebrated a mid-winter festival of lights, Chanukah, and used a symbolic seven-branched lamp which, at the time, must have been state-of-the-art illumination. In Greek myth, Apollo, the most beautiful of the gods, drove the chariot of the sun; every sunrise the world was recreated into Apollonian order; every nightfall it descended again into chaos. In Christian myth, the Godhead, in Dante's version, was 'Light Supreme' and 'Light Eternal', Christ was *Lux Mundi*, the Light of the World, and Satan, once brightest of the angels, was the Prince of Darkness who ruled over the uncanny paradox of what Milton, in the ill-lit seventeenth century, called 'darkness visible'. For both Greeks and Christians, day and night were expressions of the eternal contrasts: good and evil, form and chaos, male and female, reason and instinct, Apollonian and Dionysiac, God and the Devil.

Similarly, fire and the literal and metaphorical light that fire created were the divine gifts that separated mankind from the other orders of creation. In some Greek myths, Prometheus, the wisest of the Titans – the name means 'forethought' – fashioned man from clay in the image of the gods. He gave his creatures fire and taught them the sciences – architecture, astronomy, mathematics, navigation, medicine, metallurgy, and other useful arts. For all this, but above all for the gift of fire, a jealous Zeus condemned him to eternal torture. In Norse legend, Loki, who also stole fire from the gods, suffered equally terrible punishments for his sacrilege.

Presumably, the gods understood that fire was the first step in a process that would eventually make all of them redundant. Fire was the great enabler, the source of practical science and also the basis of society. The original social centre was the hearth, a place of safety in the perilous darkness. To the people huddled around the flames, fire provided light to see by, heat for cooking and warmth for comfort. At some crucial point in prehistory, someone took a burning log from the hearth in order to see what was going on in another part of the cave. Later, someone else realised that certain types of wood – those that contained resin – burned longer and more brightly than others. Later still, someone made the imaginative leap from fire to illumination and came up with a technical innovation: he plunged a log into resin or pitch and burned the lump on the end instead of the wood. At that point, the specially treated log ceased to be a source of fire and became a mount, a means of transporting light.

The other great prehistoric invention came about when some Palaeolithic, lateral-thinking genius noticed that a twig which fell into the grease below a roasting animal went on burning beyond its natural span. From that observation, step by slow step, the idea of the grease lamp evolved: first of a wick immersed in grease, then of a portable container for the grease. The device had been perfected at least 15,000 years ago since the paintings in the Lascaux caves in the Dordogne were illuminated by a hundred or more grease lamps. There are blackened patches on the roofs of the flint mines in Sussex which show where Neolithic miners, 4,000 years ago, stood the grease lamps they made from hollowed lumps of chalk. And in the Louvre, says O'Dea, 'there are bowl-shaped earthenware lamps retrieved from the inviolate tomb of Deir el Medineh of the New Kingdom of Egypt. These, perhaps 2,500 years old, still contain their grease and linen wicks.'[3]

In Europe, the very poor went on using grease lamps at least until the eighteenth century; in the Far East, they were still in use in this century. But grease stinks when it burns and the light it produces is unsteady. By 2,600 BC, the Sumerians, who also invented the wheel, were using oil – possibly from the seepages from petroleum deposits – for their lamps. (The earliest oil lamps were those discovered in the Royal Tombs at Ur of the Chaldees.) Mineral oils like petroleum and kerosene (paraffin) were generally hard to find, hard to modify and hard to handle, and they were not in wide-scale use until the nineteenth century. But there were plenty of alternatives: people used vegetable oils like olive oil (Exodus stipulates that the lamps before the Ark of the Covenant must burn pure olive oil), colza oil, coconut oil, groundnut oil, tea oil; they also used fish oils, especially from sperm whales and basking sharks, although some crude fish oils smelled so bad that a British Act of Parliament imposed a ban on them in 1710, with a heavy fine for those who broke it.

Some primitive communities did not bother with making lamps; they simply dried oily fish, stuck them in cleft sticks and lit them. The Indians around Vancouver Island did this to the little salmon-like candle fish, the Penobscot Indians used the sucker fish, the New Zealand Maoris the mutton fish, the Newfoundlanders the dog fish. Oily birds got the same treatment: until late in the nineteenth century, Shetlanders used to catch stormy petrels, thread a fibre wick through them, stick the feet in a lump of clay and burn them as lamps; much earlier, the Danes had done the same with the Great Auk, using a moss wick stuck in the creature's oily belly. The simplest of all natural lamps was the firefly. The West Indians used to put them in wooden cages or even stick them with gum to their big toes in order to see snakes on the path at night. Anything for a light.

Grease lamps, oil lamps, pitch torches, wax flambeaux, rushlights, candles – the drive to make night tolerable is universal and very ancient. There is evidence of domestic lighting – at least, in palaces – from about 3,000 BC: hanging earthenware and pottery lamps, lamps set in niches in passageways and at awkward turns of the stair, lamps of alabaster and gold, made around 2,600 BC and excavated from Ur of the Chaldees; copper lamps of the same period found in the tomb of Izi in Egypt. Lamps dating from 1,500 BC have been found in the area near Troy, and in 800 BC Homer made a passing reference to domestic lighting in *The Odyssey*. By the time of classical Athens, domestic lighting was commonplace – fragments have been found of more than ten thousand lamps made between the fifth and third centuries BC – and the Romans were almost as addicted to artificial light as we are now. They set up factories to make pottery lamps in vast quantities both at home and throughout the empire. Even slaves had lamps: they used snail shells to hold the oil and a tow wick. The Romans also invented the candle, another great leap in lateral thinking: solid 'oil' instead of liquid made light truly portable and eliminated the expense of a container.

The civilisation of night progressed inch by inch over the centuries, each step refining the last and producing stronger, cleaner, more convenient sources of light. By modern standards, none of them was particularly effective for a simple reason: from prehistory until the late nineteenth century, the only source of light was one form or another of fire: bonfires, flaming torches, oil lamps, candles, rushlights, gas lamps. In their different ways, they all cast a sweet, shadowy, sociable light, not much good for reading by, but enough to keep the monsters at bay. Yet fire, whatever its source, also produces smoke and odours, it burns up the oxygen in rooms, it deposits soot on cornices and furniture and clothes, it needs to be constantly tended – the wick snuffed, the reservoir of oil replenished – it is easily extinguished and, if handled carelessly, terribly dangerous. It is also a brute to light. Wooden matches that worked reliably and could be carried around safely were not available until the 1820s and, even then, lighting the hundreds of candles which were used for grand, formal occasions was a major undertaking that took hours. Before the invention of matches, getting a light from flint and tinder was an intricate and often infuriating process. One night in 1763, for instance, James Boswell decided to sit up late and write:

> About two o'clock in the morning I inadvertently snuffed out my candle, and as my fire before that was long before black and cold, I was in a great dilemma how to proceed. Downstairs did I softly and silently step to the kitchen. But, alas, there was as little fire there as upon the icy mountains of Greenland. With a tinder box a light is struck every morning to kindle the fire, which is put out at night. But this tinder box I could not see, nor knew where to find. I was now filled with gloomy ideas of the terrors of the night. I was also apprehensive that my landlord, who always keeps a pair of loaded pistols by him, might fire at me as a thief. I went up to my room, sat quietly until I heard the watchman calling 'past three o'clock'. I then called to him to knock at the door of the house where I lodged. He did so, and I opened to him and got my candle re-lumed without danger. Thus was I relieved and continued busy until eight the next day.[4]

Before electricity was harnessed, artificial light was expensive and only the leisured rich could afford the luxury of being up and doing during the hours of darkness. The poor regulated their lives by the sun: 'Working people burn no candle in the long days', Gilbert White wrote in 1789, in *The Natural History of Selborne*, 'because they rise and go to bed by daylight.' They were also unable to afford costly beeswax candles and had to make do with candles made of tallow, which stank and irritated the eyes. (Tallow candles had one advantage over beeswax: they were edible. British lighthouse keepers regularly used them to supplement their meagre rations and, as late as the mid-1960s, two modern experts in hard living, Bill Tilman and Eric Shipton, took tallow candles on expeditions to the Patagonian ice-cap in case they ran out of food.) Yet as late as the beginning of the nineteenth century, according to one social historian, 'even tallow candles were considered to be beyond the reach of most laborer families, whose houses remained dark, as they had been since the Middle Ages.'[5] At best there would be a single candle burning for an hour or two each night, with the family arranged around it, each according to his need: close for those who were trying to sew or read or play cards, further off in the shadows for those who merely wanted company or were postponing the moment when they went to bed – 'a camp-fire situation', Rayner Banham called it.[6] It was this sort of scene, in which figures crystallise out of darkness around a single source of light, that inspired artists like Caravaggio and De La Tour. To us, their paintings are about the drama of night as it used to be – mysterious, dangerous, engulfing. O'Dea, however, believes that artists exaggerated night scenes less for aesthetic reasons than because 'the paintings were made in a poor light and were to be viewed by one'. When Michelangelo painted the Sistine Chapel, lying on his back on a rickety scaffold, he designed a kind of headband with a stub of candle stuck in it in order to see what he was doing.

Usually, the poor preferred not to waste money even on a single tallow candle. Since most of them were illiterate, reading was not a problem and they got by with firelight. ('Curfew' derives from the Norman-French 'covre-le-feu', dowse the fire.) Except in the castles and churches of the ruling establishment, the luxury of domestic lighting seems to have disappeared with the fall of the Roman Empire. The Dark Ages were dark literally as well as culturally, and all through the Middle Ages and the Renaissance night was illuminated for the common people only for celebration: first by bonfires, then by fireworks to mark famous victories or special festivals, like the midsummer solstice. The illumination itself was a form of celebration; in French, *feux d'artifice*, fireworks, were originally called *feux de joie*.

In the seventeenth century, festivals of light became part of baroque courtly culture. They began after dark and lasted until dawn, and the fact that the courtiers were going home when artisans and burghers were beginning their day added a special spice to courtly pleasure. It took money to be profligate with a luxury item like artificial light; to enjoy night life was a token of social privilege, a form of conspicuous consumption. A century later, night-time pleasure gardens, like Vauxhall and Ranelagh in London, were commercial imitations of courtly festivities: illuminations, fireworks, concerts, dancing, all available for the price of a ticket. It was the turn of the middle classes to distinguish themselves from their inferiors by wasting artificial light, by getting up and going to bed unnaturally late.

Night life as an option democratically available to every-one, as a time when ordinary people can go about their ordinary business, give or take a few qualifications, is a relatively modern invention. Until less than two centuries ago, night was still a time of terrors, evil portents and violence, a no-go area where criminals, hobgoblins and all the other forces of darkness ruled, a time when law-abiding people bolted their doors and huddled together around the fire with only a candle to light them to bed.

Shakespeare's plays are full of 'deeds of darkness'. *Othello* begins with uproar in the night, bringing to Desdemona's father the mortal news of her marriage to the Moor; it ends at night with her murder by candlelight ('Put out the light and then put out the light') and Othello's suicide. By night, the ghost of Hamlet's father walks, Lear goes mad, Clarence and Polonius are murdered, the sleeping Imogen is betrayed. For Shakespeare and his contemporaries, there was nothing far-fetched or super-stitious in the association of night and evil; on the contrary, it was just another example of the poet's holding a mirror up to nature. The murderous darkness of Macbeth's castle would have been perfectly familiar to an Elizabethan audience because something very like it was waiting for them when they left the Globe. (Perhaps part of the gaiety of *A Midsummer-Night's Dream* comes from the fact that the action takes place on the shortest night of the year.) Even a couple of centuries later, the escapes and confusions of identity in *Don Giovanni*, which seem so im-plausible now and so hard to stage, would have been entirely believable to Mozart's original audience, who had only lamps and candles to light their theatres and linksmen to light their way home. The Don was like the footpads who roamed the streets, a creature of the night, a predator, an inhabitant of an alien element; darkness was part of his evil nature. (Christopher Marlowe and his companions, who dabbled in atheism, sodomy and espionage, were labelled 'The School of Night'.)

Night travellers had elementary forms of illumination: burning torches or lanterns with panels of horn, specially treated and cut thin enough for candlelight to shine through. But lights of this kind did little more than intensify the surrounding darkness and it is hard now to imagine what night life must have been like before the introduction of electricity, although sometimes, in forests or in countryside deep enough and remote enough not to have even a smudge of city glow on its horizon, you begin to understand how touch-and-go even the simple task of walking home must have been. Or rather, not walking but stumbling along potholed, muddy tracks, feeling your way through gradations of darkness in which every small noise becomes suddenly significant. Is it a sign of life, an unknown presence? Human or animal? Safe or threatening? The moon reassumes its traditional importance; it stops being a heavenly ornament, a decoration in the night sky, and becomes a blessed source of light, an aid. (Old clocks marked the phases of the moon as well as the hours, not for decoration but in order to help nocturnal travellers plan their journeys.) When Tennyson described his Princess as 'Robed in the long night of her deep hair' he was relying on centuries of real darkness to heighten the sense of dangerous erotic mystery.

Before night could be colonised and made safe for law-abiding people, two things were needed: street-lighting and a police force. Without them, night was like the original chaos out of which God created the world: 'without form and void'. In the Middle Ages, citizens prepared for nightfall like sailors battening down for a storm. First, they locked the gates of the town, then they locked their houses, then they deposited their keys with the magistrate. In properly ordered cities, curfews were enforced and nightwatchmen patrolled the streets, armed to the teeth and carrying torches – more to identify themselves than for light. Citizens who were brave enough to venture out were also required to carry torches to show they were men of good faith; those who didn't were liable to arrest. According to a statute of Edward I (1272–1307):

> none be so hardy as to be found going or wandering about the streets of the City after curfew tolled at St. Martins-le-Grand, with sword or buckler, or other arms for doing mischief, or whereof evil suspicion might arrive, nor in any other manner, unless he be a great man, or other lawful person of good repute, or their certain passengers having their warrants to go from one to another, with lanthorn in hand.[7]

The first primitive attempts at street-lighting were made early in the fifteenth century when wealthy householders were required to hang lamps from their windows. These little glimmers of light did not, of course, illuminate the streets, but at least they identified some of the houses. They were not so much street-lighting as a kind of urban cartography, points of reference in the surrounding darkness, like navigation lights at sea, to help the benighted traveller chart his way. They created an elementary structure for the town and imposed order on the otherwise uncharted chaos of night.[8]

There had been bonfires at crossroads in ancient Athens, Rome and Jerusalem, but the first properly organised attempts at street-lighting did not begin until 1662, when a shrewd Parisian cleric, the Abbé Laudati, obtained a monopoly to establish watch posts three hundred paces apart and to provide guides carrying lanterns who, at a price, would escort night travellers between them. Five years later, at the urging of his chief of police, Louis XIV issued a decree ordering the lights that hung haphazardly outside some houses to be replaced by glass lanterns suspended by ropes over the middle of every street. Each candle was of sufficient weight – three to the pound – to burn until after midnight during the five winter months. Before the end of the century, Paris alone had 6,500 lanterns and they burned 1,625 lbs of candles every night.

Street-lighting in London also began as a private enterprise. In 1694, a certain Edward Heming obtained a licence to put lights outside every tenth house from six pm to midnight between Michaelmas and Lady Day, and to charge the householders six shillings a year for the privilege of relative security. But Heming fell foul of the Tallow Chandlers Guild – he experimented with oil lamps – his licence was revoked in 1716, and London was given back to the footpads and purse-snatchers until 1736, when the City itself installed five thousand oil lamps in the streets. Within two years, that number had trebled – despite the tallow chandlers – and Oxford Street alone was said to have more lamps than the whole of Paris. Even so, the lighting was confined only to some of the streets some of the time and there was still a good living to be made by linksmen with their flaming torches and dubious connections. (In London they were often in league with criminal gangs, in Paris they were police spies.)

It was not until the introduction of gas lighting in the early nineteenth century that cities began to be illuminated regularly, reliably and on a large scale. London had gas lamps in the streets by 1807, Baltimore in 1816, Paris in 1819, Berlin in 1826. (In 1816, the citizens of Cologne objected to gaslights on the grounds that they would frighten the horses.) Electricity arrived half a century later, but only in the form of arc lights.

These were set on tall iron poles, occasionally on masts 250 feet high, and they cast a brutal glare which created more shadows than it eliminated and seemed, in its harshness, to embody everything that was most unnatural in the industrial revolution. In comparison, the light from the carbon filament bulb was subtle and adaptable, as well as cheap, efficient and clean. Swan and Edison solved the problem of the electric bulb in much the same way at much the same time – the patent litigation between them ended in a draw and they formed a joint company to exploit the British market – but it was Edison who invented and assembled the complete system to supply the lamps with commercially profitable electricity. In January 1882, when someone threw the switch for the first street lamps that used their great invention, our perception of the world changed for good.[9] Rayner Banham called it 'the greatest environmental revolution in human history since the domestication of fire'.

The painters, particularly the Impressionists who dealt in light, saw the transformation of night for what it truly was – a kind of miracle: 'The warehouses are palaces in the night,' wrote Whistler, 'and the whole city hangs in the heavens, and fairyland is before us.'[10] We take that miracle for granted now, but the ancient, awe-struck attitude to light as something festive and celebratory survives in cities specifically dedicated to pleasure. Las Vegas, for instance, is literally a city of light, with illuminated signs instead of architecture. By day, the buildings on the Strip are mostly as shoddy and functional as aircraft hangars, mere frames to hang neon on. But at night, the endless cascades of brilliantly coloured lights make them, in every sense, dazzling. They are designed to be seen in the dark, they are defined by light, they belong to the fizzing, spiralling fantasy world of celebration.

According to the sociologist Murray Melbin, night is the last frontier and since the invention of artificial lighting we have colonised it in much the same way and in much the same spirit as the Americans colonised the West in the nineteenth century.[11] Time is a dimension like space, says Melbin, and people have moved into the realm of night as the hours of daylight have become more congested. The first night people were like the trappers, hunters and drifters who went west ahead of the pioneers; they were misfits, solitaries, criminals, people who, for whatever reason, were uneasy with the straight world and had very little to lose. Then came the businessmen, the exploiters, who realised that, with the advent of gaslight, expensive machinery no longer had to lie idle for eight hours out of twenty-four, and factories could keep producing around the clock. Shift work brought other services in its wake: transport, eating places, bars and grocery stores. Gradually, as lighting improved, services expanded until now there is a whole afterhours community – everything from evening classes to supermarkets, night courts, discos and massage parlours, as well as a great army of maintenance people who service and repair the daytime world while its inhabitants sleep. The defence establishment, the financial markets, broadcasting, transport, communications now work on a 24-hour-day schedule. As Melbin sees it, night and day will soon be interchangeable; as we have transformed our environment, so we will transform ourselves – physically, socially and psychologically – to fit the new 24-hour cycle of work.

But colonising night is not the same as solving its mysteries. For those who lead night lives – everyone from shift workers to whores – what matters is the fact that, for all practical purposes, electric light has turned night into day. Night workers bring their day minds to their jobs and remain rational and analytic in their sunless worlds.

That clarity, literal as well as metaphorical, was not easily come by for anyone who had to rely on a guttering candle or an oil lamp. One gas mantle produced as much light as a dozen candles, a single electric bulb as much as one hundred.[12] Before electricity, every hour reclaimed from night was a triumph over adversity. When the youthful Milton worked late – and so took the first steps on the road that eventually led to blindness – he was marking himself down as someone special – as a thinker, Il Penseroso – and he wanted his readers to pay attention:

> Let my lamp, at midnight hour,
> Be seen in some high lonely tower.

Being seen to work at night was a source of pride and seemed to matter almost as much as the work itself. Three hundred years later, the equally youthful Billy Bathgate, in E. L. Doctorow's novel, learns the opposite lesson when he is initiated into the New York mob:

> The first thing you learn is there are no ordinary rules of night and day, there are just different kinds of light, granules of degree, and so no reason to have more or less to do in one than in another. The blackest quietest hour was only a kind of light.

Once the problem of lighting up the night had been solved and the shift workers had adjusted their body clocks to a different circadian rhythm, crime could function on a 24-hour basis, like any other business enterprise.

Yet even when night was colonised, the other kind of

darkness didn't go away; it simply shifted its ground. Night has always been a time for fear. Predators move unseen under the cover of darkness and all animals, man included, are most vulnerable to their enemies when they sleep. They are also vulnerable to dreams, those otherworldly visitations when secret fears and desires come drifting to the surface. Even with the advent of electricity, the unknowable dark side of the psyche remained as potent as it had always been. So did the drive to explain it and harnessing electricity was the necessary first step. As well as artificial light, it produced instruments with which to measure, among other things, the electrical activity of the brain. After the physical conquest of night, the search moved on into the inner darkness, the darkness inside the head. When Freud, defining the aim of psychoanalysis, said, 'Where the id was, there the ego shall be,' he was echoing, in his own way, God's first edict: 'Let there be light.'

## 2

# THE DARK AT THE TOP OF THE STAIRS

*What would the dark*
*Do without fevers to eat?*

Sylvia Plath, 'The Jailer'

*Fear at my heart, as at a cup,*
*My life-blood seemed to sip.*

Coleridge, *The Rime of the Ancient Mariner*

# I

When I was a child I was terrified of the dark. I remember this as an historical fact, but the terror itself faded long ago, and there are times now when I feel its disappearance as a loss, as some vividness gone out of my life. 'Brightness falls from the air', wrote Thomas Nashe in a time of pestilence. As you get older, fear, too, falls and vanishes, and that is not necessarily an unqualified blessing. The other darkness, the dark at the end of the tunnel that Nashe was writing about – 'I am sick, I must die – / Lord have mercy on us!' – has never bothered me much, perhaps because I have never thought of it as more than extinction, a final full stop. But there was nothing final about the darkness that frightened me as a child. On the contrary, it was teeming with possibilities, all of them undesirable.

Start with the house: built just before or just after the First World War, semi-detached, redbrick and pleasantly proportioned, with two mournful bay trees in tubs flanking the front door; a solid and spacious interior, stained-glass windows in the hall, beautifully turned banisters, heavy doors, everything fashioned to last and no expense spared. My parents moved there in 1930, when I was six months old, and both of them were still there when they died – my father in 1965, my mother in 1982. By the time my mother died, she and her ancient housekeeper-companion were the only occupants, and the place had gone to seed: the top floor shut, dry rot in the casements, fungus in the cellars. But during my childhood the house swarmed with people, all of them now dead: my parents and my two sisters, a nanny, a cook and two parlourmaids, as well as an undernurse, who stayed for a year when one of my sisters was ill, and my father's chauffeur, who lived elsewhere but was constantly in and out.

It was a three-storey house and each storey was a separate world, clearly demarcated. The ground floor – two fat Ls, joined together, three rooms to each L – was strictly for the grown-ups. The front L – dining-room, drawing-room and conservatory – belonged to my parents. The rear L was the servants' quarters: a pantry where the glasses, crockery and silver were kept and the maids washed them; a kitchen where the servants ate their meals and put their feet up (it was the only continuously warm room in the house, because it contained the coke boiler that heated the water system); and a scullery, where the cooking was done – red stone floor, twin gas ovens, a sink large enough to drown a sheep in, a big enamelled metal table with a huge stoneware jar of cooking salt, a long narrow walk-in larder. All this was the domain of Minnie, the cook; my mother was not welcome there, my father never went near it, and we children were allowed in only with Minnie's permission, which was given rarely, under sufferance and as a special mark of favour.

We lived upstairs in the day nursery, a sunny room overlooking the garden, with built-in cupboards, child-size armchairs, a friendly gas fire and a large oak table, silvery from constant scrubbing, where we ate, under Nanny's beady eye. My parents' bedroom and a big bedroom shared by my sisters were on the same floor as the day nursery – at the front of the house, separated by my father's dressing-room. The night nursery, which I shared with Nanny, was on the top floor; like my sisters' bedroom, it ran from the front to the back of the house, with views on to both the garden and the street. Across the landing from the night nursery was Minnie's bedroom and the poky little room where the two parlourmaids slept. There was a bathroom on the top floor for the children and the servants; my parents had their own bathroom, on the floor below.

Now, of course, it seems unimaginable that a middle-class Jewish family should lead this style of 'Upstairs, Downstairs' life. The domestic class barriers and carefully marked-out spheres of influence (the 'Keep Out' and 'No Trespassing' signs were invisible, but we obeyed them scrupulously) and the abiding sense of Them and Us – the sheer formality of it all – now seem more than implausible or unreal; they seem downright exotic, like the glories of the vanished Raj or the court of the Sun King. These days, you would need to be a millionaire to maintain a houseful of servants and the life that went with them. But between the wars, when wages were low and appearances cost less, the middle classes still managed to live with some of the grandeur their Victorian parents had taken for granted. (I read somewhere that during the 1930s about a third of Britain's population was in domestic service.) For a child, the relationships may have been a little remote by modern standards but, to compensate, life generally was sheltered and orderly. In other words, nothing wrong there, no obvious terrors to send the pulse racing.

Christopher Robin I emphatically was not. I was a nasty little child, the only son and much younger than my sisters: indulged, unpredictable, prone to tantrums and ill health. When I was a baby, I had had major surgery to remove a lymphatic growth from my ankle. But the operation had not been successful, the growth remained to trouble me, and my lymph system sporadically went haywire, giving me fevers, high temperatures, a good deal of pain and an unpleasant disposition. I assume the operation had also produced traumas of its own, some little shop of horrors whose contents I glimpsed only occasionally and imperfectly. Today, I would have been classified as a disturbed child and treated accordingly, but they ordered things differently in the early thirties. Fear of the dark was just one of my symptoms.

There were other conflicts in the house, seething just below the surface, and my own conflicts must have amplified them. First, there were the regional domestic politics. We children were used in a continual power struggle between nursery and kitchen, between Nannie, who favoured me, and Minnie, who favoured my sisters. Like all petty tyrants, they adopted the method of divide and rule. They set us at one another's throats to jostle for small favours, which meant that in those days there was no love lost among the three of us. (Affection came much later, after we had left home and made our own separate lives.) Nanny was stern, but not towards me – because I was delicate, because I was *her* baby. (She had arrived just after I was born and had lived with me in the hospital when I had my operation, a very rare procedure in those days.) Nanny made my sisters' lives a misery, while Minnie indulged them and terrified me. She had a wicked temper and an artistic temperament – she was an inspired cook – and, because she was deaf, she spoke in a whispering, hissing voice. She also had a finger missing from one hand – a detail that filled me with dread. Until I met her again, many years later, I thought of her as huge and menacing; in reality, she was small, almost fragile, and the whispering voice made her sound chronically shy. In my childhood, however, she was like the cook in *Alice in Wonderland*: she ruled the roost, she brooked no contradictions and no interference, and she terrorised my mother and the maids as much as she terrorised me.

We didn't see much of our parents. Like Minnie and her kitchen, Nanny considered the nursery her exclusive turf and was skilled at keeping my mother off it. And my mother, because she had been tyrannised by her father and her own nanny, assumed that this was how the world was ordered and kept docilely to her own ground-floor territory, where she drank endless cups of lemon tea and gossiped with her cousins. Occasionally, I would be brought down for their inspection, and most evenings I would be brought down again, in pyjamas and dressing-gown, bathed and combed, to say good night to my father. Until the Second World War broke out, a month after my tenth birthday, and we found ourselves suddenly thrust together without a buffer zone of servants, both my parents were remote figures, who seemed only tangentially connected with my life.

But I heard them from a distance. The power struggle between nursery and kitchen was a daytime activity. At night, a different reality took over and it had nothing to do with territory or middle-class decorum. Instead, the house was permeated by the sound of adult unhappiness. Or rather, it was permeated by two sounds, which added up to the same thing: marital rancour and classical music. Separately, my parents were good-hearted people, funny, generous and full of feeling. But they were highly neurotic in their different ways and fatally ill-matched. My father was a romantic, a great reader of travel books, a lady-charmer with a serious and educated passion for music. My mother loved food and dogs, but she was tone-deaf to music and utterly uninterested in the printed word. She was also a realist, hiding behind an eccentric façade a shrewd and sardonic view of the field of folk and its subterfuges. Both my parents were under the thumbs of their domineering fathers and both had to wait until their fathers died before they could lead their own lives without forever looking over their shoulders. It was a long wait: my father's father lived to be eighty-six; my mother's father, not to be outdone, made it to ninety-three. Until they left the stage, my parents took out their frustrations on each other and channelled their affections elsewhere – my mother into a series of ill-tempered terriers and spaniels, my father into girlfriends and music.

As a child, all I knew about was the music. My father had a vast collection of records and he played them very loud after dinner – partly for pleasure and relief, partly to shut out my mother. Most evenings, the sound of his music rose through the house, mixed with the sound of their mutual unhappiness: blurred voices shouting at each other, weeping, recriminations, and once – just once, as I remember – the sound of a blow followed by an explosion of grief. I used to sneak out of bed and listen to their distress rising confusedly up the stairwell. Always at night.

So night, I reasoned, was the time when adults showed their true natures – not something any child wants to know about. By extension – the same thing in different terms – it was also the time when monsters were abroad: ghoulies, ghosties and things that go bump in the night. I have had children of my own and they have told me about the apparitions that haunted their nights. There were marks on the wall by my daughter's bed that transformed themselves, when the lights were out, into the face of a ghost so scary that she could only sleep with her back to the wall. She and her older brother shared a bedroom when they were small. In a corner of the room was a little fireplace. The chimney had been blocked off, but the cast-iron Victorian firebasket and the chimney-breast were still in place, and the space between them, which had once led to the chimney, was inky black. It was a small space, not much more than a foot square and my son seemed terrified by it when he was very small. He used to stare at it as though he were afraid it would suck him up and engulf him for ever. For years I thought that the blackness itself was what frightened him – that he was afraid of the night within him as much as of the night about him. Not so, he told me later. His fear had a specific shape: squat shaggy monsters covered with squiggly electric black hair. The monsters appeared to him regularly in nightmares and he was transfixed by the fireplace because that, he thought, was where they lived.

He was also afraid of what he later referred to contemptuously as 'the standard shit' – snakes and other nasties waiting under the bed to snap at his toes if they stuck out from under the blankets. In the same vein, when my small daughter and her friends wanted to scare themselves they would whisper together about vampires and all the similar cloaked or bat-winged creatures that might materialise out of the night, sink fangs into their tender necks and suck their blood. There were probably other bogeys, other fears, but they were always creatures with the shapes and attributes – teeth, claws, leathery wings – of the kind that Bram Stoker might have written about or Hieronymus Bosch painted.

As a child, I must have populated the darkness in the same fashion: with witches hissing like Minnie, burglars under the bed, murderers lurking, ready to pounce, in the partly opened cupboard. Yet I remember nothing at all about them – not a single sinister face or flapping shape. My fear of darkness was a fear of dark places: of the cavernous linen cupboard on the landing outside the night nursery; of the attic above the landing, with a skylight no one ever opened; of the trapdoor in the maids' room, which gave on to four steps down and a tight space full of dusty trunks and old suitcases. Above all, I was terrified of the cellars. There were three of them, at the bottom of a flight of wooden stairs behind a narrow door in the front hall. The main cellar contained an ancient wooden icebox and a large marble slab below a wire-mesh window that led upward to a tiny barred window giving on to the garden. A door next to the slab led to a wine cellar that never had wine in it, because my parents rarely drank. At the other end of the cellar was another door, opening onto the coal cellar, into which sacks of coal and coke were dumped by means of a chute in the front garden.

The darkness of the cellars frightened me, but the spiders that haunted that darkness frightened me far more. My terror of spiders was phobic – overwhelming and unreasoning – and it outlasted my fear of darkness by several decades. Spiders seemed to me creatures that embodied, in their scuttering way, everything that was evil and venomous and impossible to escape. They were emanations of darkness itself and I was well into middle age before my phobia modified into qualified unease.

When the house was full of servants, the main cellar was regularly swept and dusted. Even so, there were always spiders' webs in the corners of the ceiling, and the unused wine cellar was full of them. But, for obvious reasons, no one ever swept the coal cellar, and its blackness was festooned with webs. My mother kept the old boiler going long after everyone else had installed central heating, and even after I was a grown man my stomach tightened whenever I went down to fetch up a scuttle of coke for her. I drew in my head, hunched my shoulders and kept my eyes rigidly to the front, in case I might see what I didn't want to see.

Spiders, cellars, attics, all those dark and secret places: an old-fashioned psychoanalyst would make a meal of them. Fear of women, I assume, and whatever fantasies of being castrated and annihilated seemed appropriate. Modern psychoanalysis is subtler, less schematic and reductive, but if the occasion were right some of the same anxieties might seem to apply. And why not? After all, it was a house full of women. When I was little, my father was around hardly at all. While my sisters and I ate our breakfast in the day nursery, he had his alone, in state, in the dining-room. Sometimes he would put in an appearance upstairs around our bedtime, but mostly we were brought down to see him – briefly. And, because life with my mother hadn't turned out how he had hoped, there was always something hesitant and uneasy about him; he seemed like a bird of passage yearning to be off to more interesting and sympathetic climes.

So I spent my days surrounded by women – seven women, to be precise, and all of them, including my sisters, much older than I. I was literally the odd man out. I was also a disturbed, difficult and demanding child. My sisters, Minnie and the maids found me hard to take and easy to resent, and my mother, as I discovered when my own children arrived, was never much good with small children – not that Nanny allowed her the chance to practise on them. Of those seven women, Nanny was the only one I loved and trusted wholeheartedly. The others were separate, confusing and vaguely hostile, and therefore, no doubt, fascinating in a slightly scary way. In the circumstances, it seems reasonable that dark places should have frightened me. I couldn't wait to get out into the male world, and I mark the beginning of a kind of happiness from the moment when I was finally packed off to a strenuous boarding school.

Blaming the women of the house is one cheapjack explanation among many. Another, equally simplistic, is that maybe my own nastiness scared me, resounding back from the darkness. But I wonder if these aren't just excuses, like the vampires and burglars – trivialisations of a dread that is far more archaic, deep-rooted and universal. Children put shapes and faces to their fear of the dark, and these shapes may be full of private meaning, dipped in what Henry James called 'the deep well of unconscious cerebration'. But the real fear is of darkness itself, and perhaps it is instinctive. Perhaps, that is, children are born with traces of primitive man's terror of night and the horrors it held for him, just as a new-hatched songbird will instinctively cower if the shadow, or the simulated shadow, of a hawk goes over it. As civilisation, with its contentments as well as its discontents, gradually takes over, the fear, like the monsters, fades away.

Spiders apart, I no longer remember how I populated the darkness that made me sweat with fear when I was small. But I remember the fear itself, particularly my fear of the darkness that shrouded the upper floor, where I slept – the dark at the top of the stairs. When I stood on the landing outside my father's dressing-room, the darkness seemed to fill the top floor even in broad daylight and roll down the staircase like fog. There were three light switches at the foot of that staircase: for the hall light below, for the first-floor landing, for the top-floor landing. Once I was tall enough to reach them, I always made a point of switching on the top light before I went upstairs, even on sunny days. Three-quarters of the way up was a small landing where the staircase turned ninety degrees. I used to pause there to summon up my courage and always took the last six steps in a rush. I did not feel safe until I was across the top landing and had the door of the night nursery shut tight behind me. Later, when I was a schoolboy and was afraid of being seen to be afraid, I managed to disguise my panic, moderate my pace, and go upstairs sedately and – I hoped – resolutely, as if I hadn't a care in the world. But it was all a fake.

The truth is that night contains whatever you care to put into it, and, because you can't see, or can see very little, it gives your imagination unlimited space to work in. The psychoanalyst W. R. Bion used the phrase 'nameless dread' to describe the meaningless fear that overwhelms an infant whose mother fails to contain its terrors and make them meaningful:

> the patient feels surrounded not so much by real objects, things-in-themselves, but by bizarre objects that are real only in that they are the residue of thoughts and conceptions that have been stripped of their meaning and ejected.[1]

Whence the ghoulies and ghosties, the bizarre objects and misshapen creatures of nightmare. The best ghost-story writers know that by night fear is a free agent, which will fix on anything that comes to hand. In M. R. James's 'Oh, Whistle and I'll Come to You, My Lad', the creature, whose 'one power was that of frightening', embodies itself in a sheet from an empty bed and confronts its victim with 'a face of crumpled linen'. In 'The Treasure of Abbot Thomas', a plump, mildewed leather bag slides forward and puts its arms around the narrator's neck:

> I was conscious of a most horrible smell of mould, and of a cold kind of face pressed against my own, and moving slowly over it, and of several – I don't know how many – legs or arms or tentacles or something clinging to my body.

Nothing is definite, nothing precise. Evil is a free-floating force and can inhabit the most commonplace objects. Fear of the dark is essentially unspecific; like darkness itself, it is formless, engulfing, full of menace, full of death. The rest is child's play: naming the demons (Satan, Beelzebub, Hecate, Lucifer) and filling in the details (fangs, claws, bats' wings, goats' horns, toad's skin, dragon's tail) are ways of sanitising the nameless dread, of containing the uncontainable. In horror movies, no matter how brilliant the special effects, the moment when the monster is finally revealed is invariably a disappointment. The creature from the black lagoon or the morgue or the pit or outer space is always easier to live with, however dangerously, than the nebulous shapes created by the imagination running free. Once you can put a face on evil, it becomes, as Hannah Arendt said, banal.

Now we have light at our command, at the flick of a switch, we have become connoisseurs of nocturnal fear and keep it constantly on tap as entertainment: horror movies, pulp novels, shock comics tailored for all age groups. It is also out there on the streets every night: the freaks and muggers and addicts, the UFO visionaries, Satanists, religious fundamentalists and political crazies, the ghouls, terrorists and perverts. The great insomniac *passeggiata* of the modern city is a walking validation of our instinctive belief that night is the time when things go wrong and lurch out of proportion, the time when values get turned around and daylight rules no longer apply.

Part of the primitive fear of darkness is connected with what happens to us when we sleep. Not only are we vulnerable to intruders and predators, we are also vulnerable to our dreams: to their obdurate strangeness; to the irrationality that seems normal at the time, even inevitable; to the overpowering terrors, griefs, rages and triumphs we did not consciously know we had. And behind all this there are other, more deeply buried anxieties.

According to Bruce Chatwin, for example, there is a concrete, historical reason that darkness and evil are inextricably linked in the human mind. For the harried and besieged first men, he suggested, the routine horrors of the night – vulnerability, loneliness and cold – were compounded by a malign predator with a taste for human flesh. In *The Songlines*, he quotes Robert Brain's hypothesis in *The Hunters or the Hunted?* that there was 'a specialist killer of the primates' called *Dinofelis*, 'the false sabre-tooth'. Chatwin writes:

> *Dinofelis* was a cat less agile than a leopard or a cheetah but far more solidly built. It had straight, dagger-like killing teeth, midway in form between a sabre-tooth's and, say, the modern tiger's. Its lower jaw could slam shut; and since, with its slightly cumbersome build, it must have hunted by stealth, it must also have hunted by night . . . Its bones have been unearthed from the Transvaal to Ethiopia: that is, the original range of man . . .
>
> Could it be, one is tempted to ask, that *Dinofelis* was Our Beast?

A Beast set aside from all the other Avatars of Hell? The Arch-Enemy who stalked us, stealthily and cunningly, wherever we went? But whom, in the end, we got the better of?

Coleridge once jotted in a notebook, 'The Prince of Darkness is a Gentleman.' What is so beguiling about a specialist predator is the idea of an intimacy with the Beast! For if, originally, there was one particular Beast, would we not want to fascinate him as he fascinated us? Would we not want to charm him, as the angels charmed the lions in Daniel's cell?

The snakes, scorpions and other menacing creatures of the savannah . . . could never have threatened our existence, as such; never have postulated the end of our world. A specialist killer could have – which is why, however tenuous the evidence, we must take him seriously.

'Bob' Brain's achievement, as I see it – whether we allow for one big cat, for several cats, or for horrors like the hunting hyena – is to have reinstated a figure whose presence has grown dimmer and dimmer since the close of the Middle Ages: the Prince of Darkness in all his sinister magnificence.

In his elegant way, Chatwin is doing for the false sabre-tooth much the same thing that Peter Benchley did for the great white shark in *Jaws*: using it to give shape and fearful presence to everybody's buried fears. The death-dealer that hunted primates by night and the shark with a taste for human flesh are both embodiments of an archaic terror. That terror lingers on in the child's instinctive fear of the dark and of the malign forces darkness hides. The terror fades as the child gets older, because, among other reasons, he learns to manipulate it by playing scary games in safety – in the cinema, at home with a book or a video – by turning it into a source of titillation and thrills and perverse enjoyment. The other form of manipulation and control, Chatwin seems to be suggesting, is abstraction. *Dinofelis* became extinct, but man, with his gift for language, gradually transformed the memory of the terror the creature once inspired into the concept of evil, turning the Beast that killed by night into the Prince of Darkness, creating morality from fear.

Scientifically, Chatwin's theory is almost certainly far-fetched; there is no sure proof that the false sabre-tooth was a specialised man-eater. But it makes poetic sense as a description of the etiology of good and evil. In other words, if the creature had never existed, we would have had to invent it because it corresponds to powerful forces in the human mind. Forces, for instance, like this:

> [It] creates a sensation in the mind of being watched by eyes from which nothing can escape. These eyes are cruel, penetrating, inhuman and untiring. They record without mercy, pity, or compassion. They follow relentlessly and judge remorselessly. No escape is possible for there is no place to shelter. Their memory is infinite and their threat is nameless. The punishment when it comes will be swift, poisonous and ruthless . . . Added to this feeling of being constantly watched and threatened there is also the sense of being acutely listened to, smelled and even having one's thoughts read, which gives some idea of the terror and hopelessness produced. These sensations create in the subject of their implacable scrutiny a feeling of being totally surrounded by irresistible forces which close in on them from all sides like the Iron [Maiden] of mediaeval tortures or the contracting room of Poe's 'The Pit and the Pendulum'.

It sounds like everybody's worst nightmare, whatever name it comes under: Big Brother or false sabre-tooth or great white shark – a creature, incidentally, that never closes its eyes to sleep and can scent blood across miles of ocean. The description is, in fact, written by a psychoanalyst and portrays the superego in its most rampant and sadistic form.[2]

Yet the same analyst, in the same article, also wrote:

> The upright stance and the development of speech, along with the presence of the super-ego [are some] of the attributes of man that [have] raised him above the animal kingdom. This structure is responsible for his conscience, his morals, his ethics, his religion, and his esthetics. It is the source of all his spiritual aspirations and endeavors.

In other words, the superego is the basis not just of conscience but of all mankind's higher values. As Freud originally defined it in *The Ego and the Id*, in 1923, the superego was a derivative of the Oedipus complex: an image of the parents installed in the child's mind, controlling it and threatening punishment. Ten years later, Melanie Klein refined this idea and made it more subtle by suggesting that the child was continually adding to this original internal image by projecting into it his own violent phantasies.[3] In this way, the superego becomes a composite force based partly on external reality – the parental figures or the child's imagination of them – and partly on the child's own frightening or intolerable internal states.

The process Klein describes is complicated, but the essential point is relatively simple: the harshness of the superego is not necessarily founded on external reality, and does not come about solely because the parents are harsh or because the child's distorted image of them makes them so or, as Freud also suggested, because it is based on some distant memory of the vengeful father of the prehistoric primal horde; it comes about also because the superego is filled up with parts of the child's own nature. The infant, that is, cannot tolerate its own sadistic, devouring, stifling phantasies, so it projects them on to the external world.★ But, once projected, they become so overwhelming that in order to control them the infant reintrojects them into the superego, where they terrorise and persecute it. But terror is a two-way street. Long before the infant can register or understand the objective dangers and malice lurking in the outside world, it can be frightened out of its senses by the violence of its own impulses, by its own imagination. The psychoanalyst Susan Isaacs wrote:

> A little girl of one year and eight months, with poor speech development, saw a shoe of her mother's from which the sole had come loose and was flapping about. The child was horrified, and screamed with terror. For about a week she would shrink away and scream if she saw her mother wearing any shoes at all, and for some time could only tolerate her mother's wearing a pair of brightly coloured house shoes. The particular offending pair was not worn for several months. The child gradually forgot about the terror, and let her mother wear any sort of shoes. At two years and eleven months, however (fifteen months later), she suddenly said to her mother in a frightened voice, 'Where are Mummy's broken shoes?' Her mother hastily said, fearing another scream- ing attack, that she had sent them away, and the child then commented, 'They might have eaten me right up.'
>
> The flapping shoe was thus *seen* by the child as a threatening mouth, and responded to as such, at one year and eight months, even though the phantasy could not be put into words till more than a year later. Here, then, we have the clearest possible evidence that phantasy can be felt, and felt as real, long before it can be expressed in words.[4]

★ Psychoanalysts distinguish between 'fantasy', in the everyday sense of *conscious* daydreams and fictions, and 'phantasy', which connotes *unconscious* mental content which may or may not become conscious.

In terms of the psychic terror they are capable of inspiring, there is nothing much to chose between *Dinofelis*, Jaws and an old flapping shoe. In one form or another, they are all devouring mouths and, as the case of the frightened little girl shows, to experience the terror it is not necessary either to have seen a devouring mouth or to be able to describe one. The phantasy and the horrors it inspires predate the reality.

It also predates practically everything else, since phantasies of this type, according to Klein, are mostly inspired by the infant's earliest experience at the breast. They fade, they change, they modify with time, but at some fundamental level they remain embedded in the psyche's structure. In full-blown psychosis, they sometimes emerge powerfully and in their most primitive forms, but traces of them appear in less disturbed patients and also, as faint as the ghost of *Dinofelis*, in the passing fancies of perfectly normal people.

Ghost-story writers, even the apparently sanest of them, maintain a permanently open hot-line to these primitive phantasies. At the turn of the century, M. R. James, Provost of Eton and Edwardian grandee, wrote a story in which a scholar of witchcraft, who is being hexed by an enemy, reaches under his pillow for his watch:

> What he touched was, according to his account, a mouth, with teeth, and with hair about it, and, he declares, not the mouth of a human being.

About ninety years later, a troubled little boy, in treatment at a London clinic and not yet able to read, told his therapist a terrible nightmare: the pillow he was sleeping on ate his head. Given a certain cast of mind, primitive phantasies, nameless dread and bizarre objects are unchanging and democratically available to everyone, regardless of age, education and social standing.

Daylight, with its routines and busyness, keep these phantasies mostly at bay. But at night, when the external world is hidden, common sense loses its points of reference, and there is space for less amenable figures to make their presence felt. As every ghost-story writer knows – including the author of *Hamlet* – evil spirits only walk after sunset and fade 'on the crowing of the cock'.

Does it follow that you need to have a punishing superego and a highly developed sense of evil to remain frightened of the dark as an adult? Or do you only need a highly developed awareness of the forces of darkness in your own psyche? Or is it the weight of the past bearing down, loosening your grip on reality? John Cheever wrote in his journals:

B. tells me Fred [Cheever's brother] is suffering from something that happened to him before his adolescence and I think it may have been my birth. I have tried for years to uncover the turning point in his life but this had never occurred to me. This is a clinical or quasi-scientific disclosure, but it seems to me as rich as any other revelation. I can readily imagine it all. He was happy, high-spirited, and adored, and when, at the age of seven, he was told he would have to share his universe with a brother, his forebodings would, naturally, have been bitter and deep. They would have been deepened by the outrageous circumstances of my birth. I was conceived mistakenly, after a sales banquet. My mother carried me reluctantly and my father must have been heard to say that he had no love in his heart for another child. These violent scenes must have given great breadth and intensity to his own conflicts. His feeling for me was always violent and ambiguous – hatred and love – and beneath all of this must have been the feeling that I challenged him in some field where he excelled – in the affections of his parents. I have felt for a long time that, with perfect consciousness, his urge was to destroy me. I have felt that there was in his drunkenness some terrible cunning.

Here then are three worlds – night, day, and the night within the night. Here are the passions and aspirations of the dead, moving freely among us with malevolence and power. Here is a world of open graves. Here is a world where our imagery breaks down. We have no names, no shapes, no lights, no colors to fill out these powers, and yet they are as persuasive as the living. Out of his window he can see the city shining in the light of day and he adores it but he will be motivated less by his vision than by his remembrance of a scream heard in a dark stairwell fifty years ago. They seem to destroy him and to counsel him to destroy me. We seem to be at one another's throats. We hear the lashing of a dragon's tail in the dead leaves, the piteous screaming of a child whose eyes are plucked out by a witch, we smell the damps of the snake pit.[5]

The night within the night and the bizarre objects that fill it come in all shapes. A woman who was scared of the dark told me a nightmare she had had when she was eight years old. Her family house had a spare room, unused except when she and her friends played there. In her dream, she went into the spare room, pulled open the top drawer of a chest of drawers and found a man's hand lying in it. There was nothing gruesome about the hand – no blood, no claws, no unnatural hairiness, no sign of its having been severed. It was horrifying for no other reason than that it was utterly unexpected. She woke screaming and it was months before she would go back into the spare room, even in company and in broad daylight. This had happened at the end of the Second World War, when her father was away in the army, and the only man in the house was her grumpy, alcoholic grandfather. Years later, she wondered if maybe her grandfather had ever tried to grope her when he was drunk. If so, it was not an incident she could remember.

The woman is now a successful middle-aged lawyer – attractive, energetic, happily married – and she is still afraid of the dark. Whenever she is alone at night, she shuts all the windows, even in high summer, checks the locks on the doors more often than is strictly necessary, and leaves all the lights on. She turns off her bedside light when she settles down to sleep but keeps the bedroom door open on to the well-lit landing. Because she is a practical woman, full of good sense, she does not believe in ghosts. It's not the supernatural that scares her, she says; it's the flesh-and-blood monsters out there on the streets, the drifting psychopaths, burglars and rapists, waiting to take advantage of other people's weakness and inattention.

'We've installed an electronic burglar alarm,' she says. 'Now I'm nothing like so worried.'

'So you turn the lights out when you go to bed?'

A shrug. An embarrassed smile. 'Not exactly.'

As for me, I wish I could remember my childish nightmares. They might be a way of recovering something valuable, a whole area of feeling I seem to have mislaid. But all I can come up with is an image from a movie: Spencer Tracy's face in the first transformation scene in *Dr Jekyll and Mr Hyde* – the features melting like wax, the lips curling back, the teeth becoming sharp and dangerous, the respectable doctor deliquescing into a monster. The film was released in 1941, so I must have been eleven or twelve when I saw it – on the edge of puberty, that is, and too late for childish terrors. Yet it gave me screaming nightmares for months, maybe years, after. On some deep level, I suppose, I must have recognised the process, if not the face. Sadistic, destructive Mr Hyde corresponded to some obscure image of myself, to impulses I was scared of and preferred not to acknowledge.

The fact that Jekyll was a doctor also helped. My parents had a knack for picking sadistic family doctors – the kind who took pleasure in lancing infected wounds without bothering to administer a local anaesthetic. Added to that was the surgery on my ankle, which had presumably caused me a good deal of pain. Not that I could remember it, but I did remember clearly a medical incident when I was about five or six. I had just started prep school and was clamouring to be allowed to play football. The doctors had forbidden it, on the ground that my ankle was too delicate and vulnerable, so my mother took me to Harley Street to see a famous specialist. Dr Cumberbach was a jolly Pickwickian figure, plump and reassuring, with a florid face and grey curls. He sat me on a high padded stool in an office full of gleaming medical machinery and examined my leg gently for a considerable time. Then he said, quite tenderly, 'You can play games if you really want, but if you get that ankle of yours kicked you might have to have your leg off.' I suppose I was terrified, but I was also outraged, and the practical effect of his warning was to make me disporportionately foolhardy on the sports field. It also provoked in me a fear and distrust of doctors that I have not yet wholly overcome. No matter how agreeable and efficient they may appear, I am always waiting for Mr Hyde to show his ugly face.

The year of *Dr Jekyll and Mr Hyde* was the year of the

London blitz, when night brought different and more obvious dangers: air-raid sirens wailing, the steady rise and fall of the bomber engines (the radio newsreaders talked about 'waves of bombers', and that was how they sounded), bombs whistling (you learned from their sound to judge their closeness with great precision), the thump of the anti-aircraft batteries on Primrose Hill, planes pinned against the night sky in a latticework of searchlights, the eerie glow over London the night the City caught fire. (I watched it from the night-nursery window until my distraught mother found me and hustled me downstairs.) At school prayers one morning, after a particularly gruelling night raid, the headmaster told us to change the words of the morning hymn from 'Oh Father, for another night of quiet sleep and rest' to 'Oh Father, for just one night . . .' He was not normally a sympathetic man or strong on humour, but, for once, he had caught the spirit both of his audience and of the moment.

For a few months, while the blitz lasted, London was a good place to be. There used to be a Cockney joke popular enough to be inscribed in poker work on ornamental wooden panels and sold in souvenir shops, along with postcards and sticks of rock, at seaside resorts like Margate: ' "Cheer up," they said. "Things could be worse." So I did and they were.' It summed up all the qualities that usually make London so trying for outsiders – the resignation, the inertia, the gloom. But during the blitz these were transformed, under pressure, into a grumbling, good-humoured stoicism, which even the children shared. It was as though we had all been enrolled into some easygoing grown-up army, with only two important rules: don't panic and don't complain. We collected shrapnel, we compared notes on how close the bombs fell to where we lived, we were sniffy about using air-raid shelters, we explored the shells of bombed-out houses, looking for trouble but pretending we were looking for treasure. And when there were casualties they did not properly register, since for most children the idea of death is more or less meaningless.

It was obviously different for adults, and it might have been different for us, too, if more bombs had fallen on north-west London or if the raids had come later in the war, when the technology of terror had been improved. As it was, the blitz was a period of wild excitement. The disruption and squalor and constant shortage of food – four ounces of butter and one ounce of cheese a week, one egg a fortnight – mattered much less to schoolboys than the nightly ration of danger. Real danger, not make-believe. For me, this excitement is fixed in an image: the brilliant aerial ballet performed, during daytime raids, by the Spitfires, Hurricanes, Messerschmitts and Heinkels. It was more than exciting, it was also beautiful, and it hooked me for ever on the adrenaline high.

It also cured me of my fear of the dark. Bruno Bettelheim, who had been a prisoner in Dachau and Buchenwald, pointed out that seriously disturbed people – especially paranoids – seemed to lose their symptoms, and even to cope quite well, in the concentration camps, because the horrors of everyday life effortlessly outstripped those of their internal worlds. Maybe this was also true for me, on a miniature scale: when every night brought violence and the threat of death, without any intervention on my part, there was no longer any need for me to be afraid of my own night within the night.

Whatever the reason, I like darkness now. I enjoy moving around the house with the lights off: the familiar shapes of the furniture shrouded by shadow, the red eyes of the burglar alarm blinking as I pass, the sound of a tap dripping in the kitchen or the rain against the windows, the tangled shadows cast by the street lamps on the ceiling. I like the privacy, the sense of being alone and unseen, even when my wife and children are sleeping quietly upstairs.

Wallace Stevens wrote a poem about reading alone at night that begins:

> The house was quiet and the world was calm.
> The reader became the book and summer night
>
> Was like the conscious being of the book.
> The house was quiet and the world was calm.

When I first read that, I thought it was about communion or communications, about the way night intensifies the silence and absorption of the act of reading: the neutral shadows at the edges of the lamplight are a kind of *cordon sanitaire* separating the reader and his book from the world outside, making them one in their single pool of light. I see now that in Stevens's world night itself is a part of that serenity, a comforting third presence, equally important.

There was a time when I could never have conceived that Stevens might be right, that the terrors of my childhood would vanish and night would be consoling and a great deal more peaceful than day. I wouldn't want those terrors back, but sometimes I miss them.

His appearances are incalculable,
His strength terrible,
I do not know his name.

Huddling pensive for weeks on end, he
Gives only random hints of life, such as
Strokes of uncomfortable coincidence.

To eat heartily, dress warmly, lie snugly
And earn respect as a leading citizen
Granted long credit at all shops and inns –

How dangerous! I had feared this shag demon
Would not conform with my conformity
And in some leaner belly make his lair.

But now in dream he suddenly bestrides me . . .
'All's well,' I groan, and fumble for a light,
Brow bathed in sweat, heart pounding.

    Robert Graves, 'Gratitude for a Nightmare'

# II

My childhood fear of the dark went on puzzling me long after I had grown out of it. I used to believe that it was just one of the many problems I had inherited from my mother. She was a great beauty when she was young – dark hair, black eyes, expressive mouth – spectacular in her way, although she herself never quite registered the fact. Others did, however. When she was doing voluntary work at the American Officers' Club in London towards the end of the First World War, a US army photographer was so smitten by her lovely face and sweet confusion that he offered to take her to Hollywood and turn her, he said, into a second Mary Pickford. (My grandfather forbade her ever to speak to him again.) But even in her bloom, the life she lived was already constrained by irrational fears and phobias, and it became more constrained and eccentric as she grew older.

She was frightened of horses and railways. She never travelled by tube because being underground made her claustrophobic and the din of the trains terrified her. Aeroplanes, of course, were out of the question. She was even frightened of opera. The only time my father persuaded her to go with him to Covent Garden was, unfortunately, to see *Turandot*. He chose it because it was Puccini and she had liked bits of *La Bohème* when he played it on the gramophone. She agreed because the opera was new and everyone was talking about it. But the princess's dramatic first-act appearance in the execution scene upset her so much that she made him take her home at the interval. That was in 1929 and, although she blamed her upset on the fact that she was pregnant, she never went to the opera again.

Behind all these daily terrors, I suspect, was another terror, more deep-rooted: she lived in mortal fear of her father. To the outside world he was a dashing figure, a dandy, a *bon vivant*, a lover of racehorses and a charmer of women, full of life, full of jokes and much admired by his high-rolling cronies. But at home he was a martinet, a Victorian tyrant who terrorised the whole household. His wife was a patient woman and she put up with him, the servants had no choice, and his two older children learned in time to fight back. But my mother was the youngest and the least confident, and he made her life a misery. She once told me that one of her earliest memories was of leaning out of the nursery window at the top of their tall house in Tavistock Square and hearing the paperboys shouting in the foggy streets below, 'Crippen caught! Crippen caught!' Crippen was a famous murderer, the current bogeyman for small children, and this occurred around bedtime. But what she felt was not excitement, she said, nor even, for once, fear; instead, she was filled with a profound relief: one monster less on the loose.

She was so absorbed in her private terrors that ordinary fears did not touch her. She ignored illness, refused to see doctors and never took pills. When she burned or cut herself, which she did continually as she got older, she wrapped up the wound any old how and forgot about it. When she fell, she picked herself up and pretended it hadn't happened. Above all, darkness left her cold. In the years between the death of my father and the onset of the particularly nasty form of arthritis that finally crippled her, she lived alone with her sullen pets, rattling happily around the big, empty house, indifferent to the shrouded rooms and spooky cellars.

So instead of blaming my mother for my childhood fear of the dark, I should thank her for showing me, by her example, that there was nothing to be afraid of and that night itself could be pleasurable. But when I was young my mother wasn't around much, and when she was around she never seemed to be someone a small child could rely on. Nanny, however, was like a rock – solid, comforting and always there. She was a handsome, energetic woman with bright blue eyes and a strong face that was surprisingly soft to touch. Like other nannies of her generation, she had devoted her life to other people's children – so much so that when she had an illegitimate child by one of her many admirers she put the baby out for adoption at birth and never saw it again. From my point of view, she was everything my temperamental parents were not: stern sometimes, but always sensible, orderly and resilient. (At the age of ninety-something she had a hip replacement. A few weeks after she left hospital, she came to see me and my family. When I asked how she was, she said, 'Right as two trivets,' and danced a jig to prove it.)

Because of my fear of the dark, I was a restless sleeper, easily woken and troubled by dreams that had the uncomfortable knack of turning into nightmares. I do not know which came first, fear of the dark or the bad dreams, but they fed on each other, just as they must have done for the first men in their caves, and the consequence was I hated sleep.

Nothing unusual about that, of course. Most children try to put off going to bed early when the adults are still up and about. I, too, resented being left out, but I resented far more the prospect of being scared. The night nursery was a big room, up under the eaves and full of shadows. Opposite my bed was a wall of built-in cupboards; because the cupboard doors were oddly angled to fit the sloping roof, they seemed to create their own shadows, and the tall poplars outside the back window were constantly on the move, adding shadows to shadows. Only the presence of my beloved Nanny got me through the nights. If I woke in the dead hours, I could hear her snoring gently in her bed on the other side of the room. If I woke earlier, what I saw was something like Wallace Stevens's poem: the nursery infused with the orange glow of the gasfire and Nanny beside it in her armchair, in a pool of lamplight, knitting and reading. She had a passion for Victorian sentimental ballads and narrative tales, and her recitations were a big hit at the social functions of the Baptist church she attended. Occasionally, as a reward for good behaviour, she would rehearse them for me, rolling them out in a ringing voice. It was like the sound of my father's records of classical music, percolating up from below – mysterious, grand and obscurely moving – and perhaps the combination of the two is where my love of poetry began. Later, at boarding school, when a marvellous English teacher called Hugo Caudwell introduced me to Donne and the Romantics and A. E. Housman, I felt I had come home at last.

Come home to what? To night and the nursery and a calming presence? I don't think so. To order, more likely, to a way of making sense of all those confusions of which fear of the dark was just one element.

But by the time I reached boarding school, I had forgotten all about my night fears. Maybe they are like Wordsworth's intimations of immortality – glimmerings, memories, faint vanishing traces of an earlier existence, though not in Wordsworth's heaven but back in the cave with our primitive forbears. Whatever the reason, I had other things on my mind at that age. Like the rest of the human race, during my teens and twenties, whatever my nominal interests and ambitions, all I really thought about was sex. (This was in the 1950s, when the sexual rules were far sterner than they are now. Maybe modern kids take sex for granted after puberty and the new rite of passage into the adult world – at least in some sections of the gun-crazy United States – is no longer losing your virginity, but taking a life.) Sometime in my early thirties, when my love life was more or less in order, the obsession with sex was replaced by an obsession with food – in London during the swinging sixties, a good restaurant was harder to find than Miss Right – and I used to comb cook books in the same spirit as I had combed novels as an adolescent, looking, literally, for the saucy bits. For me, the reign of the foodie lasted perhaps a dozen years and then was usurped by a new obsession: sleep. The ultimate, unachievable pleasurable experience became eight hours of uninterrupted oblivion.

Maybe this fitful evolution from one kind of pleasure to another was peculiar to myself, but I doubt it. As for the pleasures of sleep, I have literature on my side:

> The King, who had the air of a tired pastry-cook, sat down.
>   'We feel,' he said, 'today, we've had our fill of stares!'
>   'One little bow, Willie,' the Queen entreated, 'that wouldn't kill you.'
>   'We'd give perfect worlds,' the King went on, 'to go, by Ourselves, to bed.'

That poignant exchange is from Ronald Firbank's *The Flower Beneath the Foot*. Lawrence Sterne has another, equally heartfelt, in *Tristram Shandy*:

> Now my father . . . was musing within himself about the hardships of matrimony, as my mother broke silence. –
>
> '– My brother Toby, quoth she, is going to be married to Mrs Wadman.'
>
> '– Then he will never, quoth my father, be able to lie *diagonally* in his bed again as long as he lives.'

'To go by Ourselves, to bed', 'to lie *diagonally*': the sheer sensuality of somnolence is a secret the elderly keep from the young. Sleep and sex have bed and darkness in common and, according to the age group, they inspire a curiously similar yearning. The harassed middle aged are in love with sleep in the same way as the young are in love with love; chastity is the torment of youth, insomnia of age, and at neither stage of life does it ever seem possible to get enough of what you want.

There are other parallels:

> So restless *Cromwel* could not cease
> In the inglorious Arts of Peace,
>     But through adventrous War
>     Urged his active Star . . .
> 'Tis Madness to resist or blame
> The force of angry Heavens flame:
>     And, if we would speak true
>     Much to the Man is due . . .

When Marvell wrote his reluctant tribute to 'industrious valour' and political necessity in 'An Horatian Ode', he was voicing the mixture of admiration, resentment and disdain which the pleasure-loving majority secretly feels towards those who go places and make things happen, towards the driven few and their terrible indifference to rest. The shiftless and disheartened take comfort from the fact that those who famously spurn sleep – Napoleon, Edison, Churchill, Thatcher – all look as though they also get by with very little pleasure of any kind, apart from power and ambition. Like the rich, the over-achievers are different from us; they get off on self-denial. According to Edison:

> Most people overeat 100 per cent and oversleep 100 per cent. That extra 100 per cent makes them unhealthy and inefficient. The person who sleeps eight or ten hours a night is never fully asleep and never fully awake.

As a statement of faith, this is unusually obnoxious: self-righteous, of course, but also profoundly self-satisfied, imbued with the deep relish the abstainer derives from setting his face against the pleasures that keep the rest of mankind sane.

Yet pleasure in its different forms has been one of the great themes of this century, and not simply because the spread of wealth, comfort and labour-saving devices in the industrialised nations has produced more leisure for more people, as well as a whole industry to serve it. Edison himself was a key player in this great social shift. It was one of his inventions that lit up the night and, indirectly, made its twin pleasures, sex and sleep, available to inspection and analysis.

The century began with the publication of Freud's *The Interpretation of Dreams*; from then on, the pleasure principle, wish-fulfilment, dream-life and the many-faced ubiquitousness of sexuality became subjects of serious intellectual enquiry. Fifty years later, it was the turn of sleep research to take off as a science. It began with the discovery of rapid eye movement sleep, which coincided, more or less, with the first exploration of space. In the first flush of optimism, the same grandiose claims were being made for both new sciences:

> In the *Upanishads* of ancient India it is written that existence takes three forms, the one here in this world, another in the other world, and a third in the world of dreaming. By the second half of the 20th century scientific views of nature had nothing to say of the other world, and, with the singular and therefore highly suspect exception of psychiatry, they were equally silent about the world of dreaming. If our era will be remembered for first exploring the other world of outer space, it may be just as important that it produced the first concerted assault upon the secret workings of the brain whence comes our inner world of nightly visions . . . The physiological characteristics of [dreaming] prove so distinctive that I consider it a third state of earthly existence, the rapid eye movement or REM state, which is at least as different from sleeping and waking as each is from the other.[6]

As it turned out, the third state of earthly existence proved to be even more mysterious than it initially seemed to be, not because it was different from the first state, but because the worlds of sleeping and waking overlapped to a degree no one ever imagined.

Yet Professor Snyder's tone is typical of a great deal of the wrangling that followed: on one side, the new 'hard' science of sleep research, which would launch probes into inner space; on the other, the 'suspect' disciplines of psychiatry and psychoanalysis, with their 'unscientific' methods and 'speculative' conclusions. In practice, the two are inextricably linked. Sleep research is a subdivision of research into the neurophysiology of the brain, which ultimately revolves around the problem of what is meant by 'consciousness'. The problem of consciousness, in turn, is linked with the problem of the 'unconscious', which itself is linked to the problems of thinking, dreaming and creativity.

What is involved, in short, is night life in its private sense: the life that goes on when the lights are off and your eyes are closed, the night within the night. It is a complex subject and it has generated a vast amount of specialised literature. But specialised literature is for specialists, and neither the scientists nor the psychoanalysts seem to care much about what is happening in each others' fields. Most scientists assume that psychoanalysis has not changed since Freud wrote his early papers, and most analysts seem unaware that Freud's model of the brain and how it works is now known to be hopelessly inaccurate. So they go their separate ways, impervious to each others' subtleties. Yet from the outsider's point of view, their subtleties blend together and the state of one art illuminates the state of the other.

The section that follows is a magical mystery tour, strictly for the layman, of that night within the night. It starts, incongruously, in the staid and leafy suburb of Wimbledon, not far from the All England Tennis Club.

# 3

# THE SLEEP LABORATORY

*Some must watch while some must sleep,*
*Thus runs the world away.*

Shakespeare, *Hamlet*

*Oh sleep! It is a gentle thing,*
*Beloved from pole to pole!*
*To Mary Queen the praise be given!*
*She sent the gentle sleep from Heaven,*
*That slid into my soul.*

Coleridge, *The Rime of the Ancient Mariner*

Atkinson Morley's Hospital is a rambling two-storey mansion of grey-yellow brick. It is a sister hospital of St George's, Tooting, and it specialises in neurosurgical, neurological and psychiatric cases. It also houses – under the aegis of Professor A. H. Crisp, St George's chief psychiatrist – one of the National Health Service's last surviving sleep laboratories.

Atkinson Morley's was built in the grand Victorian manner and some of that grandeur still lingers in the spacious wards. The offices, however, have been chopped out of larger rooms, leaving some of them as high as they are wide. This makes the bedroom where the sleep laboratory's patients spend the night seem out of proportion; the window is unnaturally tall, the walls unnaturally close, the ceiling is full of shadows. The room is simply furnished: a bed with an adjustable reading-light above it, a small clothes cupboard, an uncomfortable-looking armchair upholstered in plastic, a battered writing-desk and chair. An ordinary bedroom, in fact, except for the video camera high on the wall above the desk, a microphone hanging dead centre from the ceiling, and a panel of sockets behind the bed for electrodes that the patients wear when they sleep. There is a large electric clock immediately above the bed's head, and off to one side, pointing towards the ceiling, is an infra-red lamp, a flared cylinder that looks like a giant's torch. The bedroom is insulated from the main corridor by a small room piled with junked equipment.

The sleep laboratory's observation room next door is twice the size of the bedroom and crammed with gear. A polygraph machine takes up most of the wall beneath a high window. Opposite are a steel sink, a draining board and a regiment of mugs. (Tea-drinking is part of the ritual of sleep observation.) There are waist-high kitchen units along the side walls, their tops piled with books, reprints of scientific papers and files – mostly marked 'Confidential' – along with a computer and a printer. Hanging from a rack on one wall are bunches of brightly coloured electrodes. The rest of the furniture is basic: a wooden desk, a steel filing-cabinet, two tubular-steel armchairs, a little table, a stool, a sagging easy chair without arms. In the centre of the room stand a large television set and a video recorder, both of them elderly and battered.

Sharon Borrow, who is in charge of the laboratory, is a small, thin, bird-like woman with startled eyes and a diffident voice. She looked pale and tired and there were dark circles under her eyes – understandably, given the nature of her work. She also seemed, at first, preternaturally shy, but, as the night wore on, shyness merged with something else, something to do with the job itself: watching strangers while they sleep makes her uneasy; it seems to her an invasion of privacy and she counteracts this by an intense concern to put people at their ease, to soothe their anxieties and make them feel at home.

Above all, she was concerned for the patient who, that particular evening in July, was an athletic young man in his middle-twenties. He had a round face, a large mouth, wiry hair cut short and business-like spectacles. Like everyone who finishes up at the sleep laboratory, the patient – call him Max – had been referred by his local doctor to Professor

Crisp's unit at St George's Hospital, where he was given a two-hour interview and a series of psychological tests. Max was suffering from what is called a parasomnia, which *The Encyclopedia of Sleep and Sleep Disorders* defines as a disorder 'of arousal, partial arousal and sleep stage transition', such as sleepwalking, rather than a primary sleep complaint, like insomnia or narcolepsy (excessive sleepiness).

Max's particular parasomnia, however, was different. It was a disorder quite common in very young children, but rare in adults: since long before he could remember, Max had been rocking while he slept. Sometimes he rocked himself consciously in order to get to sleep. 'It's very comforting,' he explained. 'It's like being a baby. And because it's so comfortable I associate it with home. It's not something I do in a strange bed.' More often, he rocked while he was asleep, sometimes gently, sometimes violently. This scared him, he said, because it meant he was out of control. It also upset whomever he happened to be in bed with – so much so that, by the time he arrived at the laboratory, he mostly preferred to sleep alone. 'When I'm alone', he said, 'I know I can rock and it won't upset anyone.'

Max was an articulate young man, highly intelligent and not at all reticent about his troubles, which seemed to be many. As a baby, he had been a head-banger – 'I used to bang my head so violently that I'd wake my brother in the next room' – and he had always been frightened of the dark; he slept with a night light beside his bed until he was older than he cared to say, and he still could not sleep with closed windows or drawn curtains. He talked about his troubles compellingly and in such detail that, although his manner was matter-of-fact, something else seemed to be going on between the lines:

he wanted to understand, he wanted to be helped, he wanted to be absolved from his scary night-time self.

It might even happen; in due course, perhaps, he might be referred for psychotherapy. But that was not Sharon Borrow's brief. Her job was to wire him up to her polygraph and record elements of his physiological activity while he slept. That information, suitably annotated by her, would then be fed into a computer, which would analyse it statistically, print out its findings, and also produce an elegant coloured graph of his night's sleep – the time he spent in the five stages of sleep, including his dreamtime in what is known as rapid eye movement sleep – and his periods of wakefulness. 'We are not here to cure sleep disorders,' Sharon said. 'Our role is an investigative one. All we can do is confirm a diagnosis, check out the senior registrar's clinical impression against the polygraphic evidence. We can rule things out, refine a problem and make it clearer. Then it's up to the psychiatrists to decide what to do.'

Max settled into the sagging armchair and tilted his head back warily, as though for a shave. Sharon cut nine pieces of adhesive tape and lined them up on the edge of the sink. Then she took a rope of electric leads from the rack on the wall and carefully disentangled their ends. The leads were bright pink and each had a plug at one end and a little silver-chloride cup at the other. Using what looked like a horse syringe, she injected a saline jelly into the cups, then taped them to Max's head: two under the chin, one above and one below each eye, one behind each ear, and one in the middle of his forehead. While she was doing this, she kept up a steady flow of reassuring chat, explaining each move, asking Max if he was comfortable. He replied amiably, trying to appear unconcerned, but whenever she disappeared from sight, he rolled his eyes wildly, like a frightened horse.

There were eleven leads in all and the last two had to be fixed on to the back of his scalp – a process that was not easy because his hair, though short, was thick and springy. Sharon dunked a strip of gauze into an ether-based physiological glue, parted his hair with a comb, pressed one electrode into place, slapped the sticky gauze over it, then dried it with cold air from a little compressor. By the time she had finished with the second electrode, the laboratory stank of ether and Max looked as if he were wearing two thin-spread strips of concrete on the back of his head.

At 11.15, we all trooped into the bedroom and Max, wearing his Medusa's nest of wires, climbed tentatively into bed. Sharon plugged the electrodes into the panel behind the bed, plumped his pillows, showed him a bell he could ring if he needed her, opened the curtains and window just so, switched off the light and went back to the laboratory to check the equipment. Once she was sure the polygraph, the video and the bell were working properly, she switched them off and returned to the bedroom. She told him to read until he felt sleepy, and then buzz her.

Each patient spends two nights at the hospital, the first to acclimatise him to the strange bed and stranger headgear, the second to record his sleep. But parasomnias are quirky and unreliable – sometimes they happen, sometimes they don't – so Max would be recorded both nights.

At 12.30, he rang the bell and we went back in to say good night. Sharon fussed around, making sure the bell was where it should be, the glass of water was full, the bed and the window and the curtains were how he wanted them. By then, he seemed quite easy with the electronic snakes in his hair and his eyelids were heavy. Sharon paused at the door. 'From now on, you won't be alone,' she said apologetically.

Back in the observation room, she switched on the equipment again. The image on the video monitor was cloudy, badly defined. Max, lying moodily on his back, was easy to see in the infra-red light, but you could read the clock behind his head only by comparing it with its twin above the polygraph.

The polygraph itself was an intricate-looking machine, about three feet long and shaped like a table. There were ranks of knobs and switches at one end, a broad sheet of paper unrolled itself through a slot near the centre, and between them was a row of twelve horizontal pens, of which only the farther six were in use. The first pair, the electro-oculogram (EOG), recorded Max's eye movements; the middle pair, the electroencephalogram (EEG), recorded electrical activity in his brain; the third pair, the electromyogram (EMG), recorded muscle activity from the electrodes under his chin. The polygraph paper unfolded itself from a huge box beneath the machine, moved up through the slot, across the table and over its edge, then slowly and silently folded itself back into a mobile metal tray. This would continue until Sharon was convinced that the patient was sleeping soundly. Then she would switch the recording from the polygraph to a tape machine and she herself would try to catch some sleep. In an average night, a third of a mile of paper would be covered by the pens' delicate, nervous marks.

The pattern of human sleep is more or less universal. When Max was settling down but still awake, the EEG recorded what are known as alpha waves, which are low voltage and fast (8–13 cycles per second); he blinked periodically, making the EOG jump; the pens of the EMG zigzagged wildly when he moved. After less than ten minutes, the brain waves began to slow down, blinking was replaced by slow, rolling movements of the eyes, the EMG flattened and Max drifted into Stage 1 sleep. This is a nebulous state that can as easily go back into waking as on into sleep. Real sleep, Stage 2, begins either with the first of a succession of sleep spindles or with a K-complex. Sleep spindles are short bursts of fast EEG activity and they get their name from how they look on the graph: jagged and closely bunched. A K-complex also has a distinctive EEG signature: a sharp high-voltage negative wave followed by a slow positive wave. Gradually, the EEG waves become larger and slower, eye movement stops, the EMG flattens out. When these large, slow waves – delta waves, they are called – occupy 20 per cent of one page of the graph, the subject is in Stage 3 sleep; when they take up more than 50 per cent, he is in Stage 4, the deepest sleep of all. This is the time for sleepwalking and night terrors – parasomnias – and it can last for at least forty-five minutes at a time, and often longer.

Falling asleep is like deep-sea diving: the progress is down and down, towards deeper and deeper sleep, downward from Stage 1 to Stage 4 – while the brain waves expand and slow and increase their voltage, from alpha waves to delta waves. Then suddenly, without warning, the sleeper comes up for air: blood pressure varies, heart rhythm and breathing quicken, oxygen consumption in the brain increases, its neurons fire as busily as they do during waking, and the EEG records fast, low-voltage brain waves. Although the body is still sleeping, the brain is behaving almost as it does when the body is awake.

There are two major differences between this kind of sleep

and the waking state. The first and oddest is that, although the body is almost as still as death, the eyes beneath their closed lids are moving wildly. For this reason, the phase is called Rapid Eye Movement (REM) sleep. All mammals – with a few incongruous exceptions, such as the spiny anteater and the duck-billed platypus – have regular periods of REM sleep, and so do some birds and reptiles. The discovery, in the early 1950s, of this strange, unpredicted physical characteristic was the breakthrough that changed all subsequent sleep research. The second major difference is that the EMG, which looks like the Himalayas when the patient is awake, is flat as milk in REM sleep – showing that the skeletal muscles are paralysed and movement is impossible. A second, more accurate name for this condition is paradoxical sleep: the brain is awake, but the body is asleep. It is like a car without a clutch – the engine revs, the wheels won't move. Instead of responding to the signals from the brain, getting up and going about his business, the sleeper dreams.

In a normal night, REM sleep occurs four or five times in spells of ten to thirty minutes. The first REM sleep is usually brief – about fifteen minutes in adults – but as night goes on the dreaming periods lengthen and become more frequent. The average sleeper in an average night dreams for an hour and a half or two hours. If he lives out his allotted three score years and ten, he will spend about twenty-three of them asleep and, however little of it he subsequently remembers, between five and six of those twenty-three years vividly dreaming.

The paper unfolded itself steadily through the polygraph. By 1.10, the EEG waves were spacious and slow and Max was in Stage 4 sleep. Sharon bent over the graph, studying it for long periods, checking the pens, plotting his progress aloud for my benefit. Every so often, the EEG pens zigzagged frantically, in ways that seemed unrelated to the peaceful figure on the video monitor. 'Artifacts,' Sharon said. 'Maybe someone has switched a light on somewhere in the building. It's not physiological. Believe me.'

Earlier in the evening the senior registrar, Dr Tony Katz, had told me that the polygraph is a notoriously tricky instrument to read and that Sharon is one of the few people in the country who knows how to do it accurately. It seemed as if she were proving him right.

As we watched, Max stirred and partly woke. The pens recording the EMG went briefly crazy. He settled again and lay still, but the EMG went on twitching.

'Muscle contraction,' Sharon said.

Ten minutes later, Max half woke. He drank some water, rearranged his pillows, rolled over onto his stomach, slipped partially into sleep, then surfaced again. He pulled the blanket up, pushed it back, moved fretfully from side to side. All this muscular activity provoked an insane drumming from the EMG pens. Finally, he settled on his side, one leg bent, the other straight, and seemed to sleep.

Sharon fetched a roll of foam rubber, sheets, pillow and duvet, and prepared to camp out in the observation room, if and when Max ever settled.

By 2.15 he seemed to be sleeping peacefully, but Sharon, who was constantly checking the graph, was not convinced. Whatever his state, nothing much was happening, so I called it a day and went off to the bedroom I had been allotted, opposite the laboratory. Sharon promised to wake me if he started rocking. The night sister, sitting in the corridor outside, legs propped on a chair, rug over her knees, looked up from her fat Nevil Shute paperback and smiled wearily. I climbed into bed and instantly fell asleep.

Almost immediately Sharon was knocking on the door, whispering urgently, 'It's started.'

I looked at my watch: 2.30. When I blundered back across the corridor, the night sister waved ironically.

Max was lying on his side, rocking quickly and rhythmically. To and fro, to and fro. The pens of the polygraph scratched and shuddered. While I watched the video monitor, Sharon pored over the graph. He's sleeping, she said, but she could not yet tell which stage he was in, and wouldn't know for sure until she examined the graph in detail in the morning. She checked the clock and scribbled a note on the graph, then we both stood in front of the monitor and watched, fascinated.

A sleeping presence is always a mystery, present and absent at the same time, seemingly peaceful, yet in reality off on wild adventures in strange landscapes. But this was different. Max was not dreaming. That much, at least, we knew from the polygraph. He was in the grip some archaic rhythm, to and fro, a strategy he had probably developed as an infant to allay his anxieties and soothe himself to sleep. According to Sharon, 'To go from head-banging to rocking is, in itself, a triumph of adaptation.' But gradually this adaptive strategy had acquired a life of its own and now it was taking him over when his defences were down. No wonder it scared him.

And no wonder Sharon was embarrassed by the nature of her work. I felt we shouldn't be there, watching, commenting, taking notes. What we were witnessing was something intensely private – so private that even Max didn't know about it. It was as though we were watching his doppelgänger, his secret, hidden night self.

For five minutes, he went on rocking rhythmically and obsessively. To and fro, to and fro. Then it was over, as suddenly as it had started. He sighed heavily and sank into sleep. The graph steadied.

Max was sleeping deeply when I got up at seven. At 9.30 he was still sleeping and looked set to go on until noon. I left Sharon to it.

The following evening, Sharon took the precaution of letting Max chose his own pillows – he liked them soft – but the previous night of acclimatisation had worked anyway. He seemed easy and relaxed. He had had a swim and a long walk, he said, and he felt good. Soon after midnight, he was ready for sleep.

Sharon had adjusted the video camera, so the image was clearer and sharper than it had been the previous night. Max lay on his back, hands clasped demurely over his stomach. The electrodes under his chin looked like an ornamental beard. Without moving, he was asleep within minutes.

'It's the pillows,' Sharon said. 'Comforting as well as comfortable.'

The same endless sheet of paper was unwinding through the polygraph, but this time the nearer six pens were in action, giving a parallel reading of the two nights' sleep. The differences were extraordinary – particularly the EMG, which was almost flat. Clearly, the night of acclimatisation had had an effect: the restlessness and anxiety had disappeared and Max was sleeping easily, comfortably, as though he were enjoying himself.

After about an hour, he turned on to his side and pressed the top of his head against the wall, like a baby cuddling against his mother. Then he settled back into deep sleep. The night was hot; the curtains in the observation room were closed; a little fan pushed out some breeze, but not enough. We sipped tea, Sharon read, I watched, the paper fed itself smoothly through the machine, the pens did their work in silence. The only sounds were the whirring of the fan and Max's deep, slow breathing on the monitor.

At 1.30, Max woke, drank some water, stretched, rolled on to his stomach, then on to his back, and finally settled on his side with one leg drawn up and his hands tucked beneath it. Sharon checked the graph, then watched him attentively. The expression on her face was protective. When a moth flew in through his open window, she said, in a worried voice, 'He's frightened of moths.' But, of course, although we could see the creature in the infra-red light, Max could not have, even if he had been awake.

'Night can be very threatening,' Sharon said. 'Things loom larger at two in the morning than at midday.'

I remarked that he seemed much more peaceful than he had been the previous night.

'I've heard some patients say that the sleep lab itself is the cure,' Sharon replied. 'And why not? They're being observed, measured, contained. Someone is taking them seriously.'

By 2 am, we were both sleepy. Sharon fetched in her mattress roll and unstrapped it. 'I don't think anything is going to happen,' she said.

This time, however, she was wrong. Ten minutes later, Max partly woke, yawned prodigiously, then immediately began to rock. The recording pens set up their hullabaloo. He rocked from side to side, raptly and steadily. The movement was eerie, intense, ritualistic and wholly private.

When I caught Sharon's eye she shook her head and said, 'After all these years, I still feel I'm intruding.'

The rocking continued for five long minutes. When it began, Max was technically awake. By the time it had finished, he was asleep. Ten minutes later, he woke again, drank more water, blew his nose loudly. More yawning and twisting about. He seemed unable to get comfortable and at 2.28 he started rocking again. This time, according to the polygraph, he was fully awake, but the rhythm was determined, infantile, primitive. It lasted for just one minute. Then he sighed deeply and slipped straight into Stage 2 sleep.

Sharon looked relieved. 'I don't know why he rocks,' she said. 'But it certainly does the trick. Look how sweetly he's sleeping.'

The next morning, Max was up and about by eight o'clock, cheerful and pleased with himself. 'Slept like a baby,' he announced. 'I feel great.'

When Sharon told him yes, he had rocked and it was all on the graph and videotape, he seemed doubly pleased.

'We'll analyse the material and be in touch,' she said. 'There'll be a follow-up interview in a couple of weeks.'

She, too, seemed pleased: by the good shape her patient was in on this fine summer morning, and by the fact that his parasomnia had manifested itself and she had the material she needed.

I gave Max a lift into town through the morning rush hour. He was relaxed and talkative, but what he talked about was the subject that obsesses all the young in these hard times: how difficult it is to find a job, even with the best qualifications. He did not mention his sleep problems and when I asked casually if he thought Dr Katz would recommend psychotherapy, he shrugged and said airily, 'I'm not really bothered by the rocking. In fact, I rather like it. It's comforting – it sends me to sleep. It's other people who object.'

'Then why go to the sleep lab?'

Another dismissive shrug. 'I wanted to know. I wanted to be sure. Anyway, they say it's a very rare type of behaviour. Maybe it'll be useful for them to have it on record.'

When I dropped him off in town, he strode away down the Marylebone Road, seemingly full of purpose – a man refreshed, relieved, absolved, for the moment, of his troubles. Perhaps Sharon had been right: the sleep laboratory itself was the cure.

I never found out what happened to Max. When I went back to Atkinson Morley's three weeks later, his case was filed away, like all the others, in a file marked 'Confidential'; and in sleep research, as in psychoanalysis, confidentiality is an inviolable part of the deal between the patient and the clinician. I was told just one detail and that had to do with sleep research, not with Max. Parasomnias usually start in Stage 4 sleep. 'Sleepwalkers move from deepest sleep to waking without being cognitively aware,' Sharon said. 'They are awakened by an internal event.' Max, however, rocked when he was awake and he rocked in Stages 1 and 2 sleep. He even rocked in REM sleep, which is theoretically impossible, since the muscles are paralysed in REM. But he never rocked in Stage 3 or 4. 'Academically,' said Sharon, 'it's a very interesting case.'

I was back at the laboratory to find out what it was like to have my own sleep monitored. Sleep, even when you are sleeping with someone else, is the most private of all experiences. Your dreams may be full of people and places and loony events, but you share them with no one – at least, while they are happening. And your activity – the tossing and turning and snoring, the partial waking and broken fragments of speech – all take place without your knowing anything about them. So, in principle, it seems peculiarly unnatural for a person or a machine to be watching, recording and analysing a process that is a total mystery to you yourself. But knowing that Sharon was still embarrassed by this invasion of privacy, even after years of experience, made it easier.

I sat in the beat-up easy chair while she attached the electrodes, beginning with the two under the chin. First, she rubbed the skin with industrial alcohol, 'to facilitate contact', she said. It felt like a bracing aftershave. Then the other electrodes went on: near the eyes, at centre of the forehead, behind the ears. They felt weightless, not at all uncomfortable. There was a pause while the room filled with the stench of ether. Sharon parted what hair is left on the back of my head and held the electrode in place gently with one finger. The strips of glue-soaked gauze felt icy at first, then stiff as wood when they dried. They seemed to complete a circle with the electrode in the middle of my forehead, like a hat one size too small, but within a couple of minutes the sense of restriction had gone and I was no longer bothered by them.

Sharon gathered the electrodes into a neat pink bunch and handed it to me. As we walked next door to the bedroom, she questioned me solicitously. Did I feel comfortable? Was there anything I needed? Was there anything she'd forgotten? While she checked the equipment, plumped the pillows, filled a glass of water at the sink in the junk room next door, I looked out of the enormous window at the spread of lights in the dormitory suburbs to the south. I could see cars on the A3 bypass and the brightly lit windows of a train moving briefly between two masses of shadow. But immediately beyond the hospital there was nothing but blackness. A pleasant breeze blew through the window, stirring the curtains.

I got into bed carefully, trying not to muddle the electrode leads, while Sharon plugged them into the panel behind the bed. She went next door to test the equipment, then returned, removed one of the electrodes under my chin, reinjected it with saline jelly, taped it back in place and checked it against a green-and-red dial on the panel. 'We have a problem with contact and impedance,' she said. I twisted around to watch. No matter how much she fussed with the contact, the needle on the little dial refused to shift from red to green. Finally, she said, 'I think it's the dial that's not working. The polygraph will pick it up OK.'

I asked what would happen to the electrodes when I moved around or rolled over in my sleep. 'Nothing at all,' she said. 'In a couple of minutes you won't even know they're there.'

And she was right. Going to bed with electrodes taped to your skull and knowing that they will record, while you sleep, things you yourself know nothing about – physiological events inside your brain, muscular activity, eye movements – seems like a sure-fire way of ruining a night's rest. And at first the electronic headdress felt awkward: the electrodes got in the way when I moved; they made me lie stiff-necked, like a figure on a mediaeval tomb. But we take technology for granted now; seeing yourself on a television screen, hearing your own voice played back on a tape recorder, reading off your life statistics from a computer print-out have become part of the natural process. Within minutes, I had forgotten all about the electrodes. Even so, I was glad I was undergoing only a routine recording – the kind they give to insomniacs, not to those who suffer from parasomnias – for it meant the video camera and the microphone would be switched off. No one would actually be watching me sleep; no one would hear me snore.

Sharon said good night and switched off the lights. At my request, the curtains were open and a faint sodium-orange light from the window emphasised the strange proportions of the room: long and narrow and absurdly high. The wallpaper went up to what would already have been a fair height – eight or nine feet – but the room rose, painted not papered, another six feet above that. It was the kind of misshapen space you come across more often in dreams than in waking life.

I lay watching the shadows and the stripes of orange light on the distant ceiling. I could hear the hum of traffic on the bypass and the mechanical whine of a generator, faint but monotonous, from some far wing of the building. I pictured the polygraph needles scratching away in the next room and thought guiltily but vaguely that I, too, should be writing it all down.

The next thing I knew, the room was full of morning light. I rolled over and looked at my watch; it was six o'clock. I had had no dreams that I could remember, the glass of water by the bed was untouched, the electrodes on my head were all in place. I was grateful for such a sweet night's sleep, but I also felt that I had somehow missed the point of being there.

Sharon had told me she always woke at seven, however late

she went to sleep, and I could see no reason to disturb her. I turned away from the window and the next time I woke it was seven o'clock. Sharon, looking scrubbed and cheerful, came in when I rang the bell and carefully untaped the electrodes from my head. When I told her I'd had a great night's sleep, she seemed relieved as well as pleased.

The day was warm and bright and I went to the window to sniff the morning air. The bedroom was at the back of the hospital. Beyond was a little field with a marquee and a red windsock. (Atkinson Morley's is the regional headquarters for neurosurgical injuries and the field is a landing strip for air ambulances.) As I watched, a hawk landed in one of the trees surrounding the field and settled down to eat its breakfast. Beyond the field were a gasometer, a short section of bypass, scattered houses and trees, then the rolling Surrey hills.

I showered and dressed and joined Sharon in the observation room for coffee and cornflakes. She said that it would be at least a month before the computer had analysed the polygraph readings and produced a graph of my night's sleep. She pulled a section of folded paper from the metal tray at the instrument's foot and spread it out. The peaks and dips and nervous squiggles appeared to have nothing to do with my deep, dreamless sleep, but she studied them carefully and seemed satisfied.

'Look at this.' She pointed to a sequence of curves on the EOG that looked like the kind of waves a surfer dreams about. 'That's a really classic rolling eye movement.' From the way she spoke, I realised she was paying me a compliment.

And why not? I thought. I've done everything a model patient should do; I've slept like a baby.

But not according to the computer, which eventually

produced a print-out and a statistical analysis of the various stages of my sleep, as well as a coloured graph. What had felt like a long night's rest had in fact lasted just over six and a half hours, and in that period I had awakened and fallen back to sleep twenty-three times before my final waking. Most of those wakings were so brief that they hardly registered on the graph's horizontal time scale, but one had lasted a full ten minutes and the grand total for the night was forty-three minutes. Yet the only time I could remember waking up was when I rolled over and looked at my watch at six o'clock. I thought that on that occasion I had gone straight back to sleep, but according to the polygraph I had been awake for a full five minutes. I had awakened momentarily from Stage 4 sleep a couple of times and from REM five times; the rest of the wakings were from Stage 2. Stage 2 does not count as deep sleep, but it is still real sleep, unlike Stage 1, so perhaps that is why I knew nothing about my waking episodes.

I also remembered nothing about my dreams, although I had had the standard five periods of REM sleep – two of them broken by momentary wakings and relapses to Stage 2. I had also been dreaming for ten minutes immediately before I woke at six, and was having a fragmentary dream when I woke for good an hour later. But none of the dreams had left a trace behind them.

In other words, the scientifically recorded reality of my night's sleep bore no relationship at all to my subjective experience of it. I had had the impression of a long night of dreamless and undisturbed rest. In reality, the time from my first dropping off to my final waking up was a mere six hours thirty-two minutes, and during that period I had really slept for only five hours forty-nine minutes, including sixty-five minutes in REM. According to the computer, this gave me a 'sleep efficiency' of 89 per cent.

Statistically, this was about right for my age group, whose sleep efficiency averages 90 per cent. I was awake for longer than the average (11 per cent of the time instead of 8), spent less than average time in Stage 1 (2 per cent instead of 10), about average time in Stage 2 (56 per cent), far longer in deep sleep, Stages 3 and 4 (15 per cent instead of 3), and a little below average in REM (17 per cent instead of 23). There was just one very brief episode of 'movement time' and eight tiny 'minor arousals', which are scarcely more than muscular twitches. (Technically, a 'minor arousal' is defined as a burst of muscular activity that occupies at least 20 per cent of an 'epoch', or page of the graph; a burst of 50 per cent or more is called 'movement time'.) Together they amounted to less than one minute. (Each page is a third of a minute.) That meant that the computer rated the movement time and its percentage as zero. So at least my impression of having slept peacefully was justified.

But if I hadn't tossed and turned, I hadn't slept much, either. I was dismayed by the number of times I had apparently woken and I put it to Sharon that an insomniac's graph would not have looked much different from mine. Not true, she said. It was just a question of age: as you get older, you need less sleep; you spend progressively more time awake and in light sleep, less in deep sleep and REM. But that was not how it had felt and I have had enough bad nights in my time to know the difference.

I slept badly when I was young, woke often and was troubled by my dreams. Briefly, when I was around thirty and my life seemed to be coming apart in my hands, I had a period when I was unable to sleep more than a couple of hours each night. But that is a classic symptom of depression and thirty years later I was no longer depressed. Or rather, no longer clinically depressed. Instead, as I grew older I seemed to sleep better, more deeply, more gratefully each night. By the time I reached my middle fifties, I could hardly wait to go to bed at night and often found it hard to think of a good reason for getting up the next morning. Maybe that, too, was a symptom of depression. If so, it was a different kind of depression and one I had less trouble living with. Now, in my sixties, I find that what may once have been a symptom has settled into habit and I have given up making excuses for my partiality to sleep. The fact is, I am addicted to it, the way I'm addicted to coffee, and will take whatever is on offer: eight hours is fine and seven seems nothing like enough. I drop off quickly and usually remember nothing – not even my dreams – until the alarm buzzes. Of course, I don't wake altogether refreshed. After a certain age, someone has said, if you wake up without any aches and pains, it means you are dead. But at least I don't feel cheated. And that is precisely how I felt when I learned from the polygraph that my good night's sleep had in fact been an hour and a half shorter than usual, and for 11 per cent of the time, an astonishing forty-three minutes, I had been awake.

My first reaction was disbelief: I felt I'd slept well, the machines said I hadn't; one of us had to be wrong. Or perhaps we were both reporting accurately two quite different events and the problem with sleep research was the same as the problem with most literary biographies, even those of the recently dead: no matter how accurate the facts and painstaking the methods – all the survivors interviewed, the sources double-checked, the footnotes amazing – the results are always insidiously skewed. What is missing is everything that makes the writer's work his own: the constantly shifting give-and-take between him and the other people in his life, allied to the feel and the tone of a specific place at a specific time – Paris in the twenties, London in the sixties. What is missing, in other words, is how it felt to be that person in that world – all the details and overtones that are simply not available, whatever the goodwill and faultless research, to someone who wasn't there and can't make the necessary leap of imagination. That was also true in the sleep laboratory: with an event as subjective as sleep, the polygraph recording and the computer-generated information were bound to be partial, and leaps of imagination were not appropriate to graphs, print-outs and statistical analyses.

Yet I wasn't imagining how I had felt. A good night's sleep is restorative – among other reasons, Sharon explained, because during slow-wave sleep there are massive secretions of anabolic hormone that help tissue synthesis and regeneration – and when I woke I had felt restored. When I told Sharon I would have probably been feeling lousy if I'd known I'd had so little sleep, she said, 'We all wake more than we think we do.'

It was an answer that deepened the mystery instead of explaining it. After all, it is a curious kind of wakefulness which can occur without your being aware of it. Sharon and I seemed to be using the same ordinary words to mean utterly different things. So I looked up 'wakefulness' in *The Encyclopedia of Sleep and Sleep Disorders*:

A brain state that occurs in the absence of sleep in an otherwise

84

healthy individual. It is the state of being awake that is characterized by EEG wave patterns dominated by alpha rhythm, or electrocortical activity, between 8 Hz and 13 Hz. This alpha activity is most pronounced when the eyes are closed and the subject is relaxed . . . In addition to the characteristic alpha activity of wakefulness, there are also beta rhythms, which occur particularly with increased alertness, motor activity and in response to environmental stimuli. Wakefulness is often subdivided into quiet wakefulness, where an individual is resting in a relaxed condition, compared with a period of active wakefulness, when the individual is more alert and may be engaged in talking or other motor activities.

So now I knew. In Sharon's terms, most of the wakefulness I had experienced was not subjectively real; it was technical, a mere change of brain rhythm, a neurological event so brief that it registered as no more than a double vertical line on the computer graph. For the layman, the kind of waking that sets the pens of the polygraph jiggling is as 'paradoxical' as REM sleep seemed when it was first discovered.

That in itself was no surprise. It is one of the truisms of sleep research that many insomniacs, when wired up to a polygraph, will swear they never got a wink of sleep, although the machine registers a near-normal night's repose. It is also true that the brain remains almost as active during sleep as it is when awake. Earlier in this century, physiologists like Sherrington and Pavlov assumed that the purpose of sleep was to rest the brain as well as the body. This has now been shown to be untrue. In his brilliant study of sleep, *The Dreaming Brain*, Professor J. Allan Hobson writes:

When microelectrodes were inserted into the cerebral cortex . . . investigators . . . observed that as many neurons turned on as turned off during sleep, and that almost all the cells in the brain were spectacularly active during REM sleep. Clearly, a general theory of neural rest during sleep can be only partially correct and is particularly controverted.[1]

In other words, sleep itself is paradoxical, a condition in which none of the waking rules apply, including the rules about waking itself. Waking, dreaming and all the other mental events that take place while we sleep leave, at best, only a passing trace on the memory – a trace that usually vanishes unless you write it down straight away.[2] Mental life goes on in a pure culture, as it were, unconnected with the senses. It is often deeply tinged with emotion, but that, too, is in a pure culture; it only connects up with your waking life later, when you think about it – when you take it literally to heart.

And that is precisely the area that cannot, as yet, be measured in a laboratory. Sleep is a comparatively new field of research because it depends on a sophisticated technology that has been developed only recently, and is still developing. Neuroscientists now have extraordinarily refined techniques for recording what happens in the brain, when it is both awake and asleep, but there are still no precise methods for measuring subjective experience. Until there are, sleep researchers and laymen are going to have trouble understanding each other. 'He sleeps well,' wrote Francis Bacon, 'who knows not that he sleeps ill.' We laymen define wakefulness in terms of consciousness – of being awake to the fact that we are awake. Sharon and her colleagues define it as something else entirely.

From my experience in the sleep laboratory, I assumed that the something else was highly technical, something registered in microvolts and recorded on graph paper and computer print-outs. But when I asked Sharon, 'You mean sleep is nothing like we imagine it?' all she said was, 'It's very subjective.'

# 4

# DREAMING

*I dreamed that I seduced L.E. and believe me it took some doing and I do not understand the capricious lewdness of the sleeping mind.*

John Cheever, *Journals*

*The mind, everyone's mind, is forever unstill, is a continual restlessness like light, even in sleep, when the light is inside and not outside the skull.*

Harold Brodkey, 'Dying: An Update'

*The Sleep of Reason Breeds Monsters.*

Goya

## THE PHYSIOLOGY

*'I have only a bare working knowledge of the human brain but it's enough to make me proud to be an American. Your brain has a trillion neurons and every neuron has ten thousand little dendrites. The system of intercommunication is awe-inspiring. It's like a galaxy that you can hold in your hand, only more complex, more mysterious.'*

*'Why does this make you proud to be an American?'*

*'The infant's brain develops in response to stimuli. We still lead the world in stimuli.'*

Don DeLillo, *White Noise*

## 1 The Discovery of REM Sleep

'It's all very subjective' is a variation on a truth first formulated by Heraclitus: 'For the waking there is one common world only; but when asleep, each man turns to his own private world.' For the next two and a half thousand years, mankind's attitude to the world of sleep stopped at Heraclitus: it was death's image, an impenetrable mystery, approachable only through the interpretation of dreams, which has been a common pursuit at least since the beginnings of literature (The first significant poem, *The Epic of Gilgamesh*, written in Assyrian in the third millennium BC, is punctuated by meaningful dreams that help the plot along.) The scientific investigation of this private world – sleep research and the neurophysiology of the brain – has taken off only in the last half century.

The discovery of REM sleep in 1953 was a turning point, much like the discovery of DNA in the same year. Rapid eye movement, of course, had been there to be seen by anyone who ever watched a sleeping dog, eyes rolling, feet twitching, as it chased a dream rabbit. There is even a passing reference to REM in the first great work of popular science, Lucretius's poem *De Rerum Natura*. But observation, as scientists say, is always theory-driven – you only see what you are looking for – and nobody had ever focused on the phenomenon or thought about what it meant.

The breakthrough was made by Eugene Aserinsky, a graduate student who had never graduated, a drop-out *avant la lettre*; he had dropped out of college without a degree, served in the Army, dropped out of dental school and dropped out of social work before he found his way to the University of Chicago, where he was taken in – 'like a stray cat', he has said – by Nathaniel Kleitman, one of the founders of sleep research.

Aserinsky had noticed that the eyes move during sleep and he wanted to study the physiology of this curious phenomenon; he was interested, that is, in the *how*, not the *why* of what was eventually called REM sleep. It was an idea no one else had bothered with, and to study it he resurrected a junked electroencephalograph from the university's basement and wired up one of his eight-year-old son's eyes while the child slept. But the broken-down machine went on breaking down, no matter how often Aserinsky fixed it, and even when it seemed to be running properly, recording the slow waves of the boy's rolling eye movements, its pens intermittently went wild, tracing jagged peaks and troughs similar to those of the waking brain. Naturally, Aserinsky assumed the machine was malfunctioning, so he double-checked it by wiring up his son's other eye with a second EEG in tandem with the first. When he still got the same improbable results, he realised that he might have stumbled on a significant discovery.

The next question was inevitable but tricky: what was happening in his son's sleeping brain that made the pens go wild? But that involved a step from physiological change to mental event, and Aserinsky took it reluctantly since it contradicted everything that was then thought to be true about the restorative nature of sleep. Within five years of publishing their original article, however, Aserinsky and Kleitman, along with another distinguished sleep researcher, William C. Dement, had established beyond doubt that there was a connection between REM sleep and dreaming. They repeated Aserinsky's experiment 343 times in carefully controlled laboratory conditions and discovered that when sleepers were woken while the polysomnograph was registering Rapid Eye Movement sleep, between 80 and 95 per cent of them reported vivid dreams, compared with only 6.9 per cent of those woken from non-REM sleep.

The discovery said less about dreaming than about sleep and the way the sleeping brain behaves. It put paid once and for all to what had seemed the self-evident truth that sleep rests the brain just as it rests the body. Until the discovery of REM sleep, physiologists had believed that consciousness, in Charles Sherrington's beautiful image, was a shuttle-loom bright with the twinkling lights of neuronal activity which gradually extinguish during sleep until 'the great knotted headpiece of the whole sleeping system lies for the most part dark. Occasionally at places in it lighted points flash or move but soon subside.'[1] It seemed a perfect metaphor for the body's stillness and the mind's oblivion, but now experimental evidence had proved Sherrington wrong: for four or five relatively lengthy periods every night, all the lights switch back on and the brain is as active as it is while awake. But instead of waking, the sleeper dreams.

Like Lucretius's passing observation of Rapid Eye Movement, the idea that mental life is continuous in all stages of sleep had already been formulated, without benefit of neuroscience, in Diderot's *Encyclopedia*:

Dreams occupy us during sleep, and when a dream comes to us, we emerge from the kind of total lethargy into which deep sleep had plunged us, and perceive a sequence of images which are more or less well-defined, depending on the intensity of the dream; this is the popular conception of dreaming. We can only be said to be dreaming when we become conscious of these images, when these images imprint themselves on our memories and we are able to say we have had such and such a dream, or at least that we have been dreaming. But, in the strictest sense, we are dreaming all the time, that is to say that as soon as sleep has taken possession of our mental operations, the mind is subject to an uninterrupted series of representations and perceptions; but sometimes they are so confused or so dimly registered, that they do not leave the slightest trace, and this is in fact what we call 'deep sleep'; but we would be wrong to regard it as a total absence of any sort of perception, as complete mental inertia.[2]

This was a revolutionary idea, brilliantly perceptive and original, but so far ahead of its time that it was virtually ignored. Diderot had nothing to go on but his own insights into his own experience and it was another two hundred years before there were scientific instruments and techniques to show that he had guessed right. Once started, however, the technology developed fast.

The basic sleep research machine, the polysomnograph (the EEG, EOG, EMG), is a kind of robot laboratory assistant, a tireless observer you plug into the wall, and in terms of brain research it is a crude device. The best the EEG can do is measure general electrical activity from the brain's surface. To understand the true working of the brain something far more accurate and sophisticated was needed. Microelectrodes, which began to be developed in the same year as the discovery of REM sleep, were eventually refined until they became instruments precise and sensitive enough to enable scientists to communicate directly with individual brain cells. Allan Hobson has called this

> the neurobiological equivalent of the astronomer's ability to discern individual celestial bodies, and is analogous to the recognition, in physics, of the atom as an essential organizational element of matter. Neurobiology, and the study of the relation of brain to mind, had, for want of such an analytic technique, lagged far behind the other physical sciences. But now, after thirty years of experience, we can begin to understand how brain activity may be organized.[3]

Using microelectrodes, neurophysiologists began to map the universe within the head, and also to understand the physiology of sleep.

On the simplest level, for instance, charting the neurons in the brain demonstrated in detail and beyond doubt that Aserinsky had got it right with his beat-up EEG: a man sleeps in a pitch-dark room, eyes shut tight, muscles paralysed, a very picture of death; but in his dreams he is busily up and about; he sees people and goes places, he runs, flies, talks, weeps, makes love, and all without stirring a muscle, because the brain cells that have to do with seeing and moving are as vividly active in REM sleep as they are when he is going about his business by day. (He rarely tastes or smells things, since the taste and olfactory neurons are quiescent.) In other words, 'paradoxical' sleep is truly paradoxical.

Sleep research has come a long way since Aserinsky, Kleitman and Dement, and the theories that go with it are a great deal more sophisticated and comprehensive. Allan Hobson, of the Harvard Medical School, is one of the key, and most controversial, players in contemporary sleep research and the cluttered walls of his office at the Massachusetts Mental Health Center are hung with tropies of his research. They look like framed examples of computer-generated abstract art – brightly coloured, intricate and dramatic. In fact, they are enormously magnified photographs of brain cells and synapses. The infinitely small elements that go to make up the darkness of the brain are now open to scientific inspection.

Hobson himself is a rangy, balding and energetic man, fiercely argumentative and well informed. Unlike many of his colleagues, he has read a great deal of Freud and has a highly competitive love-hate relationship with the great man. Too competitive, perhaps. Although *The Dreaming Brain*, Hobson's history of the neurobiology of dreaming and exposition of his own theories, is stylishly written and powerfully argued, he wastes a disproportionate amount of ammunition blazing away at early theories of Freud which all but a handful of unreconstructed classical Freudians aban-doned years ago. But that, as he explained it to me, is because his goal is much the same as Freud's: 'a codified scientific theory', he called it, based on the belief that 'the brain never does anything without trying to find out what meaning means'.

As part of that quest, Hobson and his colleagues have developed a model for the neurophysiology of dreams. They have, for example, located clusters of REM-on and REM-off cells in the brainstem – the reticular neurons in the pontine giant cell and the aminergic neurons in the locus ceruleus, respectively – and have plotted their interaction over time in a graph with curves which Hobson, whose aesthetic taste is unusually eclectic, called 'very beautiful'. The REM-on cells do their work by releasing a chemical called acetylcholine and Hobson has triggered artificial dreams by injecting volunteers intravenously, while they sleep, with a substance that imitates acetylcholine. For a week or more, their REM sleep increased by 300 per cent. 'I think', he told me, 'we've found the dream nerve.' The REM-off cells, however, have so far proved to be less amenable to his experiments and less predictable in their behaviour. Among his colleagues, the jury is still out on Hobson's model of the dreaming brain.

What is not in dispute is the fact that the microelectrode was the key to exploring what the neuroscientist Gerald Edelman has called 'the most complicated material object in the known universe'.[4] The human brain weighs a mere three to four pounds, but it contains as many neurons as there are stars in the Milky Way – about one hundred billion of them. Each neuron is made up of a neuronal cell body, or soma, from which emanate a spider's web of dendrites and axons; dendrites collect information, axons convey it. The neurons generate their own energy, produce their own signals and communicate with each other through chemicals, called neurotransmitters, which are released from the endings of their axons by electrical signals, called action potentials. The communication takes place at cell-to-cell junctions called synapses. In the cerebral cortex alone – the corrugated sheet that covers the dome and sides of the head and is the seat of the higher brain functions, like speech and thought and complex movement – there are about ten billion neurons. But there are also about one million billion synapses. 'If you were to count them, one connection (or synapse) per second,' writes Edelman, 'you would finish counting some thirty-two million years after you began.' In other words, each of the ten billion neurons of the cerebral cortex communicates simultaneously with at least ten thousand of its neighbours, and each neuron generates between one hundred and three hundred messages a second, continually, day and night.

Hobson describes this activity as a nightmare of teenage chatter: 'It is as if each person in the world were in constant and simultaneous telephonic communication with ten thousand other people!' For the layman, this is like the black holes in space that astrophysicists talk about; it describes an order of complexity beyond comprehension, unfathomable even in the age of super-computers. But there is a crucial difference: black holes are theoretical constructions, which may or may not exist somewhere out there in the far reaches of the universe. The brain, however, is right there behind the eyes. 'There is much promise / in the circumstance / that so many people have heads', wrote the Czech poet and scientist, Miroslav Holub. Much promise perhaps, but also great mystery and frustration in the fact that what goes on inside the head is as strange and baffling as what goes on in remote corners of remote galaxies.

## 2 The Trouble with Consciousness

*The human being . . . is a book reading itself.*

P. N. Furbank on Diderot

The neuroscientists themselves are not immune to the mysteriousness of what they have discovered, but their understandable reaction is to push the argument one step further and claim they have unlocked one of the ultimate secrets. According to Hobson, the product of this perpetual and self-generated communication of brain cell with brain cell, which continues whether or not there is input from the external world, is consciousness itself:

> We know that the internal communication from nerve cell to nerve cell is a continuous process: night and day it goes on and on and on. And we know that this ongoing nervous activity is spontaneous: it changes in relation to signals from the external world, coding them in its own way into its own language. But it is not created by – nor is it dependent upon – external inputs. And we know that during sleep the ratio of external to internal signaling changes; during dream sleep, there is just as much activity going on within the system as there is during waking. In other words, during dreams the system is literally talking to itself . . . this incessant activity all proceeds silently, with only relatively peaceful consciousness as its product. The music of these spheres from the galaxy within our head is our consciousness. Consciousness is the continuous subjective awareness of the activity of billions of cells firing at many times a second, communicating instantaneously with tens of thousands of their neighbors. And the organization of this symphony of activity is such that it is sometimes externally oriented (during waking),

sometimes oblivious to the outside world (during sleep), and sometimes so remarkably aware of itself (during dreams) that it recreates the external world in its own image.[5]

This is eloquent and persuasive, particularly as a description of the mechanics of dreaming. But it is not strictly logical and this illogicality is central to the limitations of Hobson's understanding of the mind. The problem is not in his evocative description of the working brain but in his conclusion: 'Consciousness is the continuous *subjective* awareness of the activity of billions of cells firing at many times a second.' Either this is a tautology – if 'subjectivity' is what he is trying to define – or he is saying that consciousness is created by those billions of cells ceaselessly communicating with each other – which may well be true but has not yet been scientifically proved. At the present time, all that scientists know for sure is that 'subjective awareness' is an infinitely intricate amalgam of the mental and physical, internal and external. But what it most assuredly is *not* – in my experience, at least – is an awareness of the neurons firing in the brain. Sometimes, of course, the reverse seems to be true: at a certain low point in middle age when your memory begins to fail, there are quiet moments when you imagine you can hear the brain cells snuffing out. But, even with the wildest leap of the imagination, there is no moment at all when you can ever hear them firing. As a scientist, however, Hobson knows what is happening in the brain; he has observed the neurons firing in laboratory experiments and has plotted the results. But that is not the same as proving a connection between neuronal activity and the consciousness of reality. Understanding the physiology of the brain, even the physiology of dreaming, is different from understanding the mind.

Perhaps Hobson prefers to ignore this because, despite all the evidence to the contrary – his intellectual passion and artistic taste – he belongs to the hard-headed tradition of scientific materialism and has the appropriate hidden agenda: to eliminate abstractions and mystification from his descriptions of how we perceive the world. Naturally, he will have nothing to do with the concept of 'soul' as a spiritual entity and, covertly, he also seems to be trying to dispense with the soul in its contemporary disguise – the psyche. He wants a mind that he can measure and test and describe scientifically, a mind that is also a thing. Because dreaming is a mental event and the activity of the dreaming brain seems almost indistinguishable from that of the waking brain, he concludes that 'brain' and 'mind' are essentially one and the same, a physical entity he calls the 'brain-mind': 'Our brain-mind has a dynamic life of its own with which it interacts with the external world. Thus our psyche is *materialized*, and thus our brain is *animated*.'[6]

Not all Hobson's colleagues would agree. The brain may be 'the most complicated material object in the known universe', and neuroscience may have gone a long way towards describing how it works and mapping out the ways in which its various regions interconnect, but complexity itself is still not an adequate explanation of mind. The case for a wider view has been put best by another Harvard professor, the neurobiologist Gerald D. Fischbach:

There is more to mind than consciousness or the cerebral cortex. Urges, moods, desires and subconscious forms of learning are mental phenomena in the broad view. We are not zombies. Affect depends on the function of neurons in the same manner as does conscious thought . . . The liver probably contains 100 million cells, but 1,000 livers do not add up to a rich inner life.[7]

Research into the physiology of the brain, then, has not yet solved the mystery of mind or even consciousness. It has, however, undermined the traditional view of the brain as a 'passive reflex' machine, capable only of responding to the external world and not able to generate its own states. When William James talked about 'the stream of consciousness' he sounded as though he were describing something very similar to Hobson's neuronal telephone exchange; in fact, he was describing the opposite process. For James, 'the stream of consciousness' meant the brain states which are generated by the flow of *external* stimuli through the nervous system and which serve as representations of *external* reality. Neuroscientists now believe that the brain is essentially a closed system – 'a closed loop' – which functions happily whether or not there is any input from the world outside.

This means that although waking and dreaming seem to be worlds apart, they are uncannily alike in terms of brain activity. According to a recent summary of the state of the art in current brain research, wakefulness and REM sleep are almost indistinguishable. Both are 'intrinsic brain functions', similar in terms of how the brain works – its electrophysiology – differing only in terms of the material it is working on – sensory input when awake, memories when asleep:

REM sleep can be considered as a modified attentive state in which attention is turned away from the sensory input, towards memories . . . wakefulness is nothing other than a dreamlike state modulated by the constraints produced by specific sensory inputs.[8]

Because this comes from an article which is learned, technical and authoritative, the last sentence is confusing. To the uninitiated, the idea that 'wakefulness is nothing other than a dreamlike state' constrained by external reality reads like a scientific excuse for the highly unscientific belief that life itself is a dream – shadows thrown by an ideal reality on the walls of Plato's cave, an illusion we wake from. On a more technical level, a British psychoanalyst might take it as a vindication of his belief that waking consciousness is inextricably mixed with fantasy, hallucination and dream, and is constantly shifting between them.

In practice, however, neuroscientists distinguish carefully between the different ways in which the mind works – its formal rules of operation – in dreaming and waking. According to Hobson, this difference can be explained in terms of neurophysiology: the chemically specific neurons that are thought to be important to attention, learning and memory go down to 50 per cent in non-REM sleep and turn off completely in REM sleep. The brain then has to cope with full activity without the instruments it needs to analyse this chaos, compare it with previous experience and put it in order.

It sounds very like 'the stream of consciousness' as the layman understands it: the disjointed mental chatter of Molly Bloom's monologue in *Ulysses*, the white noise the mind makes when it wanders. This is not the same as daydreaming or fantasising, although daydreams and fantasies are part of it. But so, too, are memories, partially registered inputs from the senses, verbal waste-disposal, half-remembered snatches of music and song – the whole conflicting, drifting background of mental stuff that clears only in those moments when you concentrate.

Explaining the neurophysiology of this white noise, however, is not necessarily – or not yet – the same as solving the problem of subjectivity, although that does not seem to have deterred some brain scientists from jumping to conclusions. There is little noticeable difference between Hobson's version of consciousness – as 'the subjective awareness' of billions of nerve cells, each communicating simultaneously with thousands of its neighbours – and the conclusions reached by Professors R. R. Llinás and D. Paré in their learned analysis of the electrophysiology of wakefulness and dreaming. Both states, they suggest, share the same fundamental mechanism: a ceaseless dialogue between the cerebral cortex, the seat of vision and higher thought, and the thalamus, a central brain structure that contains nuclei that connect sensory and other brain signals to the cortex. They describe this 'inner talking' in great technical detail and then conclude:

> if consciousness is a product of thalamocortical activity, *it is the dialogue between the thalamus and the cortex that generates subjectivity*.

The italics are theirs and, within their own terms, the note of triumph is justified; the research is subtle, wide-ranging and meticulous, and their synthesis of it is invigorating even to the layman. But the implication that they have solved a deep philosophical problem that has puzzled thinkers at least since the beginnings of classical philosophy is plainly not true. To show that the brain is a closed-loop system, which generates its own energy and continually communicates with itself, regardless of the external world, is only a preliminary step in understanding subjectivity – necessary, of course, but still a long way from being sufficient.

Philosophically, the problem of subjectivity – of the privacy of the mind – is not a scientific problem at all. It is a conceptual problem, larger, different and more manifold than scientists allow, and the answers to it have nothing to do with neurophysiology. For philosophers, subjectivity is, among other things, an epistemological problem, a question of knowledge and possession, and it arises in its basic, simplest form with the sensations – pain and pleasure, hot and cold. Philosophers say, for example, that when you feel pain you know it with utter certainty; you alone are the final authority on whether or not something hurts. But no matter how great my empathy or subtle my intuitions, *my* knowledge of *your* pain is quite different from yours and radically open to doubt. Even the most skilled, dedicated and imaginative torturer can only surmise what his victim feels; he himself can never suffer the same pain in the same way because he himself can never have his victim's own sensations. In other words, the world of the mind is private and each individual has a privileged access to it that no one else possesses. The scientist with his microelectrodes may eventually be able to detect with some certainty the activation of the neurons that cause pain, but the epistemological problem of pain – knowing what that particular pain feels like to someone else – can only be solved by *having* the other person's pain, and that, in principle, cannot be done. This is the core of the philosophical problem of subjectivity, and when the neurophysiologists describe how the brain works physically they are solving a different kind of problem based on a different kind of intellectual activity.

Gerald Edelman, who believes that 'consciousness arose in the material order' and that a science of the mind is possible only if it is based on biology, has discussed this problem in terms of what he calls 'qualia':

> Qualia constitute the collection of personal or subjective experiences, feelings, and sensations that accompany awareness. They are phenomenal states – 'how things seem to us' as human beings. For example, the 'redness' of a red object is a quale. Qualia are discriminable parts of a mental scene that nonetheless has an overall unity . . . Given the fact that qualia are experienced directly only by single individuals, our methodological difficulty becomes obvious. *We cannot construct a phenomenal psychology that can be shared in the same way as a physics can be shared.* What is directly experienced as qualia by one individual cannot be fully shared by another individual as an observer. An individual can report his or her experience to an observer, but that report must always be partial, imprecise, and relative to his or her personal context . . . phenomenal experience is a first–person matter.[9]

D. H. Lawrence said much the same in his poem 'Red Geranium and Godly Mignonette', although he put it in racier language:

> Imagine that any mind ever *thought* a red geranium!
> As if the redness of a red geranium could be anything but a sensual experience,
> and as if sensual experience could take place before there were any senses.
> We know that even God could not imagine the redness of a red geranium
> nor the smell of mignonette
> when geraniums were not, and mignonette neither.
> You can't imagine the Holy Ghost sniffing at cherry-pie heliotrope.

Or the Most High, during the coal age, cudgelling his mighty
    brains
even if he had any brains: straining his mighty mind
to think, among the moss and mud of lizards and mastodons
to think out, in the abstract, when all was twilit green and muddy:
'Now there shall be tum-tiddly-um, and tum-tiddly-um,
hey-presto! scarlet geranium!'

We know it couldn't be done . . .

However you put it, subjective experience, like sensual
experience, is unique and ultimately unsharable. To add to the
problem, brains, too, are unique, right down to their finest
microscopic details: each neuron and its relationship to every
other neuron is different, even in identical twins and genetic-
ally identical animals. Moreover, as Edelman describes it,
brain development and mental activity are themselves as
unique and as infinitely complex as the brain itself:

> It begins with molecules and goes on to genes. It involves vast
> numbers of cells with electrical activity and chemical diversity, an
> enormously intricate anatomy of blobs and sheets linked in rich
> ways, and maps that receive signals from sensory input and send
> signals to motor output. These structures undergo continual
> electrical change, driving and being driven by animal movement.
> This movement is itself conditioned by animal shape and pattern,
> leading to behavior. Some of this behavior involves communi-
> cation with an animal's memory, which is in turn affected by its
> own products.[10]

Quite simply, mind and body are inextricably interconnected at every level, from the most basic to the most
sophisticated; the brain is not just communicating with itself,
it is also involved in a constant and infinitely complex

interchange with the body, the memory and the external world in which they all exist.

Presumably, there is little in any of this that Allan Hobson would argue with, yet somehow his neurophysiological account of subjectivity leaves out this larger dimension in which mind and body and the external world react together, shifting, changing, modifying, adapting each to each, and creating in their subtle dance the 'strange loops' which the computer scientist Douglas Hofstadter described so eloquently in his book on the mysterious, paradoxical ways in which the mind works, *Gödel, Escher, Bach*. And strange loops are not only more intricate, they are also different in essence from the closed-loop model of the brain talking to itself.

A simple example: Hobson says of sleep, 'Nature is much too economical to waste hours of biological time doing nothing but simply saving energy and idling the brain.' He also points out that, for the brain, sleep is not rest; even at the deepest level of sleep – Stage 4 – there is only a 5–10 per cent decrease in neuronal activity in the brain. So what is the brain doing during sleep? Hobson's answer is that 'a night of sleep is as much preparation for the subsequent day's activity as recovery from that of the previous day'. More precisely, during REM sleep a selected group of neurons – those essential to learning, attention and memory – are resting. By being shut off electrically, though not metabolically, they can top themselves up with whatever they need to equip the rest of the brain with the chemicals necessary to the most important faculties in the waking state. And that, he says, is how it feels in the morning: you can sense the cognitive gain; you are intellectually sharper when you wake, as well as more energetic. To prove this, he set up experiments to show that sleep produces a net gain in the faculty of attention.

But the reverse is also true: sleep may refresh the brain cells, but it also refreshes the body, and the body itself is deeply implicated in our sense of self. 'The shape of an animal's body is as important to the functioning and evolution of its brain as the shape and functioning of the brain are to the behavior of that body,' says Edelman. Hobbes said much the same in *Leviathan*: 'That which is not body is nothing and nowhere.' So did Blake in *The Marriage of Heaven and Hell*, although he put it differently:

> How do you know but that ev'ry Bird that cuts the airy way,
> Is an immense World of Delight, clos'd by your senses five?

Delight, that spiritual grace, is a bodily condition, a pleasure of the senses as well as impalpable happiness. For Blake, body and spirit were as much one as brain and mind are for Hobson.

Blake's language may be imprecise scientifically, but in terms of how we experience the world it seems faultless. On the most elementary level, most people function better intellectually when they feel in good shape physically; they think more clearly when they are healthy and fit. But this is not a fact academics and intellectuals necessarily take into account, since they tend to assume that everything begins and ends in the head. When D. H. Lawrence, whose sensibility was closer to Blake's than to Hobson's, heard someone enthusing about the lucidity of Bertrand Russell's mind, he snapped irritably, 'Have you seen him in a bathing dress? Poor Bertie Russell! He is all Disembodied Mind.'

A second simple point: however busily the mind-brain functions independently of the outside world, consciousness itself is not an isolated phenomenon. The word itself derives from the Latin 'knowing something with others', and there is now good scientific research which indicates that its etymology is justified. Child developmentalists, for example, have shown that, although babies are born with astonishingly sophisticated mental equipment already in place – they can think abstractly and have a concept of three-dimensionality – an infant's sense of its self develops through shared experience with other people; 'inter-subjectivity', as they say, swiftly changes into 'intra-subjectivity'.[11] In other words, consciousness is a two-way street; you can't have 'self' without 'the other'.

You also can't have love and marriage, hatred, ambition, loyalty, or any of the other concepts which form the substratum of our consciousness of the self and dictate how we act in the world. You can't, in fact, even have language, since language is intentional, a two-person activity, a communication with someone else, even if that someone is no more substantial than an imagined, interior listener.

A philosopher has suggested that maybe we think of 'mind' as a thing because we use a noun to describe it, whereas in fact mind is the way we live our lives, or what we live our lives through. Behind the neurophysiologists' idea of the mind-brain as a material entity is, I suspect, the shadowy belief that, sooner or later, it may be possible to localise love, loyalty and the rest in the neuronal circuits of the brain. They may, just conceivably, be right; as Blake also wrote, 'What is now proved was once only imagined.' But those circuits, if they exist, are likely to be infinitely more sophisticated, both in themselves and in the way they operate, than anything the closed-loop model of the brain's activity allows for. In the meantime, the understanding of how the brain communicates with itself and how dreams are switched on and off, and the discovery that, in terms of brain activity, waking and dreaming are profoundly similar states, are startling enough concepts to be getting on with.

# THE INTERPRETATION OF DREAMS

*There seems to be something in dream images that has a certain resemblance to the signs of a language, as a series of marks on paper or sand might have. There might be no mark which we recognised as a conventional sign in any alphabet we knew, and yet we might have a strong feeling that they must be a language of some sort, that they mean something.*

Ludwig Wittgenstein

*I've always had access to other worlds. We all do because we all dream. What I don't have access to is myself.*

Leonora Carrington, Surrealist painter

## 1 Artemidorus and the Ancient World

The idea that the waking brain and the dreaming brain behave in much the same way goes against common sense and common experience, as well as against the sturdy belief, much admired by poets, in sleep as a release and a restorer: Sir Philip Sydney's 'certain knot of peace', Shakespeare's 'innocent sleep, /Sleep that knits up the ravell'd sleave of care', Keats's 'soft embalmer of the still midnight! / Shutting, with careful fingers and benign, / Our gloom-pleased eyes'. It also contradicts the equally enduring belief that there is only a fine line between dreaming and madness:

> The five cardinal characteristics of dream mentation may also be seen in the hallucinations, disorientations, bizarre thoughts, delusions, and amnesias of patients with mental illness. These mental symptoms collectively constitute delirium, dementia, and psychosis. Thus, were it not for the fact that we are asleep when they occur, we would be obliged to say that our dreams are formally psychotic and that we are all, during dreaming, formally delirious and demented . . . Dreaming could thus be the mental product of the same *kind* of psychological process that is deranged in mental illness . . . since all of the major signs of mental illness can be imitated by normal minds in the normal state of dreaming. The study of dreams is the study of a model of mental illness. [12]

Those are Allan Hobson's clinical variations on a traditional theme, but Hobson is just one of many. Freud listed some of the others in *The Interpretation of Dreams*: 'The madman is a waking dreamer' (Kant); 'Insanity is a dream dreamt while all the senses are awake' (Kraus); 'Dreams are a brief madness, madness a long dream' (Schopenhauer); 'We ourselves, in fact, can experience in dreams almost all the phenomena to be met with in insane asylums' (Wundt). Over the centuries, the craziness of dreams has been a permanent source of uneasiness for everyone who has ever woken in a sweat and thought about where he has just been in his dreams and what he has been doing.

Dickens expressed this unease best, perhaps because he was fascinated by that shadowy area where madness enters daily life and becomes eccentricity. He was also fascinated by night and the life that goes on under the cover of darkness. On one of his nocturnal rambles through London he found himself outside the Bethlehem Insane Asylum:

> Are not the sane and the insane equal at night as the sane lie a dreaming? Are not all of us outside this Hospital who dream, more or less in the condition of those inside it, every night of our lives? . . . Do we not nightly jumble events and personages and times and places, as these do daily? Are we not sometimes vexed by our own sleeping inconsistencies, and do we not vexedly try to account for them or excuse them, just as these do sometimes in respect of their waking delusions? Said an afflicted man to me, when I was last in a hospital like this, 'Sir, I can frequently fly.' I was half ashamed to reflect that so could I – by night . . . I wonder that the great master who knew everything, when he called Sleep the death of each day's life, did not call Dreams the insanity of each day's sanity.[13]

There is not much difference between Dickens's premonition of madness as a close companion we visit secretly every night and Freud's conception of the psychopathology of everyday life, his understanding of the way the irrational, the uncomprehended and the unexpected intrude into daytime behaviour. The real difference is one of emphasis: for Dickens, it was a passing insight; for Freud, it was the basis of his life's work.

Being mad means living in a closed, hallucinatory world so powerful that reality simply cannot get through, and that is precisely how the dreamer feels in the grip of his dream. But the dreamer wakes and is left with the irredeemable strangeness of what, in his dreams, had seemed perfectly rational. The utter discontinuity between the two worlds – the familiar world the waking dreamer opens his eyes to and the distorted, disorientated fantasy land of dreams, populated by strange and vivid presences, where time implodes and impossible events seem perfectly normal – has been a perpetual source of trouble for as long as people have been telling their dreams. Shakespeare's proposition that 'The lunatic, the lover and the poet/Are of imagination all compact' ruffles nobody's feathers because nobody takes the lover or the poet seriously. But the idea that sleep is everyman's gateway to madness is altogether harder to live with.

Hence the fascination with dreams and the urge to make sense of them, both of which seem to be as old as mankind. There are interpretations of dreams in fragments of papyri dating from the second millennium BC and in Assyrian cuneiform; there was even a book called *The Interpretation of Dreams* seven centuries before Freud wrote his. When Artemidorus of Dalis compiled his *Oneirocritica* in the second century AD, he gathered his material from the whole Mediterranean basin – Greece, North Africa, the Middle East – where dream-interpretation was a full-blown art, a sub-division of both soothsaying and medicine which, then as now, were prestigious, lucrative professions, swollen with their own mystery. Freud described the typical procedure in a footnote to his own dream book:

> In Greece there were dream oracles, which were regularly visited by patients in search of recovery. A sick man would enter the temple of Apollo or Aesculapius, would perform various ceremonies there, would be purified by lustration, massage and incense, and then, in a state of exaltation, would be stretched on the skin of a lamb that had been sacrificed. He would then fall asleep and would dream of the remedies for his illness. These would be revealed to him either in their natural form or in

symbols and pictures which would afterwards be interpreted by the priests.[14]

That sounds much like a modern health farm, complete with swimming pool, gymnasium, massage, aromatherapy, controlled diet and counselling. It has nothing at all to do with psychoanalysis for the simple reason that, in ancient times, dreams were not considered to be personal, perhaps because the personal life counted for very little in rigidly hierarchical religious societies. Instead, dreams were messages from the gods; their interpretation was the business of priests and the dreamer was merely a vehicle, a channel for supernatural forces that – officially – had nothing much to do with him. 'The Greeks never spoke of "having" a dream, but of "seeing" one,' writes Liam Hudson, 'and dreams were said not only to "visit" the dreamer but to "stand over" him.'[15] They were impersonal presences, beyond his control.

That did not lessen the mystery of sleep and its impalpable world within the perceived world, differently organised and with a logic that only sporadically obeyed that of waking life. On the contrary, it seemed to deepen it. The ancient belief in dreams as messages from the gods was so universal and profound that it makes the myths of creation seem like an upside-down way of explaining the mystery of dreams: instead of the gods inventing mankind in their image, man invented the gods in the image of his dreams in order to account for the strangeness of the sleeping world. Like dreams, the gods were not restrained by any of the rules of waking life, physical or moral; they could change at will into swans, bulls, showers of gold or pillars of fire; they could put a girdle about the earth in forty minutes, strike sinners dead with bolts of lightning, speak in voices of thunder and erupt, raging, from volcanoes. Yes, despite all their bewildering transformations, they remained eerily familiar with our inner thoughts and desires.

They could also read the book of the future. Since dreams were messages from the gods, then dreams were prophetic. Consequently, dream interpretation, with its mysteries, its rites, its elaborate symbolism, was considered a kind of high-toned fortune-telling, catering for the same yearnings and superstitions as astrology does now.

That did not mean that ancient dreaming was any less erotically charged or perverse than modern dreams or that the interpreters failed to notice this. Artemidorus, for example, devotes an eloquent section of his book to the interpretation of dreams of incest in all its possible variations: what it means when the dreamer (usually male) sleeps with his son, his daughter, his mother, his father. Each category is then subdivided into age and circumstance: whether the child is under five, under ten, or grown-up, whether the mother or father is living or dead, and so on. For Artemidorus, however, incest and all the other forms of sexual perversion were not in themselves interesting. Instead, they were ways of assuaging a different but equally perennial lust, the lust for fortune in every sense – for riches, luck and what the future holds in store:

To possess a son who is not yet five years old signifies, I have observed, the child's death. That the dream should have this meaning is quite understandable, since the small child will be corrupted and we call corruption 'death'. But if the child is more than five years old but less than ten, he will be sick and the dreamer will be involved in some disgrace as the result of some thoughtless undertaking. The child, because he has been possessed while he is still too young, will suffer pain and, in this way, will be sick. The dreamer will be disgraced because of his foolishness . . .

But if the son is more than a child, it has the following meaning. If the father is poor, he will send his son away to school and pay his expenses, and will strain off his resources into him in this way. If a rich man has this dream, he will give and transfer to his son considerable property, and in this way spend part of his resources on him.

To have sexual intercourse with one's son, if he is already a grown man and living abroad, is auspicious. For the dream signifies that they will be reunited and live with one another . . . But if the son is not far away and is living with his father, it is inauspicious. For they must separate because intercourse generally takes place between men when they are not face to face . . .

If [the daughter] is ready for marriage, she will enter her husband's house and the dreamer will furnish a dowry and spend his substance on his daughter in this way . . . It is good for a poor man to have sexual intercourse with a rich daughter. For he will receive great assistance from his daughter and, in this way, take pleasure of her. [16]

Artemidorus translates sex, as he translates almost everything else in dreams, into terms of fortune – into money and luck, getting and spending. And perhaps this was typical of the ancient world, since in any poor or unequal society money is usually sexier than sex; *les petits plaisirs des pauvres* are freely available to everyone, but wealth generates an erotic power all of its own.

It was also typical of the era that Artemidorus should have

taken incest and child-abuse as a matter of course. He assumes these things happen – in waking life as commonly as in dreams is the implication – but they don't mean a great deal to him, at least in terms of how the world is ordered and the wheel of fortune turns. For Artemidorus and his readers, the stuff of dreams mattered much less than the spin the interpreter put on them in terms of wealth and worldly happiness.

This, for example, is how Artemidorus dealt with the cornerstone of Freudian psychology: copulating with one's mother is 'auspicious', he says, providing the mother is living and the copulation takes place in the 'natural' way, face-to-face, 'because we ordinarily call a person's trade his "mother", and what else would having intercourse with her mean if not to be occupied with and earn one's living from one's art?' In other words, like a proto-Marxist interpreting history, he was not looking at what the dreams said about the dreamer or his inner life, but at what they could be made to say about economics and social power.

There was nothing original about any of this. Artemidorus did not invent a technique of dream interpretation, he simply collected and codified the received wisdom about how these troublesome phenomena should be dealt with: optimistically and with great care not to give offence to the dreamer. And these same rules applied even to the bad dreams that heralded great disasters, such as the assassination of Julius Caesar. According to Suetonius, 'When on the following night, much to his dismay, [Caesar] had a dream of raping his own mother, the soothsayers greatly encouraged him by their interpretation of it: namely, that he was destined to conquer the earth, our Universal Mother.'[17] In Shakespeare's *Julius Caesar*, this premonitory incestuous dream is cleaned up for public consumption. Caesar decides to stay home on the fatal day because his wife, Calphurnia, has dreamt that she saw his statue spouting blood, while smiling Romans bathed their hands in the gore. He is dissuaded by the smooth-talking Decius:

> This dream is all amiss interpreted;
> It was a vision fair and fortunate:
> You statue spouting blood in many pipes,
> In which so many smiling Romans bath'd,
> Signifies that from you great Rome shall suck
> Reviving blood, and that great men shall press
> For tinctures, stains, relics, and cognizance.
> This by Calphurnia's dream is signified.

Shakespeare may have Bowdlerised his sources, but the effect is the same: the interpretation of dreams, old-style, was governed by what was acceptable and convenient to the dreamer.

This anodyne optimism, apparently, was what the audience wanted at the time, and also what they continued to want. The *Oneirocritica* was translated into Arabic in the ninth century, then into European languages during the Renaissance, and Artemidorus's transformational method of decoding messages from dreamland into waking life survived, in one form or another, well into the twentieth century. George Seferis, in his introduction to a 1970 Italian translation of the *Oneirocritica*, recalls pedlars hawking popular versions of the book in the streets of Smyrna in the first decade of this century. Thirty years later, when I was a child, there was an annual publication called *Old Moore's Almanac*, which included a simple system for demystifying dreams, *à la* Artemidorus, along with astrological predictions of what the year held in store. Most households had a copy. In grander establishments, the servants usually kept it below stairs in the kitchen, but it was always somewhere 'upstairs' people could find it in time of need. *Old Moore's Almanac* is still going strong.

## 2 Freud

Artemidorus's dream interpretations prove yet again the truth that observation is always theory-driven; you see only what you are looking for. The ancients recorded every possible polymorphous perversion, but seemed not to think them important. Freud looked at similar dreams in a similar way, as he himself acknowledged, but he changed the perspective:

> Artemidorus . . . insisted on the importance of basing the interpretation of dreams on observation and experience . . . The principle of his interpretative art . . . is identical with magic, the principle of association. A thing in a dream means what it recalls to the mind – to the dream-interpreter's mind, it need hardly be said . . . The technique which I describe . . . differs in one essential respect from the ancient method: it imposes the task of interpretation upon the dreamer himself. It is not concerned with what occurs to the *interpreter* in connection with a particular element of the dream, but with what occurs to the *dreamer*.[18]

Freud's innovation was to read dreams as messages from the dreamer's unconscious self instead of from the gods. Yet that did not make him any less a traditionalist. For Freud, as powerfully as for Artemidorus, dreams were still messages full of secret meaning (he called it 'latent content') that needed to be interpreted before it could be understood. He was also a traditionalist in his early belief that, since 'most of the dreams of adults are traced back by analysis to *erotic wishes*' (his italics), practically any object can be interpreted as a sexual symbol:

> There are some symbols that bear a single meaning almost universally: thus the Emperor and Empress (or the King and Queen) stand for the parents, rooms represent women and their entrances and exits the openings of the body. The majority of dream-symbols serve to represent persons, parts of the body and activities invested with erotic interest; in particular, the genitals are represented by a number of often very surprising symbols, and the greatest variety of objects are employed to denote them symbolically. Sharp weapons, long and stiff objects, such as tree-trunks and sticks, stand for the male genitals; while cupboards, boxes, carriages or ovens may represent the uterus.[19]

Freud wrote that in 1911, as an addition to *On Dreams*, a potted version (he called it a 'brochure') of the great dream book. By that time, he had already added 'an express warning against overestimating the importance of symbols in dream-interpretation, against restricting the work of translating dreams merely to translating symbols and against abandoning the technique of making use of the dreamer's assocations'.[20] But in the first innocent rapture of uncovering the profoundly sexual nature of unconscious urges, neither Freud nor his disciples seem to have taken much notice of that caveat. There was very little which touched on the world of fantasy that they could not interpret in sexual terms.

Charles Rycroft, a psychoanalyst who is critical of Freud, quotes approvingly an aphorism by the German poet Jean Paul Richter: 'Dreams are an involuntary kind of poetry.'

Conversely, some poems are an involuntary kind of dreaming and so, involuntarily, become fair game for dream interpretation. For example:

My long two-pointed ladder's sticking through a tree
Toward heaven still,
And there's a barrel that I didn't fill
Beside it, and there may be two or three
Apples I didn't pick upon some bough.
But I am done with apple-picking now.
Essence of winter sleep is on the night,
The scent of apples: I am drowsing off.
I cannot rub the strangeness from my sight
I got from looking through a pane of glass
I skimmed this morning from the drinking trough
And held against the world of hoary grass.
It melted, and I let it fall and break.
But I was well
Upon my way to sleep before it fell,
And I could tell
What form my dreaming was about to take.
Magnified apples appear and disappear,
Stem end and blossom end,
And every fleck of russet showing clear.
My instep arch not only keeps the ache,
It keeps the pressure of a ladder-round.
I feel the ladder sway as the boughs bend.
And I keep hearing from the cellar bin
The rumbling sound
Of load on load of apples coming in.
For I have had too much
Of apple-picking: I am overtired
Of the great harvest I myself desired.

There were ten thousand thousand fruit to touch,
Cherish in hand, lift down, and not let fall.
For all
That struck the earth,
No matter if not bruised or spiked with stubble,
Went sure to the cider-apple heap
As of no worth.
One can see what will trouble
This sleep of mine, whatever sleep it is.
Were he not gone,
The woodchuck could say whether it's like his
Long sleep, as I describe its coming on,
Or just some human sleep.

'After Apple-picking' is a sweet and innocent poem, salvaged from the edge of sleep and heavy with nostalgia, repletion and a vague uneasiness. Robert Frost wrote it some time before 1914, and had he presented it, or a dream like it, to a strict Freudian of that period he would not much have cared for the interpretations he might have been offered. In crude parody form, they might have run something like this: 'What we seem to have here are fantasies of sexual omnipotence (a long ladder, barrels filled, fruit picked) masking castration anxiety (the ladder is two-pointed, a sure sign of defensive doubling) and Oedipal fantasies (the apple is associated with Eve, mother of us all). Tell me, is it only your foot that aches from the exertion? And that "rumbling sound of load on load of apples coming in". Do I detect a note of anxiety? You hear in it, perhaps, the voice of the menacing father? Apple-picking, harvest and creativity are all very well, but let's not forget your Oedipus complex, your fear of retribution, your dread of impotence.'

By the time 'After Apple-picking' was published, however, sexual symbolism was no longer the only method of decoding dreams used by psychoanalysts. Jung, for example, who had quarrelled with Freud and gone his own way before 1914, would have come at the dream/poem from a less reductive, more respectful angle – one with which even a poet as private and touchy and unforgiving as Frost might have found harder to take offence. For Jung, there was never much difference between dreams and poems; both talked a symbolic language and the business of the analyst, he said, was not to translate them, like the Freudians, 'semiotically, i.e., as signs and symbols of a fixed character, but as true symbols, i.e., as expressions of a content not yet consciously recognized or conceptually formulated'.[21] On those terms, the fact that the ladder is two-pointed or sticking through a tree is of no great importance; what matters is that it is aimed towards heaven. In short, forget the Oedipus complex; concentrate, instead, on the difference between the poet's youthful aspirations and his adult understanding that, sooner or later, he has to let ambition go and come back down to earth. In other words, Jung would probably have read the poem as an expression of the mid-life crisis – a subject of perennial interest to him, since his own mid-life crisis had precipitated a kind of breakdown – all very necessary and sensible, except for one detail: the poet is, after all, scarcely forty years old. Maybe Jung might have wondered if that were not rather young to be embracing old age, especially when there seemed to be so much delectable fruit still waiting to be picked. And that intimation of mortality at the end: wasn't it perhaps a little premature? It is as though the poet felt uneasy with his fruitful vision of the world, with his own creative powers as well as his appetites.

Both these interpretations, of course, are parodies of the real thing. If the Jungian seems to make more sense, that is because it reads the poem/dream as a statement about how things really are in the poet's emotional world, whereas the early Freudian begins with the premise that dreams never talk straight. They are like spies reporting from deep cover; they speak in code; what they really mean is not what they seem to mean; the latent content is different from the manifest content, and it is the business of the psychoanalyst to break the code and decipher the true meaning. And behind this is another premise: there is only one code-book and the Freudians have it.

In fact, there are as many code-books as there are interpreters. 'There is no algorithm, no certain method for discovering the true meaning of a dream. The kinds of meaning given to dreams vary according to the person to whom the dreamer tells the dream – priest, sage, psychoanalyst, philosopher,' wrote the psychiatrist Morton Schatzman.[22] This must have been apparent even in the early days of psychoanalysis, since it was conflicting interpretations of a dream that destroyed Freud's friendship with Jung. On their journey across the Atlantic, Jung dreamed he was exploring his house. It was a two-storeyed building; on the upper floor was a salon, full of grand rococo furniture; the ground floor was mediaeval and 'rather dark'; below it was an ancient Roman cellar, and below that 'a low cave cut into the rock. Thick dust lay on the floor, and in the dust were scattered bones and broken pottery, like remains of a primitive culture. I discovered two human skulls, obviously very old and half disintegrated. Then I awoke.'[23] For Jung, the dream was about levels of consciousness, 'a kind of structural diagram of the human psyche', he called it. Freud took it altogether more personally; the skull in the cave was his and the dream showed that, unconsciously, Jung wished his mentor dead.

Each of them was right on his own terms and according to his own preoccupations. Jung was concerned with working out his mystical vision of the unconscious and its connections with the world of primitive beliefs. He was also younger than Freud and fretting to assert his own intellectual and emotional independence. Freud himself had no time for mysticism. He was a profoundly worldly man, a scientist both by training and temperament, and still hopeful that psychoanalysis would eventually be recognised as a science. But because he was greatly perturbed by the outrage his theories had provoked among his fellow scientists, he was particularly alert to the faintest threats to his authority or signs of disloyalty among his followers.

In different circumstances, there might have been room for both interpretations, without bad blood or loss of face on either side. Freud, however, was convinced that he alone held the key to the secret of dreams, although he knew from clinical experience that the whole secret even of his own dreams was inevitably beyond him. The discipline of psychoanalysis is based on the premise that dreams, and all the other ephemeral manifestations of the unconscious, are like the glittering fragments in a kaleidoscope, constantly shifting and re-assembling themselves when the instrument is passed from hand to hand. The attentive, sympathetic, but disinterested outsider is bound to see in them a pattern different from the one perceived by the dreamer, even when the dreamer is as self-aware as Freud himself.

The classic example is his 'Dream of the Botanical Monograph':

> I have written a monograph on a certain plant. The book lay before me and I was at the moment turning over a folded coloured plate. Bound up in each copy there was a dried specimen of the plant, as though it had been taken from a herbarium.[24]

The dream itself is brief and curiously lacking in emotion. Freud seems to be using it merely to illustrate his theory that dreams make use of the previous day's experience. Accordingly, the analysis begins simply and factually:

> That morning I had seen a new book in the window of a bookshop, bearing the title *The Genus Cyclamen* – evidently a monograph on that plant.
>
> Cyclamens, I reflected, were my wife's favourite flowers and I reproached myself for so rarely remembering to bring her flowers, which was what she liked.

It seems a natural response to the recollection of a passing impression, but in the world of the unconscious nothing is simple. The botanical monograph on his wife's favourite flower was an image packed with meaning for Freud and he draws from it a dense web of associations – about his colleagues and their wives, his professional career and rivalries, his ambitions and disappointments, his childhood misdemeanours. The analysis runs to more than seven pages and is a marvel of intricacy. Slyly, inevitably, one association leads to another, and each thread is separated so delicately from the central knot that, by the end, the reader is over-whelmed by Freud's subtlety, his patience, and also by the honesty with which he lays bare what seems to be the secret of the dream's latent content: his devouring professional ambition, resentments and guilt.

It is a disarmingly frank revelation but, for two reasons, it doesn't quite ring true: first, the frankness puts Freud in an unnaturally good light ('How admirable of him to admit to such shabby failings!'); second, it in no way explains why a dream so brief and non-committal should have provoked in him such a fever of associations. Maybe they were an excuse – a 'screen', he would have called it – for something he found less easy to talk about and altogether less fetching.

Erich Fromm has suggested what that something might have been:

The central symbol of the dream is the dried flower. A dried and carefully preserved flower contains an element of contradiction. It is a flower, something standing for aliveness and beauty, but in being dried it has lost this very quality and has become an object of detached scientific study. Freud's assocations to the dream point to this contradiction in the symbol. Freud mentions that the flower, cyclamen, the monograph about which he had seen in the bookseller's window, is his wife's favourite flower, and he reproaches himself for remembering so seldom to bring her flowers. In other words, the monograph about the cyclamen stirs up his feeling that he fails in that aspect of life which is symbolized by love and tenderness . . . The dream, then, seems to express a conflict which Freud feels sharply in the dream while he seems not to be aware of it in his waking life. He reproaches himself for having neglected that side of life which is expressed by the flower and by his wife for the sake of his ambition and his one-sided intellectual scientific orientation to the world. In fact, the dream is expressive of a deep contradiction in Freud's total personality and his lifework. The main subject matter of his interest and studies is love and sex. But he is a puritan; if anything, we notice in him a Victorian aversion against sex and pleasure combined with a sad tolerance for man's weakness in this respect. He has dried the flower, made sex and love the object of scientific inspection and speculation, rather than leave it alive.[25]

As it happens, Fromm may have been speaking even truer than he knew. According to Liam Hudson, who has read all the recent biographies, 'Freud had abjured sexual relations with Martha', his wife, around the time he began work on *The Interpretation of Dreams*. Flowers always had erotic meanings in Freud's code-book; in the circumstances, the cyclamen, his wife's favourite, would have been especially poignant.

But the simple point is that Fromm not only views the dream from the cooling perspective of half a century, he is also, as every good psychoanalyst is supposed to be, an attentive, dispassionate outsider who can see what Freud, for all his ingenuity and rigour and pertinacity, leaves out. In other words, there is no one definitive interpretation of a dream, even when the dreamer and the interpreter, the analysand and the analyst, are Freud himself. For every dream there are as many interpretations as there are interpreters. Some interpretations may be better than others and no one, not even Freud, can make them entirely by himself.

---

Freud's emphasis on sexual symbolism was part of a larger and more serious intellectual enterprise. In his definition, sexuality did not just mean genital activity and genital pleasure; it encompassed a far wider range of excitements and activities than could be properly explained in terms of basic physiological needs – desire or hunger or excretion. This diffused sexuality, he believed, was particularly prominent in infant life; and infant experience, in all its unreconstructed, primitive force, was what lay behind the complexities of adult dreamwork:

> a dream might be described as *a substitute for an infantile scene modified by being transferred onto a recent experience*. The infantile scene is unable to bring about its own revival and has to be content with returning as a dream . . . What once dominated waking life, while the mind was still young and incompetent, seems now to have been banished into the night – just as the primitive weapons, the bows and arrows, that have been abandoned by adult men, turn up once more in the nursery. *Dreaming is a piece of infantile mental life that has been superseded.*[26] [Freud's italics.]

In Freud's upstairs-downstairs geography of the mind, these primitive or infantile wishes are confined to the basement of the unconscious, the Id, and are never allowed up into the civilised drawing-room where the conscious ego holds court. But when the ego relaxes its grip and lapses into sleep, the creatures in the basement come banging on the drawing-room door, clamouring to be let in. Since the ego needs its rest, a guard is posted at the door, a dream censor whose duty it is to tame these unruly intruders, turn them into acceptable dreams and so preserve sleep. The primitive urges, Freud thought, are combined with fragments from the previous day's experience, the 'day residue'; they are condensed, displaced, made representable and detoxified; they are also subjected to a 'secondary revision' which makes them intelligible. In this way, the dreams we dream, duly sanitised by the censor's blue pencil, become 'the guardians of sleep' instead of its disturbers.

'What man in his dreams has not slept with his mother?' cried Jocasta as her secret unravelled in *Oedipus Rex*, and Plato wrote, 'In all of us, even in good men, there is a lawless wild beast nature that peers out in sleep.' Freud thought so, too, and, for him, dreaming had a specific function, similar to that of a neurotic symptom. Both were what he called 'a compromise function', a manifestation of a wish and a protection against it.

It is a subtle point, but easily misinterpreted. One implication of his theory is that the real stuff of dreams, their latent content, is invariably a forbidden wish – usually Oedipal – unacceptable to the virtuous waking ego. But if dreams are the disguised expressions of intolerable erotic impulses, then dreaming itself is akin to sickness. And that, according to Charles Rycroft, is a self-defeating argument:

> by categorizing dreams as 'abnormal psychical phenomena' [Freud] succeeded in explaining them to his own satisfaction as analogous to neurotic symptoms, but at the cost of obliterating the distinction between health and illness. If dreams are both universally occurring experiences and abnormal psychical phenomena, then the healthy are virtual neurotics, and the distinction between health and wholeness on the one hand and illness and lack of integration on the other goes by the board.[27]

Sixty years after Freud published *The Interpretation of Dreams*, sleep researchers had proved conclusively that dreaming is universally part of the natural process of sleep. If

I no longer remember how I populated the darkness, but I remember the fear itself, particularly of the darkness that shrouded the upper floor, where I slept.

*Roger Parry, 'Untitled'*

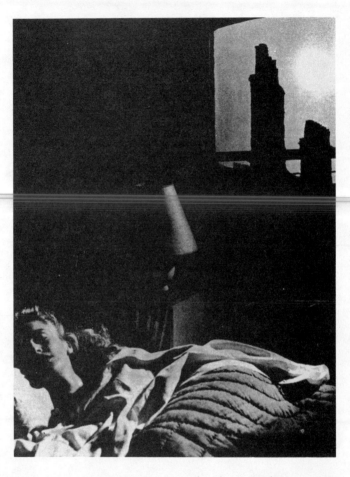

Night has always been a time for fear. Predators move unseen under the cover of darkness and all animals, man included, are most vulnerable to their enemies when they sleep. They are also vulnerable to dreams, those other-worldly visitations when secret fears and desires come drifting to the surface.

*Bill Brandt, 'Nightwalk', 1941*

*Goya, 'The Forcibly Bewitched', 1797-8*

The drama of night as it used to be – mysterious,
dangerous, engulfing.

*Georges de la Tour, 'The Repentant
Magdalene with the Night-light', 1636-8*

Wherever the turning lane of light becomes stationary for
a moment, some sleeper appears at the end of it, submits
himself to be scrutinised, and fades away into the darkness.

*Gustave Doré, 'The Bull's Eye', 1871*

The great packed sweep of Manhattan is one of the wonders of the
world – delicate, variegated, dazzling, the future come true –
especially at night.

*Berenice Abbot, 'Nightview, New York', 1932*

'It was no dream: I lay broad waking.'

*Edward Hopper, 'Night Windows', 1928*

There is the other darkness, the darkness of death, the night that gets us all in the end, the night that no amount of electric light will ever illuminate.

Bill Brandt, 'The Magic Lantern of a Car's Headlights', 1945

REM sleep is synonymous with dreaming, then everybody dreams: not just the neurotics and the healthy, but all vertebrates – with the curious exceptions I mentioned earlier: the spiny anteater and the duck-billed platypus. Normal adults pass between a fifth and a quarter of their sleep in REM sleep, small babies about one half, and the thirty-week-old infant in the womb may spend virtually 24 hours a day in REM. In other words, dreaming is a basic biological process, not a neurotic symptom, and Freud had the problem the wrong way round: dreams are not the guardians of sleep, sleep is the guardian of dreams. We don't dream – even if the Freudian censor has done its work and we dream successfully – in order to preserve our sleep; we sleep in order to dream because dreaming is a natural and necessary bodily function.[28] When volunteers in laboratory experiments are deprived of REM sleep they undergo what researchers call 'REM rebound' – that is, they make up for lost dream time directly their sleep is undisturbed. And they do so far more urgently and thoroughly than when they are deprived of deep sleep. In short, it is more important to dream than to sleep.

There were two good reasons why Freud should have misunderstood the nature and purpose of dreaming. The first concerns the nineteenth-century model of the brain on which he based his theories. Freud, after all, had started out as a clinical neurologist and, before he embarked on *The Interpretation of Dreams*, he had attempted to bring together what was then known about how the brain works in a grand synoptic theory called *Project for a Scientific Psychology*.[29] He was not finally satisfied with the results and never published the book but, as his disciples James Strachey and Ernst Kris said, 'The ghost of Freud's project haunts all of his subsequent work.' The project was based squarely on late nineteeth-century neurophysiology, which viewed the activity of the brain in relatively simple mechanical terms that had more in common with the workings of the steam engine than with those of the sophisticated, multi-layered, multi-pathed electronic devices which even the most rigidly mechanistic behaviourists now take for granted.

Like his contemporaries, Freud believed that the brain could respond only to stimulus from the outside world, that it was, in Hobson's words, 'a passive receptacle of both energy and information; able to create neither and to get rid of either only via some motor action'. In simplest terms, this meant that the brain's neuronal circuits received stimulus-energy from the external world and either discharged it as motion – lifting a hand to ward off a blow – or stored it, like a pressure-cooker, for later discharge – when, for example, a painful experience expresses itself in a dream or a neurotic symptom. Neither Freud nor anyone else at that time could conceive of the brain as 'a galaxy that you can hold in your hand', a self-contained universe of billions of inter-communicating neurons, which can create and cancel its own energy and information, and which continues to function as busily in sleep, when there is no input from the external world, as it does in waking. However sophisticated Freud's theory of the mind and its workings eventually became – and it became very sophisticated indeed as he constantly adjusted it to his clinical insights – it was based on simple push-me-pull-you nineteenth-century mechanics.

The contemporary model of the brain and its activity is infinitely more intricate, as different from Freud's as quantum physics is from the physics of Newton. Although psychoanalysis never developed into a science, as Freud originally hoped, it has not remained altogether science-proof. Modern psychoanalysts don't have to know about the latest research in neurophysiology in order to understand that Freud's model of the brain, and how it works, was inadequate. Rather than reducing the mind to the simple nineteenth-century steam-powered mechanism, they now assume, like the research scientists, that the brain is at least as complex as the mind.

There is a second reason why Freud misunderstood the nature of dreams: his real business was not with dreams and dreaming *in themselves*; it was with dreams as they reappear in waking life, translated from visual images into language, drenched in feeling and bristling with what the psychoanalyst Donald Meltzer has called 'little fish hooks' that catch on to the patient's unconscious life. For scientists, REM sleep is a physical condition, a neuronal and chemical activity. Dreaming, however, is a mental experience and many psychoanalysts treat it as a way of speaking, a form of communication. They are not interested in the dreams as dreams: they are interested in how patients tell their dreams – in what they include, emphasise, gloss over, leave out – and in the out-of-the-way and seemingly irrelevant places their narrative takes them. When Freud called dreams 'the royal road to the unconscious', he was not referring to dreaming itself, but to the patients' associations to their dreams. What he learned from dreams, above all, was a clinical technique – the technique of free-association – from which all subsequent psychoanalytic techniques developed. Someone once called Freud 'the surgeon of the night'; free-association was the scalpel he used to lay bare the unconscious.

Freud was not concerned with what dreams are or where they come from, only in where they lead. Although he believed, like Artemidorus, that dreams had something to say, that they contained messages, that there was 'material underlying' them that got disguised, displaced and condensed, he was never interested in interpreting dreams *as dreams*. He was *using* dreams to interpret character, motives, states of mind, neuroses, and whatever else goes to make up the infinite deviousness of the human psyche. In other words, the title of the book is misleading. A good deal of popular misunderstanding might have been avoided if he had called it *The Uses of Dreams*.

Freud was partly inspired by another, more flexible tradition of dream interpretation that had come down through literature and the arts, disciplines for which he always maintained a profound respect. Lionel Trilling called psychoanalysis 'one of the culminations of the Romanticist literature of the nineteenth century', and he quoted Freud's famous disclaimer when, on his seventieth birthday, an admirer called him the 'discoverer of the unconscious': 'The poets and philosophers before me discovered the unconscious. What I discovered was the scientific method by which the unconscious can be studied.'[30]

According to that other tradition, dreams carried, in intense and concentrated form, the burden of the dreamer's emotional preoccupations. Shakespeare took this attitude to dreams for granted and used it everywhere: for example, the appearance of Caesar's ghost to Brutus on the night before Philippi (the others in the tent are asleep and it is only a theatrical convenience for Brutus to be awake; if Shakespeare had been writing a movie, the visitation would have been a dream); Clarence's dream premonition of his death by drowning in *Richard III*, and Richard's dream before the battle of Bosworth, when the ghosts of his victims visit him one after the other, repeating 'Despair, and die!', then appear to the opposing general saying, 'Live, and flourish!' In each instance, Shakespeare was following his historical sources – Plutarch, Holinshed – but also using dreams for a double purpose: as a conventional way of predicting the future, *à la* Artemidorus, and to dramatise a character's overpowering sense of guilt for the crimes he has committed, *à la* Freud. But when Lady Macbeth walks in her sleep, re-enacting the murders and washing imaginary blood from her hands, as though her dream itself were a play within the play, Artemidorus goes out the window and dreams become wholly what Freud took them to be: a translation into dramatic, visual terms of a guilt-infested mind. Lady Macbeth's sleepwalking is a dream transformed into drama, and the watching doctor becomes the listening analyst: 'Infected minds', he says, 'to their deaf pillows will discharge their secrets. More needs she the divine than a physician.'

Freud was exceptional among scientists because he was willing to acknowledge that the arts, which scientists usually regard as the lesser of two cultures, also had access to valid truths. Maybe that is why his standing in the scientific community has remained so low, while artists of every kind have tried to co-opt him as one of them. Robert Lowell once remarked that reading Freud's case histories was like reading a great Russian novel. For Freud himself, the apparent literariness of his clinical studies – or perhaps his own powerful literary talents as a narrator and stylist – was an ambiguous virtue: 'it still strikes me myself as strange that the case histories I write should read like short stories and that, as one might say, they lack the serious stamp of science'.[31]

The truth the arts were willing to acknowledge – or made it their whole business to reveal – was that 'the desires of the heart are as crooked as corkscrews', and the more Freud understood this in his clinical work, the less adequate scientific empiricism began to seem:

> the essential dream-thoughts . . . usually emerge as a complex of thoughts and memories of the most intricate possible structure, with all the attributes of the trains of thought familiar to us in waking life. They are more infrequently trains of thought starting out from more than one centre, though having points of contact. Each train of thought is almost invariably accompanied by its contradictory counterpart, linked with it by antithetical association.
>
> The different portions of this complicated structure stand, of course, in the most manifold logical relations to one another. They can represent foreground and background, digressions and illustrations, conditions, chains of evidence and counter-arguments. When the whole mass of these dream-thoughts is brought under the pressure of the dream-work, and its elements are turned about, broken into fragments and jammed together – almost like pack-ice – the question arises of what happens to the logical connections which have hitherto formed its framework. What representations do dreams provide for 'if', 'because', 'just

as', 'although', 'either-or', and all the other conjunctions without which we cannot understand sentences or speeches.[32]

What Freud is talking about here is the mind itself in all its exasperating complexity, doubleness and contradictions. He is a rationalist trying to cope with something that is fundamentally irrational, and his image of the fragments jammed together like pack ice is uncannily close – in spirit if not in detail – to the neuronal cacophony invoked by the neurophysiologists.

The passage is typical of *The Interpretation of Dreams* and of one of the qualities that makes it continually fascinating, even to the layman: the sheer intellectual persistence with which Freud worried away at his insights and observations. He may have been wrong in his premises and pig-headed about the correctness of his system, but no one has ever thought about the universal experience of dreaming more subtly or with more rigour.

That, however, is not enough to redeem his work for the scientists. There is traditional antipathy between science and the concerns of psychoanalysis which seems to be as old as science itself:

> Around the year 500 B.C. natural science began with a repudiation of the dream. Heracleitos of Ephesos issued a scientific manifesto in the two sentences: 'We must not act and speak like sleepers, for in our sleep too we act and speak' and 'The waking have one world in common, but the sleeping turn aside each into a world of his own.'[33]

Scientists find it particularly hard to forgive Freud's claim that what he was doing was science. Since he had started as a clinical neurologist, doing serious research in histology, they argue, he should have known better. As a true scientist, he should have recognised that his theories were speculative – not properly scientific, not empirically based. Hobson, in particular, gets a lot of indignant mileage out of this. Not only was Freud's picture of the brain wrong, he says – it could hardly have been otherwise at that time – but his data were subjective – the dreams he analysed were either his own or based on second-hand reports of other people's dreams – and his theories 'are not logically constructed in such a way as to be amenable to experimental test'. The psychoanalysts reply that most scientists treat human beings as machines and ignore all the depths and contradictions that make them human. Both sides are equally correct or misleading, depending on whether you look at dreaming as a neuronal and chemical activity or as a form of communication.

But the argument is not properly to the point: in the early decades, Freud himself was ambivalent about the scientific status of his work. When he was still feeling his way into this vast and unexplored territory, his claims to scientific truth and his attitude to his theories were curiously tentative. He called them 'conventions', and the more he understood the trickiness of the mind, the less certain he was of the strictly scientific validity of what he was up to:

> The scientific results of psychoanalysis are at present only a by-product of its therapeutic aims, and for that reason it is often just in those cases where treatment fails that most discoveries are made.[34]

By any standards, that is written in a spirit of true scientific doubt. Unfortunately, it didn't stay that way. Freud's attitudes hardened in his later years because what he had to say about the power and ubiquity of sexuality opened a great can of worms – for him personally as much as for everyone else.

Someone has described the effect of his work as 'merely the most recent in a series of painful humiliations that human narcissism had suffered since the advent of the scientific age. After Copernicus and Darwin displaced humanity from a privileged place in the universe and the hierarchy of creation, Freud had dealt a third blow by showing that the ego was not even master of the human psyche.'[35] As a result, what Freud had to say not only offended scientists, it was also an offence against his own society, whose approval he sought, whose values he believed in and, as a non-believing but unassimilated Jew at a deeply anti-Semitic time, whose conventions he adhered to with particular fervour. Just as Freud's upstairs-downstairs picture of the psyche reflected the upstairs-downstairs society in which he lived, so the censor he put into the dreamer's head mirrored the censorship at work around him, and the tribulations it caused him. In pursuit of his own particular brand of scientific truth, he could not avoid the suppressed material, the erotic latent content he found hidden behind apparently innocuous dreams.

Yet, in some ways, that ubiquitous sexuality was as unacceptable to him as it was to the rest of the medical establishment of his time. He was a doctor and a family man, middle class and correct, and however ambitious he was to break new ground in his arcane discipline, subversion was not on his agenda; the idea of appearing disreputable appalled him. Whence the *cordon sanitaire* of both disinterestedness and scientific rigour which he erected around the psychoanalytic project as a whole. Then as now, the social life and comportment of psychoanalysts was the most scrupulously proper – i.e., dullest – of all the professions. Then as now, the wild men were invariably ejected from the charmed analytic circle. Otto Gross, for example, whom Freud initially considered one of the most gifted of all his disciples, went on to preach free love to the writers and artists of Schwabing, the bohemia of Munich, spectacularly practised what he preached, was disowned by Freud, became a drug addict and died, literally, in the gutter.

But all the social propriety in the world was no defence against the moral prudery of the time or against the shock and outrage which Freud's insights into the power and omnipresence of human sexuality provoked in his readers. 'People are in general not candid over sexual matters,' he said in his 1909 Clark Lectures. 'They do not show their sexuality freely, but to conceal it they wear a heavy overcoat woven of a tissue of lies, as though the weather were bad in the world of sexuality.'[36]

## 3 Modern Psychoanalysis

The weather stayed bad until at least a quarter of a century after his death in 1938, and Freud, as he grew older, became progressively more embattled. He equated disagreement with disloyalty and sought to have his theory cut in stone – a curious fate for a discipline that enquires into that most fluid of subjects, the human condition. Yet he also went on developing his theories, and over the years his model of the mind became increasingly more sophisticated. Anxiety, guilt and conscience replaced sex and wish-fulfilment as the motive forces of the psyche. Late Freud himself was not strictly a Freudian.

After his death, as the groups splintered, the theories proliferated and the tablets of the law were gradually re-written, until what survived was, above all, the intellectual example Freud himself set – his probing, dissatisfied, scientific curiosity. Ninety years on, there are mercifully fewer primitive, unreconstructed Freudians, who believe un-flinchingly in the omnipotence of the Oedipus complex and the libidinal forces or in the mechanics of dreaming as set out in *The Interpretation of Dreams* – the dream censor, wish-fulfilment and the rest. The most interesting trends in modern psychoanalysis are now altogether more flexible. They are concerned, above all, with what goes on between the patient and the analyst in the here-and-now of the session.

Freud was a great collector of ancient artifacts and his attitude to his discipline was correspondingly archaeological. He believed that, deep below the accretions of culture and social habit lay some kind of primal fault – some crucial, usually sexual, conflict – which had provoked the symptoms that brought the patient to his consulting-room, and which could eventually be uncovered, layer by layer, through patience, hard work and intuition. In other words, he believed in a one-person, 'intra-psychic' psychology in which every-thing begins and ends with the patient and his unique, private history.

Modern analysis, in contrast, is founded on a two-person, 'object-relations' psychology. It assumes that psychic life, like language, is always directed towards someone else, even if that someone exists mostly as a spectral presence in the patient's mind, as what the followers of Melanie Klein call an 'internal object'. Consequently, the process of psychoanalysis shifts from the archaeological past to the conversational present. It is less concerned with exhuming the patient's early life than with the transference and the counter-transference – with the way the patient talks and feels in his relationship towards the analyst, and with the reactions aroused in the analyst by the patient. At this point, dreams become just another element in an already complicated interaction.

At the same time, that interaction itself is just another kind of dreaming. Jung once said, 'It is on the whole probable that we continually dream, but that consciousness makes such a noise that we do not hear it.' Melanie Klein thought so too, except that what Jung called 'dreaming' she called 'unconscious phantasy', and she conceived of it as a continuous process taking place in the internal world. This, in turn, gave a new meaning to dreams:

> Dreaming could not be viewed merely as a process for allaying tensions in order to maintain sleep; dreams had to be seen as pictures of *dream life* that was going on all the time, awake or asleep. We may call these transactions 'dreams' when we are asleep, and 'unconscious phantasies' when we are awake. The implication was that this internal world must be assigned the full significance of a *place*, a life-space, perhaps *the* place where meaning was generated . . . We would consider dreaming to be as continuous in the mind as digestion is in the body, but concentrated more fully on its task when the other mental processes of dealing with the outside world are in abeyance during sleep.[37]

If you substitute 'mentation' for 'dreaming', you have a picture of mind very similar to the 'closed-loop' system of the modern neurophysiologists.

The difference is that scientists are interested in the chemistry of the brain, while psychoanalysts are concerned with mental life and feelings. Or rather, less pompously and like the dreamers themselves, psychoanalysts are concerned with the poignancy of dreams. Freud made the crucial distinction when he wrote, 'large numbers of dreams appear to be indifferent, whereas it is never possible to enter into the dream-thoughts without being deeply moved'.[38] For analysts and dreamers alike, dreams are like libraries: your whole life is packed away on the shelves, forgotten, but when you take down a book and start to read – that is, to free-associate – everything is suddenly present again: the experiences and feelings you once had and then mislaid; all of them complete, all with the fears and heart-break still in place.

One function of the analyst is to comprehend this lost world and take account of the shadows it casts on the present. His other function is to comprehend the dream as something happening now, not just in the transference, but also in the patient's life. At a seminar held by the great psychoanalyst Wilfred Bion, shortly before he died, a child-analyst was discussing the case of a rather academic young patient who told her that he yearned, above all, 'to touch a piece of history'. Soon after, he dreamed he dug up a fossil and was filled with such delight that when he woke, knowing it was only a dream, he wept. For the child, the dream was packed with feeling and significance, and the analyst, too, was profoundly moved by it. This was in London, in 1978, when old-style Freudian sexual symbolism had gone out of fashion and had been replaced in some circles by an equally cumbersome lingo of 'part objects', a kind of parody of Melanie Klein's early theories. One enthusiast in the seminar promptly suggested that the fossil, of course, was really 'a dead baby wrapped in faeces'. This was as schematic a simplification, blindly indifferent to the emotional content of the dream, as anything Artemidorus ever managed, and the child's analyst seemed struck dumb by its inappropriateness. Finally, an exasperated unbeliever rose to the bait, protesting that reductionism of that order missed the whole point of the dream. Bion listened to the squabble in his usual Sphinx-like silence. Then he said mildly, 'But he *did* touch a piece of history.' The dream, he meant, was not a passing fantasy; it was a real event in the child's life – as real, in terms of feeling and meaning and even consequence, as any waking experience.

It is this dimension of emotional or existential truth that is missing in scientific accounts of how the brain works when it dreams. In Hobson's 'activation-synthesis hypothesis', for example, the dreaming brain is making its brilliant best of a bad job in REM sleep. (First, it is activated; then it synthesises its own sensory and motor information.) Because it is working flat out in isolation, while the doors of perception are shut tight against the external world and the body is effectively paralysed, it has to make sense of its own internally created activity with whatever means it has at its disposal. The abrupt shifts in time and place, the bizarre transformations of people and scenery, the flouting of natural laws – 'Sir, I can frequently fly' – all these, according to Hobson, are related to the brain's intense but random neuronal activity, and to the way the eyes swivel and slide and rotate in REM sleep. And all these the mind, with its rage for order, tries to translate into a language it can understand. For Hobson and his colleagues, in short, the brain is like the scientist: it seeks to make sense of what it experiences, to create order out of the randomness of what is given.

This is a sophisticated advance on the attitude of the so-called 'pure' scientists for whom, ultimately, the brain is an advanced computer that will eventually be outstripped by the scientifically designed real thing. There are numerous variations on this materialist theme, but the most florid is that of the molecular biologists Francis Crick and Graeme Mitchison, who dismiss dreams as mere mental waste-disposal; we dream, they say, in order to get rid of 'spurious memories' – parasitic thought patterns that serve no purpose and actively hinder the brain's efficiency – which would otherwise overload the storage capacity of the computer-brain.

In contrast to other 'hard' scientists, Hobson believes that dreams do have meanings and can be interpreted. Jung said, 'The dream is its own interpretation', and Hobson agrees, although he prefers the term 'transparent'. For him, dreams mean exactly what they say; the wishes and drives they express are as stated; nothing is hidden or veiled or suppressed. When he dreams of finding Mozart playing a concerto at the Boston Museum of Fine Arts, Mozart is not a symbolic substitute for his father; Mozart is Mozart, someone whose music Hobson adores, whom he would love to have met and with whom, he admits, he secretly identifies. For Hobson, in other words, dreams are what is known in computer-babble as WYSIWYG: What You See Is What You Get.

This is one way of avoiding the Artemidorus trap of over-ingenious interpretations – above all, those classical Freudian interpretations of Oedipal conflict which Hobson holds in particular scorn. In practice, however, theories of interpretation are not the issue. Whatever system a psychoanalyst adheres to by training and temperament is no concern of the patient. A dream means what it says *in the context of the session.*

More important, the handful of dreams that linger on into waking life are different from the enormous number you dream and then forget each and every night of your life. Some acquire meaning and are coloured with emotion because you remember them; others you remember because they are coloured with emotion and are telling you something you need to know. That, in fact, is the basic premise of psychoanalysis: when a patient recounts a dream he is telling the analyst indirectly something urgent which he cannot tell him straight. Dreams may be enigmatic, but they do not necessarily speak in riddles. Instead, they speak in images; their language is oblique and metaphorical. In the circumstances, 'transparent' is a curious word to describe such a rich and densely packed phenomenon.

## A NOTE ON CHAOS THEORY

Jung postulated a collective unconscious whereby myths – stories woven from mankind's most primitive and universally recurrent experiences and preoccupations – are hard-wired into the basic structure of the brain. But myth is just one way of imposing structure on apparent chaos, and chaos of a kind is precisely what is at stake. After all, the inner world of unconscious fantasy comprises, in principle, *everything* that an individual has over experienced. This means that it is at least as complex as the densely intercommunicating neurons of the brain.

Both are strong examples of what are called 'non-linear systems' – dynamic systems whose behaviour can be described 'only by considering the *interaction* of the components *within* the system, and not simply by the *addition* of the system's qualities'.[39] In other words, the sum of a non-linear system is *qualitatively* different from its parts because its parts act on each other to produce complex and unpredicted behaviour. Non-linear systems also show, as they say, 'sensitive dependence on initial conditions'; that is, the smallest variation at the start has wildly unexpected consequences in the distant future: witness the famous swarm of butterflies whose wing-beats over the Gulf of Mexico produce storms over Iceland.

Chaos theory is the science of non-linear systems, and its purpose is to demonstrate, often with great elegance, that even chaos has its own form of order. The guiding principle of this order is what mathematicians call 'the strange attractor'. In ordinary dynamic systems – dynamics being the study of the way in which systems change – an attractor is either a fixed point where a trajectory ends – as life ends in death – or it is a 'limit cycle', the point at which the trajectory becomes periodic – as in the to-and-fro movement of the pendulum in a grandfather clock. But because the components of a non-linear system act on each other, their trajectories evolve differently, the system's equilibrium is unstable, and the attractor works in undetermined ways. A strange attractor is strange because it makes this happen – because it induces the phenomenon of 'sensitivity to initial conditions' – and also because it imposes order on non-periodic trajectories. For the layman, this means, quite simply, that a strange attractor is strange because it works in mysterious ways and is itself strangely complex.[40]

The psychoanalyst Michael Moran believes that the mind, too, has its own strange attractor, and it is his business as an analyst to understand it. It is 'the fixed collection of the patient's unconscious fantasies, his unconscious story (or collection of stories) about himself', and it manifests itself in every detail of every session: in verbal associations, slips of the tongue, tone of voice, even in the way the patient lies on the couch. But above all, this psychic strange attractor manifests itself in dreams, and this suggests to Moran that neuronal activity during REM sleep, and the nonsensical, purposeless dream images it produces, may not be quite as random as neurophysiologists like to think:

The strange attractor of a neurosis can be seen not only as the determining force for mental activity, but as a characteristic (for the patient) *limit of random activity*. In this way, the experience (and the meaning of the experience) resulting from what indeed may be random pontine neuronal firings would be limited by the strange attractor, whose experiential features these firings would then *randomly* 'illuminate', much as an erratic electronic television gun might allow the display of only part of the *determined* broadcast picture. The strange attractor lays out the limits of dream meaning that can be activated by the neurologic events, just as the attractor does with the experiences of waking life.

In other words, dreams may be dotty, but only within limits – the limits laid down by the strange attractor of the dreamer's inner life and personal history. And because they are products of a non-linear system, even recurrent dreams can never be the same twice since, second time around, the dreamer himself has been changed, both by what has happened to him in the interval and by the dream itself.

There is another limit to the craziness of dreams: in order to be salvaged from night they have to undergo what Freud called 'secondary revision'; this is, they have to be translated into language. But since language is 'intentional' – a means of communicating with someone else – the only way to translate the seemingly random patchwork of dream images is to impose on them a narrative structure. 'This happened, then that happened' makes sense of even the most demented fantasies.

Maybe Jung was right about myth and the collective unconscious; maybe story-telling is as basic an instinct as sex. If so, however much we learn about the physiology of dreaming, the true, unmediated, pre-linguistic nature of dreams will always be just beyond the reach of our understanding – at least until the technology that has enabled scientists to record the activity of individual neurons in the brain is developed to the point where they can make videos of our dreams.

## HYPNAGOGIC HALLUCINATIONS

Although we can reconstitute our dreams only by turning them into narrative, dreaming in its turn changes the way we tell stories. When Freud reinstated the interpretation of dreams as a serious topic of discussion, he also reinstated dreams as a source of artistic inspiration, and not just for the Surrealists. There is a great mass of twentieth-century literature – from at least Kafka to Márquez – which begins with the same disjunctions from reality that the dreamer takes for granted. On one level, Kafka's novels and tales are pure dream: the eternal supplicant at the impenetrable castle, the hunger artist in his cage at the circus, the nightmare machine in the penal settlement which carves the transgressor's sentence on to his back, the man who wakes 'from uneasy dreams' to find himself transformed into a gigantic insect. All of them are dream situations followed through with a terrible waking logic. For Eugène Ionesco, in whose plays it seems quite normal for a corpse to grow in the bedroom or for people to turn into rhinoceroses, dream is the basis of art:

> The dream is pure drama. In a dream, one is always in mid-situation. To be more concise, I think that the dream is a lucid thought, more lucid than any one has when awake, a thought expressed in images, and that at the same time its form is always dramatic.[41]

Even by Allan Hobson's rigorously scientific criteria, it

makes sense that dreams should be the place where art begins, since dreaming, he thinks, is fundamentally an artistic process, a universal form of creativity: 'Each of us is a surrealist at night during his or her dreams: each is a Picasso, a Dali, a Fellini.'[42] This cheerful belief that art is democratically available to everyone, regardless of race, colour, creed and natural ability, does not take into account the sheer hard labour of true creativity or the artist's realistic understanding of his medium or the richness of his inner world. Even so, imposing a structure on random neuronal events, turning them into stories and filling them with emotional significance may be as close as most of us ever get to the real thing.

But there is another kind of dreaming, a dreaming un-mediated by language and wholly impervious to art, narrative and interpretation. I mean the flickering images and voices that well up just before sleep takes over. Their technical name is hypnagogic hallucinations, and they occur, according to the manuals, 'as the control of ideas escapes us'. They have no apparent structure at all and, with one exception that I know of, they seem to be outside the range of literature. The exception is Don DeLillo, a novelist who has always been fascinated by what happens around the edges of experience:

> Just before I went to sleep I imagined myself fighting with Brand. We hit each other dozens of times. Then something else moved across my mind, possessions, things in my home, shapes of objects unfondled of late, the Olivetti Lettera 32, the Nikon F, and then girls in purple stockings rolling across a paper plain, and James Joyce and Antonioni and Samuel Beckett sitting in my living room, six legs crossed at the ankles, Tana Elkbridge naked on Riverside Drive while her husband read *Business Week* at thirty thousand feet, and Jennifer naked in the West Eighties, something

touching about her hipbones, and Meredith naked in Gramercy Park, and Sullivan naked in the bath. Then we were fighting again. I backed away from a long right and came back with a left to the cheekbone and a short straight right square on the point of the chin. Brand went to his knees and hung there, breathing blood. I kicked him in the stomach and went to sleep.[43]

DeLillo captures the stop-frame, strobe flicker of hypnagogic hallucinations, but only by *seeming to* impose on them a spurious continuity. Whether DeLillo is elegantly fantasising or faithfully reporting what he experiences is not important because hypnagogic hallucinations are so quirky, anarchic and fragmentary that they are even further beyond the rules of waking life than dreams. They also vanish so fast that some people never properly register their subliminal, ghostly presence. A clinical psychiatrist once assured me that he had hypnagogic hallucinations no more than once or twice a month, and they were always the same: he was walking in a familiar landscape – always the same landscape from month to month – then he slipped, fell, awoke with a myoclonic jerk of his leg, and sank back instantly into sleep.

But for most people hypnagogic hallucinations are a freak show, a zoo of distorted faces, voices talking at full pitch but just out of focus, explosions of light and colour, strange images dissolving into each other, shifting and reassembling themselves. And, unlike dreams, all this happens in an emotional vacuum, with a total absence of feeling. We are spectators, not players – all eye and no ego – unshocked, unsurprised, uninvolved.

'Those Whispers just as you have fallen or are falling asleep – what are they and whence?' Coleridge wrote in his notebooks. Half a century later, the Marquis Marie Jean Léon Hervey de

Saint-Denys, an authority on Chinese culture and an obsessed student of dreams, provided an answer of sorts. Hervey was born in 1822 and suffered the galling loneliness which at that time came, as though by birth-right, to an aristocratic only child: educated at home by tutors, surrounded by servants, yet with no one to play with and no one to talk to. To amuse himself in his isolation, or perhaps to people it, he took up drawing. Then, when he was thirteen, he 'conceived the idea of drawing a picture based on my recollections of a curious dream which had made a strong impression on me'.[44] This was the beginning of an illustrated dream journal which he kept up for years, and which eventually filled twenty-two notebooks. The notebooks have disappeared but, in 1867, Hervey published a distillation of his lifelong obsession with dreaming in a book called *Dreams and How to Guide Them*.

Hervey's dream-life was so rich and consuming that, like some modern psychoanalysts and neurophysiologists, he became convinced that dreaming was a continuous process, that 'there can be no sleep without dreams, any more than there can be waking consciousness without thoughts'. He seems to have had a kind of genius for dreaming and he worked at it deliberately, training himself to remember his dreams as strenuously as a gymnast, he said, trains for the trapeze or trampoline. He also developed, to a prodigious degree, his gift for what is called 'lucid dreaming' – for knowing *in his dreams* that he was dreaming, and then behaving as though he were awake.

He became so proficient in this strange skill that he was not only able to control the course of his dreams while he slept, he was also able to move so deliberately between dreaming and waking that dreams became, he claimed, 'elements of my

ordinary intellectual life . . . part of the body of reminiscences
my mind could draw upon while I was asleep'. One night, for
example, he dreamt of 'a golden-haired young woman talking to
[his] sister'. He seemed to know her well in the dream, and was
convinced he had met her several times before. Then he woke
up. The image of her face was clear before him, yet he was
wholly unable to recognise it. So he went back to sleep, re-
entered the dream, approached the young woman and asked her
politely if he had had the pleasure of meeting her before.
' "Certainly," she replied. "Don't you remember? We went
bathing together at Pornic?" '[45] He then woke again, remembering contentedly everything about their first encounter.

This is closer to wizardry than to dreaming, like the Magus
Zoroaster who met his own image walking in the garden. But
because Hervey describes it as though it were the most natural
thing in the world, it is hard to decide what is strangest about
this strange interlude: his ability to invade his own dreams at
will or his uncanny control over dream-events and dream-
people? Not only can he remember in his dream to ask a
question that had puzzled him when he was awake, but the
figures in his dream answer him promptly, willingly and
correctly. Strangest of all is his bland assumption that this is
how dream-life really is if you train yourself for it.

Hervey became a distinguished orientalist, a professor at
the Collège de France, where he taught Chinese and Tartar-
Manchu, and President of the *Académie des Inscriptions et
Belles-Lettres*. Yet his scholarly career was only one half of
what was, in fact, two separate lives: a daytime life laden with
academic honours and a second life lived while he slept, which
was equally vivid and, for him, as deliberate and as subject to
free-will as his waking life.

The ease and inevitability with which he moved from one life to the other was uncanny:

> First, I dreamed that, on coming out of a theatre, I got into a hackney carriage, which moved off. I woke up almost immediately, without remembering this insignificant vision. I looked at the time on my watch; I picked up a lighter that I had knocked over; and after having been *completely* awake for ten or fifteen minutes, I fell asleep again. It was here that the strange part of the dream began. I dreamed that I woke up in the carriage, which I remembered perfectly well having entered to go home. I had the impression that I had dozed off for about a quarter of an hour, but without remembering what thoughts had passed through my mind during that time. Thereupon I reflected that a large part of the journey must already be over, and I looked out of the window to see what street we were in, having thus interpreted as time asleep the very time when I had stopped sleeping.[46]

This is not the double life of schizophrenic Dr Jekyll and Mr Hyde. Instead, it is two lives lived in parallel, and both subject to the same strenuous intellectual rules. It is as though Hervey had abolished the craziness of dreams, along with the blessed unconsciousness of sleep. As he describes them, his dreams owe very little to the imagination. He was convinced – and produced elaborate dreams to prove it – that every visual detail, however bizarre, was based on something he had once seen in his waking life, stored away in his memory, and then apparently mislaid until he came across it again in sleep.

Like Freud, Hervey believed that the key to dreams was the association of ideas but, for him, ideas in dreams were always images, images developing logically, one from the other, in a kind of shadowland version of rational thought:

I am having lunch in a café. On the table I put a small spoon which I have been holding. The spoon somewhat resembles the silver-plated key to my lodging. Immediately it becomes a key. That gives me the idea of going home. And from there it is only a moment before I find myself outside my door. My key turns in the lock – I have been instantaneously transported from the café to my home.[47]

For Hervey, with his Gallic belief in the power of the intellect, dreams were problems that could be solved rationally. He worked out the logic of their imagery with the same glassy persistence as he controlled the direction of his lucid dreams. Naturally, this unremitting intellectual effort did not leave much room for feeling. Despite his meticulousness and occasional brilliance, he was immune to precisely those aspects of dreams that made them important to Freud: their obscure private significance and terrible emotional pull.

Hervey's rigorously disciplined dream habits, however, worked perfectly with hypnagogic hallucinations. He not only trained himself to remember them, he also drew delicate pictures of them, described them in vivid detail, and then explained how and why one hypnagogic image led to another:

I was very tired, having spent the previous night travelling. Foreseeing that I would go to sleep quickly, I asked a friend to sit by my bed and wake me up five or six minutes after I seemed to be asleep. Everything happened as I had hoped. I was woken up at the moment I was dreaming that I was preventing a dog from eating a wounded bird. The dream was completely coherent, and on waking I retained a clear impression of it. I followed the train of thought back and discovered it to be as follows: among the initial shapes which appeared to me, the first I remember was a sort of bundle of arrows standing on end, which seemed to open out to form one of those long baskets in which linen is kept warm in the bathroom. White towels could be seen through the wickerwork. Soon the pieces of cane seemed to narrow, to twist and curl up, and finally to turn into a leafy thicket, from the middle of which rose a bushy tree. A white dog (obviously metamorphosed from the white towels) was running to and fro on the other side of the thicket trying to get through it, while a wounded bird lay on the grass at my feet. The dog had managed to get through the bushes, and I was fending it off with my stick when I was woken up. The dreaming state had already been established for some moments.[48]

This is analytic in the literal and pre-Freudian sense – a matter of close observation, discipline and logic, a triumph of precision over hallucinations which are, by their nature, fleeting, imprecise and bafflingly elusive. 'I regard the continuous application of attention as practically impossible', Hervey wrote, 'in that transitory period between waking and sleeping in which anarchy reigns among our ideas and confusion among the images representing them.'[49] Yet one of his greatest contributions to the understanding of dreams was to have done what he said was impossible; he brought order to the pure chaos of hypnagogic hallucinations by setting them down on paper in pictures and careful prose. That in itself justified all those other qualities which seem so inappropriate when applied to dreams: his obsessional, top-heavy logic, his curious emotional blandness, his remorseless insistence on control.

Freud may have disclaimed the honour of having discovered the unconscious, but he established beyond doubt that consciousness contains a great deal we know very little about, that what we say is often at odds with what we seem to think and feel, and that the unconscious expresses itself obliquely, slyly, in ways beyond our control – in slips of the tongue, in body language, in tone of voice. Hypnagogic hallucinations, which are purer than dreams because they are less structured, show that the mind is packed not just with feelings we are unaware of, but also with images of places and people and things we have never seen, with the sounds of voices we have never heard, with mouthings and fragments which are proof of nothing other than the continual spontaneous creativity of the brain.

Cognitive psychologists believe that the hallucinations which come as we fall asleep are very like those induced by sensory deprivation, meditation and psychedelic drugs.[50] I myself believe that this deranged kaleidoscope is a pure culture of the mind, a partially conscious version – like a blurred and evanescent rough sketch – of what happens in REM sleep when the neurons of the brain are firing away while the senses are shut down. It is not the control of ideas that escapes us, but our perception of external reality, as though the outer world itself were a strange attractor that steadies the conscious mind, gathers our wits together and provokes the mental faculties we need to cope and survive: attention, learning, memory. So far as the workings of the brain are concerned, sanity is a convention, like mathematics or religion, a way of imposing order on the chaos which the brain produces when left to its own devices.

We are back, in short, to the uncomfortable likeness of dreams to madness: 'Dreaming permits each and every one of us to be quietly and safely insane every night of our lives.' Charles Fisher's aphorism is elegant but not strictly true. Dreams may be the acceptable face of insanity, but dreams are artifacts, reassembled after the event, translated into language, constrained by narrative, and then brought, washed and brushed and decently clothed, into the light of Heraclitus's 'common world'. The physiological process of dreaming itself, however, and the brain's fragmentary neuronal firework display, which we glimpse fleetingly in hypnagogic hallucinations, are nothing like so cosy or orderly or safe.

# PROBLEM-SOLVING IN DREAMS

*It is a sleepy language, and thou speak'st*
*Out of thy sleep. What is it thou didst say?*
*This is a strange repose, to be asleep*
*With eyes wide open: standing, speaking, moving,*
*And yet so fast asleep.*

Shakespeare, *The Tempest*

*Dreams sometimes useful by giving to the well-grounded*
*fears & hopes of the understanding the feelings of visual*
*sense.*

Coleridge, *Notebooks*, 1796

None of them last, neither hypnagogic hallucinations nor even the dreams we rescue from sleep, unless we translate them into language by telling them or writing them down. 'Well, dreams are all lost,' says a character in one of Isaac Bashevis Singer's stories. 'Each day begins with amnesia.' Freud thought we forget dreams because most of them are too unsavoury to remember. Hobson thinks we forget them because the neurotransmitters necessary for memory – the aminergic neurons in the brain stem – are switched off in REM sleep. Whatever the reason, however deep and significant, however saturated with feeling, dreams without language are like the ghost of Hamlet's father; they fade 'on the crowing of the cock'.

But the language of dreams is different in kind from the language of thought; it is concrete, visual, dramatic. 'The image of the dream is to the idea which calls it forth exactly what the image of the magic lantern is to the lighted glass-plate which produces it,' wrote Hervey, who was as overwhelmed by the new science of photography as some contemporary theorists of the brain are by computers. In dreams, he meant, ideas are expressed in images, not in words. Freud thought so too, although he preferred a theatrical metaphor:

> Here we have the most general and most striking psychological characteristic of the process of dreaming: a thought . . . is objectified in the dream, is represented as a scene, or, as it seems to us, is experienced . . . two almost independent features stand out as characteristic . . . One is the fact that the thought is represented as an immediate situation with the 'perhaps' omitted, and the other is the fact that the thought is transformed into visual images and speech.[51]

Later, in *The Ego and the Id*, Freud remarked that visual memory is closer to the unconscious processes than thinking in words, and 'unquestionably older than the latter, both ontogenetically and phylogenetically'. In other words, the dreaming brain thinks, but it expresses its thoughts in an archaic form, one that preceded abstract language, as hieroglyphs preceded the phonetic alphabet. This fits with current brain research which has shown that in REM sleep the right hemisphere is more active than the left, and the right hemisphere is visual rather than verbal.[52]

This is where the two main pieces of the puzzle begin to

come together: the physiological fact that the activity of the brain never ceases, even in deep sleep, and the psychoanalytic belief that remembered dreams, no matter how bizarre and disjointed, seem full of personal meaning. The brain goes on working, mentation – which is one step down from thinking – continues, even in non-REM sleep, *but it continues in different terms*. The sleeping brain thinks symbolically, in concrete images rather than in words and ideas. Thinking symbolically, however, does not mean that all we need to interpret dreams is access to the right code-book – Freud's, Jung's, Klein's, Artemidorus's, Old Moore's. Dreams are enigmatic and have as many symbolic meanings as there are dreamers and interpreters. The code is unimportant; what matters is the thinking itself and where it leads. What matters, in short, is the point where dreams enter waking life and interact with it.

The conviction that we think in our sleep has been around far longer than neurophysiology or psychoanalysis. 'Let me sleep on it' is not always a way of postponing a decision; it may also be a recourse to the folk wisdom that knows there is more than one way to think about a problem. In 1920, for example, the German-born biochemist Otto Loewi was working on an experiment to show whether the nerves – specifically, the *vagus* nerve from the brain to the heart – send their messages electrically or chemically. On Easter Sunday, Loewi dreamed an experiment that would give him the answer he was looking for. He woke, scribbled it down, then went back to sleep. But by morning the dream had vanished and he could not decipher his nocturnal scrawl. The next night, he went to bed still thinking about the problem. At three o'clock, the dream returned and this time he was ready for it. 'I got up immediately,' he wrote later, 'went to the laboratory and performed the experiment.' The experiment was simple, but with the kind of simplicity only genius can achieve. Loewi prepared two frogs, stimulated the *vagus* nerve of one, causing its heart-beat to slow down, then transferred the blood from the first frog's heart to the second's; when that slowed too, Loewi had his answer: nerves were not like tiny wires conducting electricity, they transmitted their signals chemically. Later, it was shown that the chemical in question, Loewi's *vagustoff*, was acetylcholine, the neurotransmitter that triggers dreams. A dream, in short, had provided a clue to understanding the chemistry of dreams.

Loewi, who was awarded the Nobel Prize for his work in 1936, never explained how the solution presented itself in his dream, but other scientists and inventors have been less reticent about their discoveries. Elias Howe, an eminently practical man, laboured for years unsuccessfully over the design of his sewing machine, until a dream solved the problem for him. In all his failed prototypes, he had positioned the eye of the needle in the middle of the shaft. Then, one night, he dreamed he was captured by a tribe of savages. He never mentioned what emotions the savages aroused in him, although they may well have echoed the fear and rage and frustration that continual failure sometimes provokes. All he said later was that the savages gave him the answer he was looking for: their spears, he noticed, had eye-shaped holes near the tips.

At a scientific convention in 1890, the German biochemist August Kekulé von Stradonitz claimed that the solution to the problem of the structure of the benzene molecule – it was a ring – came to him in a dream:

Again the atoms were juggling before my eyes . . . my mind's eye, sharpened by repeated sights of a similar kind, could now distinguish larger structures of different forms and in long chains, many of them close together; everything was moving in a snake-like and twisting manner. Suddenly, what was this? One of the snakes got hold of its own tail and the whole structure was mockingly twisting in front of my own eyes. As if struck by lightning, I awoke . . . Let us learn to dream, gentlemen, and then we may perhaps find the truth. [53]

Kekulé's vision had no characters, no situations, none of the essential drama of dreams. It seems, instead, to have been a hypnagogic hallucination that came to him while he dozed in front of the fire. He had been thinking about the problem when he nodded off and, in much the same way as a dozing reader continues to read in his sleep, he went on thinking about it in terms of the flickering shapes of the flames he had been staring at. Although what he saw may not have been strictly a dream, the thinking was unquestionably dream-thinking – ideas transformed into images.

In 1983, Morton Schatzman went public on the subject of problem-solving in dreams. In the course of an article in the *Sunday Times*, he posed two brain-teasers: first, What is curious about this sentence: 'Show this bold Prussian that praises slaughter, slaughter brings rout'?; second, Which of the following verbs does not belong in this group: bring, catch, draw, fight, seek, teach and think? He asked his readers to think about the problems when they went to bed, and to try to solve them in their dreams. This is one of the many replies he received:

On Tuesday night (two days after the article appeared), before going to sleep, I memorized the problems, without much expectation of success. Between 3.00 and 3.30 am, I woke up aware of terrible indigestion and of having had a rather weird dream. In my dream I'm watching Michael Caine in one of his spy roles, possibly *The Ipcress File*. He's in the Centre, or whatever spy-headquarters is called.

He walks up to a door marked Computer Room and opens it; behind the door is a heavy wire-mesh screen. He passes a folded copy of the *Sunday Times* to someone behind the screen.

From the Computer Room come sounds of whirring tapes, clickings and other computer-type noises. I see that through a slot in the grille is being pushed a coloured comic postcard with a caption at the bottom. Michael Caine takes it, looks at it, chuckles briefly and hands it to me.

The postcard comes to life and I'm sitting in an audience watching a stage show. On the stage, a comic Elizabethan figure in doublet and hose, wearing a hat with an enormous feather, is kneeling with his head in a guillotine. He looks apprehensively at the audience and rolls his eyes. The audience rocks with laughter, and the comic figure struggles to his feet, comes to the front of the stage and says, 'Sh-she-sh! Laughter is a capital offence!' More riotous laughter from the audience. The comic figure doffs his hat with a flourish and bows extravagantly.

For some reason I feel very grateful to Michael Caine, and turn to thank him. He says nothing, but points over his shoulder to indicate that he must 'dash', and with a friendly wave walks off.

I woke up, turned on the light and from my bedside table picked up the *Sunday Times*, which was open at the article on dreams. At no time during the dream had I been aware that it might relate to the problems, but now I found that I knew one of the answers: if the first (or capital) letter in each word is lopped off . . . [the sentence becomes 'How his old Russian hat raises laughter, laughter rings out.'] . . . I turned off my bedside lamp and started drowsing again. In my rather sleepy state I wondered what had happened to the answer to the other problem, which I felt I should know.

Before actually falling asleep again, I saw Michael Caine looking rather irritable and repeating the pointing gesture over his shoulder. I realised that he was performing a mime and that . . . pointing over his shoulder indicated past tense.

Again I switched on my bedside light and looked at the problems. I saw that the only one of the verbs whose past tense doesn't end in '-ght' was 'draw'.[54]

It is a remarkable dream, and not just because it comes up with both the right answers: first, lop off the first letters of the words in the trick sentence; second, look at the past tense of the verbs. It also reiterates its message in several forms, as though to make sure the dreamer gets the point: the Elizabethan actor, who is about to have his head chopped off, also doffs his ridiculous hat and calls laughter 'a capital offence'; Michael Caine repeats his past-tense gesture, first amiably, then irritably.

But there are other layers, other subtleties. The uproarious laughter expresses in mime what the transformed sentence says: 'laughter rings out'. In other words, the problem has already been unconsciously solved, the solution is present *before* the dreamer has discovered it. Added to that, the dream mimics itself: the processes of the mind busily working away become the whirrings and clickings of the code-breaking computers.

Jacques Lacan once said that dreams are 'like a charade where the participants must guess an utterance known to them, or its variant, with the sole help of a mimed scene'. Lacan had a gift for going too far, but for once he seems not to have gone far enough. Dreams are not *like* charades, they *are* charades – inner dramas in which mental activity expresses itself physically in signs and gestures. They are ideas in dumb show, thinking in mime.

***

Schatzman chose brain-teasers to illustrate how we think in dreams because brain-teasers have clear answers, and clear answers are persuasive, even to sceptics. But there is another kind of thinking in dreams, the kind that is full of meaning for the dreamers, the kind that interests psychoanalysts. These are the dreams which, in Emily Brontë's words, 'go through one's life like wine through water', the dreams which change your perspective and either help you to make decisions or show you the decisions you have already unwittingly taken. They, too, are the outcome of dream-thinking and, although sceptics are not always convinced by them, nearly everyone has experienced them at some time or other.

Not everyone, of course, is willing or able to hear what their dreams are telling them. But sometimes, when the message gets through, a dream changes the dreamer's life. When that happens, it ceases to be a dream and becomes a life event, something that stays on in the dreamer's conscious memory, as vivid and indelible as any waking landmark.

Here are two interconnected examples. The first was told to me by an American woman, now middle-aged and living in London:

When I was in my early twenties, doing graduate work in Chicago, I got engaged to a young man from South Carolina. We had parted for the summer, planning to be married in the fall. He'd gone home to Charleston, I'd gone back to New York. I have a feeling that it was the distance that enabled me to have the dream.

I dreamt that the wedding was taking place and, of course, his parents, whom I knew and liked, were there. They were charming Southerners but, despite all their culture and learning and good manners, I think they were racially prejudiced, like most other Southerners at that time. I was bothered by that, although my fiancé himself was not at all prejudiced. In the dream, his parents and his sisters and my family were all present. I guess the wedding had just taken place and I knew in my dream that it was the most terrible mistake. That's all I can remember. I think there was also something bothering me about the two families – probably because mine wasn't as respectable as his. On the other hand, I loved my rather disreputable parents, so it wasn't as simple as insecurity or envy over inferiority. It was something deeper: I just knew that the marriage was absolutely wrong. The real truth is, although we loved each other in a sisterly-brotherly way and we had a really good friendship and the sex was fine, there was something missing in our relationship – some kind of electrical charge, some buzz.

When I woke up, I knew the dream was telling me the truth: the feeling of misery and hopelessness and desperation that I felt at the wedding meant that I could never go through with it. So I broke off the engagement.

A couple of years later, the woman settled in London. The man she eventually married takes up the story:

In the early sixties, when I was between marriages and grimly playing the field in London, I had an on-and-off affair with an

American girl. For the most part, it was more off than on. We lived together for a few weeks, sometimes a few months, then we fought – or got tired of fighting – broke up and found other partners to live with. The usual routine. After about two years of this, I had a dream. She and I were off at that point and hadn't seen each other for months. I hadn't even thought much about her since I was preoccupied with another young woman – very attractive but very elusive – who was giving me a hard time. And because she was giving me a hard time and because I, being slow to grow up and stubbornly romantic, believed that true love was always doomed and unhappy, I imagined I was in love with her. In my dream, however, the American girl and I were dancing, something we always did well together and with pleasure. We were smiling at each other; I made a joke, she laughed. And then, still dancing, I pushed her out to arm's length and looked at her. I saw that her hair was white and I realized that mine, too, was white. We're old, I thought in my dream, and we're together. And I was perfectly happy.

I woke up still happy and I couldn't understand it. I knew I found her enormously attractive, I knew I enjoyed her company, but somehow I imagined that was not enough. It was too easy, too natural, not sufficiently doomed. (I suspect she felt the same.) But the dream was telling me what I refused to know: that I wanted to spend the rest of my life with her.

A few days later, I met the American girl on the street and told her the dream. Soon after that, we got back together again. We were married six months later.

All this took place nearly thirty years ago. The couple are still married – happily, in fact – and, although neither of them is prone to superstition or magical thinking, both are still convinced that without their dreams their lives would have been different because the dreams helped them understand choices they had already unconsciously made.

There is nothing eerie or far-fetched about this. On the contrary, what they experienced, at different times and on different continents, was the natural and inevitable outcome of what neurophysiologists now know to be true: the brain goes on working in sleep when we are not aware of it. The two young people were not receiving coded messages from an unknown source, they were simply thinking about their lives while they slept – not with words, not with abstractions, not with the left hemisphere of their brains, but concretely, dramatically and in images.

Roger Penrose, the Rouse Ball Professor of Mathematics at the University of Oxford, believes that this is how true thinking is done. He is a fierce and eloquent critic of the proponents of what is called 'strong AI' (Artificial Intelligence), who believe that the mind functions algorithmically, like an electronic computer, in a well-defined sequence of operations, and it is only a matter of time before computers will equal or surpass human intelligence. Penrose, who has been called 'one of the world's most knowledgeable and creative mathematical physicists', will have none of this. His case against AI is intricate and often dense, but in the course of it he quotes a letter by Albert Einstein:

> The words or the language, as they are written or spoken, do not seem to play any role in my mechanism of thought. The psychical entities which seem to serve as elements of thought are certain signs and more or less clear images which can be 'voluntarily' reproduced and combined . . . The above mentioned elements are, in my case, of visual and some muscular type. Conventional words or other signs have to be sought for laboriously only in a second stage, when the mentioned associative play is sufficiently established and can be reproduced at will.[55]

Penrose has other famous witnesses for the prosecution – they include the mathematician Henri Poincaré and the geneticist Francis Galton – all of whom agree that insight and inspiration have almost nothing to do with language, and that painstaking, logical, verbal thinking is, literally, the last thing they do. Schopenhauer wrote, 'thoughts die the moment they are embodied by words', and Penrose says of his own mathematical discoveries, 'Rigorous argument is usually the *last* step!' In other words, real thinking is a kind of physical process – 'visual and . . . muscular' were Einstein's words – deeply embedded in the structure of each individual's unique body-mind, just as John Donne once described it:

> wee understood
> Her by her sight; her pure and eloquent blood
> Spoke in her cheekes, and so distinctly wrought,
> That one might almost say, her body thought.

By these lights, thinking in dreams is a democratic version, freely available to all, of the kind of subliminal, instinctual, pre-verbal thinking that, in creative people, is called inspiration. The latter, however, then have to go through the laborious process of translating their intuitions into logical, communicable forms: mathematical equations, philosophical statements, music, paintings, poems, chess moves. The interpretation of dreams is just another variation on that painstaking theme.

# ART AND DREAMS

*O God, I could be bounded in a nutshell and count myself*
*king of infinite space, were it not that I have bad dreams.*

Shakespeare, *Hamlet*

*Duchess: I am Duchess of Malfi still.*
*Bosola: That makes thy sleeps so broken . . .*

Webster, *The Duchess of Malfi*

When Morton Schatzman asked his readers to try to solve brain-twisters in their sleep, he also posed the more general question, Why do we dream? One of his correspondents, a music lover, answered with an eloquent letter about 'a glorious musical dream'. She was child again, she wrote, back in the school chapel, listening to the girls sing Monteverdi's Vespers. The headmistress, a hateful woman who despised the pupils, was conducting, but she was standing sideways-on to the choir instead of facing them. The dreamer felt triumphant that these apparently contemptible little girls – herself included – could produce such beauty. She hoped that the headmistress was humbled by it, and ashamed.

My rational, conscious, intellectual self, is now feeling as thoroughly awed by this dream as, in the dream, I imagined the Head would be by the music! Surely I *am* now the 'head', listening to what the music as a whole – that is, the dream

173

itself – adds up to. The dream music was an impressive work of art, produced as it were unconsciously (in that each singer was singing only her own little part, unaware of what the music was like as a whole) – without any directing or control by the Head, who only had to listen. In other words, what the dream was saying was that dreaming itself is an art, to be 'listened to' with suitable humility by the overweening intellect. It seems to me, therefore . . . that I have produced a dream answer to your question, Why do we dream?, in a dream that illustrates and embodies itself![56]

When the mind dreams, she is saying, the body speaks without benefit of the head. It is like a variation on Donne's beautiful line 'That one might almost say, her body thought' – a line which, with its pausing, hesitant movement, embodies its own meaning by being itself thoughtful. Dreams are thinking without the intellect, thinking in bodily terms. And because dreaming is a purely mental experience which occurs mostly in REM sleep, when the body is out of action – the muscles virtually paralysed, the motor responses inhibited – it makes paradoxical, compensatory sense that dreams should speak a concrete, physical language, that thoughts and feelings should be expressed as actions and things, in mime and images, rather than abstractly in words.

But that, of course, is also how the arts work – even the arts whose medium is language. They make thoughts thinkable and feelings apprehensible by using words or paint or clay or marble or musical notation or film to give, among other things, a kind of physical immediacy to the mental and emotional world. So it also makes sense that dreams should figure large as a source of creative inspiration.

In one traditional view, dreams and art were almost inter-changeable. Consider, for example, Herman Gombiner, the hero of Isaac Bashevis Singer's story 'The Letter-Writer'. Awake, he leads a life reduced to the barest essentials: without family – they all died in the Nazi extermination camps – without friends, without lovers, without physical pleasures; he eats almost nothing and, once his meagre job has gone, he scarcely ventures out of his tiny apartment. But Herman is a man of premonitions and intuitions, in touch with the strangeness of things, and with a taste for the occult. His inner world is like Aladdin's cave, packed with exotic treasures, and his real life happens mostly in dreams:

> The greatest works began when Herman dozed off. As soon as he closed his eyes, his dreams came like locusts. He saw everything with clarity and precision. These were not dreams but visions. He flew over Oriental cities, hovered over cupolas, mosques, and castles, lingered in strange gardens, mysterious forests. He came upon undiscovered tribes, spoke foreign languages. Sometimes he was frightened by monsters.
>
> Herman had often thought that one's true life was lived during sleep. Waking was no more than a marginal time assigned for doing things.[57]

For Herman, as for the psychoanalyst Wilfred Bion, dreams are life events, and what he experiences while he sleeps is as charged with meaning as his waking life. But his shyness, frailty, weariness and pathetically constrained circumstances are permanently at odds with his wildly adventurous dream-life. The only place where his dreaming and waking meet is in his compulsive letter-writing to other aficionados of the occult, most of them women and all of them inaccessible. And maybe that, by implication, is Singer's view of the writer's fate: a rich fantasy, a pinched life, a nervous disposition and an unreliable audience whom he never sees.

But dreams are not simply a fantasy world to which the artist escapes, they are also part of the nature and fabric of art. To put it another way, art is the place where dreams and imagination cross and, long before the Romantics re-discovered the nightmare or Freud the unconscious, the business of art was to infuse waking reality with the power and vividness and drama of dreams:

> They flee from me, that sometime did me seek
>    With naked foot, stalking in my chamber.
> I have seen them gentle, tame, and meek,
>    That now are wild, and do not remember
>    That sometime they put themselves in danger
> To take bread at my hand; and now they range
> Busily seeking with a continual change.
>
> Thankéd be fortune it hath been otherwise
>    Twenty times better; but once, in special,
> In thin array, after a pleasant guise,
>    When her loose gown from her shoulders did fall,
>    And she me caught in her arms long and small,
> Therewithall sweetly did me kiss
> And softly said, 'Dear heart, how like you this?'
>
> It was no dream: I lay broad waking.
>    But all is turnéd, through my gentleness,
> Into a strange fashion of forsaking;
>    And I have leave to go of her goodness,
>    And she also to use newfangleness.
> But since that I so kindly am servéd,
> I would fain know what she hath deservéd.

Sir Thomas Wyatt wrote that poem sometime around 1535, probably about the elusive Anne Boleyn, who had been his mistress until she dumped him abruptly when she took the king's fancy. Whoever inspired it, the poem is about love, lust, frustration and outrage, and, like a dream, it presents the whole slithering, tangled mass of emotions with all their contradictions intact.

Like a dream too, nothing is fixed or stable; the scene switches to and fro, from forest to courtly chamber and back, while the identities of the hunter and the hunted shift and elide. The predator stalking in the poet's bedroom changes into a shy quarry that can be coaxed into taking bread from his hand. (This in itself is a dream transformation of words into things; behind it are what, even then, were conventional literary puns: dear/deer, heart/hart). In the second stanza, the scene switches again and there is another sudden dream transformation – from wild creature to temptress, from deer to dear. The seduction that follows is also pure dream; not a narrative, but a series of vivid details which together add up to a kind of erotic epiphany: the nightgown slipping from the woman's shoulders, 'her arms long and small' (slender), the sweet kiss and single, whispered sentence – 'Dear heart, how like you this?' (Miss Foxwell, a Victorian editor of Wyatt, responded to this supreme provocation with a helpful footnote: 'A common 16th century form of salutation'!)

'It was no dream: I lay broad waking.' The more Wyatt denies the dream, the more dreamlike the poem becomes. It is as though the memories of what had happened were so confusing – so vivid, strange, tantalising and outrageous – that he himself could no longer distinguish dream-life from reality. For Wyatt, however, 'it was no dream' in the formal, literary sense because at that time deliberate dream poems, visions of this and that, were schematic and simple-minded, in the manner of Artemidorus. The poem is *like* a dream, but it is not *about* a dream; it is about an intensely waking seduction and the poet's subsequent inability to get out from under its spell. In other words, it is about an experience which aroused in Wyatt emotions so tangled and conflicting that the only way to express them was through the techniques that dreaming takes for granted – through condensation and elision, through thoughts expressed as images and thinking as drama. Poetry, in short, does not necessarily come from dreams, but the language and methods of dreaming come naturally to poetry.

They also come naturally to other creative processes. In judging the validity of mathematical inspiration, '*aesthetic* criteria are enormously valuable', writes Roger Penrose, and the italics are his:

> In the arts, one might say that it is aesthetic criteria that are paramount . . . It could be argued that in mathematics and the sciences, such criteria are merely incidental, the criterion of *truth* being paramount. However, it seems impossible to separate one from the other when one considers the issues of inspiration and insight. My impression is that the strong conviction of the *validity* of a flash of inspiration . . . is very closely bound up with its aesthetic qualities. A beautiful idea has a much greater chance of being a correct idea than an ugly one.[58]

The same is true of dreams, except that the aesthetics of a dream are emotional rather than formal. There is nothing inherently beautiful about the dream of the young man and his girl dancing happily together when they are old or of the studious child digging up a fossil. Like the flash of mathematical inspiration, the dreams are beautiful because they are simple and they feel right. Each weaves together a complicated web of feelings and then transforms it into a single dramatic image which is moving in two senses – because it is enacted and because it is emotionally true.

Maybe this is what all aesthetic judgments boil down to: not rightness of form, since forms change and what is ugly to one generation – tribal art, for example – is beautiful to another, but rightness of feeling. In poetry, feelings – not the grand emotions aspired to, but the altogether subtler sense of being emotionally awakened – are expressed less in the imagery than in the inner rhythm of the language, in the way a line moves. The line itself may have no visual elements at all – Coleridge's 'And the spring comes slowly up this way' – or the imagery may be suppressed and at a remove – 'Busily seeking with a continual change' – but if you listen properly you can hear it stir and pause and breathe.

When I. A. Richards said rhythm was the one thing the poet can never fake, he was not referring to the regular, mechanical thumpity-thump – 'The Assyrian came down like the wolf on the fold,/ And his cohorts were gleaming in silver and gold' – he meant the inner rhythm, the natural breath. When the poet is genuinely disturbed or aroused, it is this inner rhythm of the lines that shows it. And when the rhythm is dead, no amount of invention can disguise the fact. In this respect, poetry is like music, which is a kind of mathematics of the emotions: the rhythm – the way the sounds move, combine, separate, recombine – is the vehicle for the feeling. I know from my own experience that it is sometimes possible to hear a poem before you know what it is about, to get the movement before you get the words. And without that inner movement or disturbance, the words, no matter how fetching, remain inert. In this way at least, the dynamics of poetry – and probably of all the arts – are the same as the dynamics of dreaming. They share the same methods, they have the same underlying structure.

## COLERIDGE

*In a distempered dream things & forms in themselves common & harmless inflict a terror of anguish.*

Coleridge, *Notebooks*, 1797

For the Augustans, the proper study of mankind may have been man, but man only in his role as a social animal. What happened in the private world or the world of sleep was not on their agenda for the arts. Late in the eighteenth century, however, a change occurred. From the moment when the Romantics turned away from polite society and re-established the private self at the centre of the world, dreams ceased to be disturbing curiosities on the periphery of literature and became a major preoccupation. Not only were they authentic manifestations of the inner world, they also neatly fitted the Romantics' idea of the artist as a vessel for inspiration, an Aeolian harp blown on by forces he did not properly understand. What could be more fickle or ephemeral, more impossible to predict or provoke – in a word, more romantic – than a dream?

The Romantics courted dreams and cultivated them – mostly dreams of themselves as tormented outsiders or, in one guise or another, of *belles dames sans merci*. They were also enamoured of what Shelley called 'the tempestuous loveliness of terror' and, in the pursuit of it, they courted nightmares with the same absurd solemnity as the bards of the drug culture in the 1960s courted out-of-body experiences:

> The painter Fuseli, who thought that 'one of the most unexplored regions of art are Dreams', ate large quantities of raw meat before going to bed. Anne Radcliffe, who domesticated the Gothick novel in the 1790s, also resorted to indigestible food and spent her waking hours explaining the nightmares her diet induced. Southey preferred laughing gas . . . Charles Robert Maturin's *Melmoth the Wanderer* and Matthew Lewis's *The Monk* both contain long descriptions of horrible dreams which have little relation to the central plots . . . Sometimes [the Gothick fantasies] were stimulated by opium. Byron took Black Drop, a popular compound, as a tranquillizer; Shelley took laudanum for nervous headaches . . . Minor Gothick neophytes, of the type satirized in *Northanger Abbey*, had been trying to emulate Horace Walpole's success for years, by stimulating nightmares of their own: they ate bad meat after long periods of vegetarianism, read as many worm-ridden tomes as they could find and tried to let their blinkered imaginations run riot. But they soon discovered that nightmares *in vacuo*, created by numbers, were not really frightening at all – plenty of romance, not much agony, save perhaps indigestion.[59]

The Gothick novel and its associated fantasies were the penny-dreadful aspect of Romanticism. But there was nothing at all sensational about Coleridge's nightmares. He had been a martyr to them since childhood, he remained a martyr for the whole of his life and, in the catalogue of his tribulations, nightmares outranked even his disastrous marriage and his addiction to what he modestly called 'stimulants' – i.e., opium:

my marriage – constant dread in my mind respecting Mrs Coleridge's Temper, &c – and finally stimulants in the fear & prevention of violent Bowel-attacks from mental agitation/ then (almost epileptic) night-horrors in my sleep/ & since then every error I have committed, has been the immediate effect of the Dread of these bad most shocking Dreams – any thing to prevent them.[60]

Nightmares made him 'dread to go to bed or fall asleep', and when he did they woke him screaming night after night, with his terrified family gathered around his bed. 'With Sleep my Horrors commence . . .' he wrote. 'Dreams are no shadows with me; but the real, substantial miseries of life.'[61] Unlike the scribblers of Gothick novels eating rotting meat in order to induce nightmares, Coleridge poisoned himself with opium in order to prevent them. But it was his nature to be fascinated by whatever troubled him most. He was an analysand *avant la lettre*, an analysand without an analyst, and his scrupulous attention to his inner world richly compensated for the fecklessness of his daily life.

Above all, he studied his dreams. His notebooks are full of subtle comments on the bizarreness of dreams, on their relationship to waking life, on the mechanics and levels of dreaming, on the *ego diurnus* and the *ego nocturnus*, the day self and the night self. And because he was a poet, he was particularly shrewd on the difference between 'the language of Dream=Night [and] that of Waking=Day'. Like a modern dream-researcher describing the predominance of the brain's right hemisphere activity in REM sleep, Coleridge believed that the night self spoke 'a language of Images and Sensations, the various dialects of which are far less different from each other, than the various (Day-) Languages of Nations'.[62]

When Coleridge wrote that note in 1818, I think he was recollecting – in comparative tranquillity – his own youthful experience with dream-language, as he had described it in the preface to 'Kubla Khan', the greatest of all dream poems:

> The Author continued for about three hours in a profound sleep, at least of the external senses, during which time he has the most vivid confidence, that he could not have composed less than from two to three hundred lines; if that indeed can be called composition in which all the images rose up before him as *things*, with a parallel production of the correspondent expressions, without any sensation or consciousness of effort.[63]

'Kubla Khan' is all images, all 'things' that Coleridge had absorbed in the course of his omnivorous reading, then dredged up again, transformed and suffused with feeling, so that the strange landscape they create has the urgency of a powerful dream – the kind that stays on after the dreamer wakes and seems to insist that it has something important to say.[64] An old-fashioned Freudian could have a field-day with the 'caverns measureless to man' and 'sunless sea', the walled paradise garden, 'that deep romantic chasm' with a 'mighty fountain' spurting from it, the 'demon lover' and 'ancestral voices'. But the primal scene, I think, was not the creativity Coleridge had (even unconsciously) in mind. The landscape of 'Kubla Khan' sounds, instead, very like the imagination as Coleridge later described it in the famous chapters of his *Biographia Literaria*: as a river, a living force that 'dissolves, diffuses, dissipates, in order to re-create', or, as he depicted Shakespeare's genius, as two rivers, his creative powers and his intellectual energy, 'that, at their first meeting within narrow and rocky banks, mutually strive to repel each other and intermix reluctantly and in tumult; but soon finding a wider channel and more yielding shores blend, and dilate, and flow on in one current and with one voice . . . diverging and contracting'.[65] In other words, in the same way as dreams are often about themselves and the process of dreaming, 'Kubla Khan' can be read as a dream poem about poetry and the poetic imagination.

Coleridge was a great literary critic, prodigiously intelligent and well read. But he was also prodigiously loquacious, and his reading, particularly his appetite for metaphysics, played in with his long-windedness and his tendency, as a poet, to run on and on long after his inspiration had subsided. The poet who wrote a perfect quatrain like

> The moving Moon went up the sky,
> And no where did abide:
> Softly she was going up,
> And a star or two beside . . .

was also guilty of:

> She felt them coming, but no power
> Had she the words to smother;
> And with a kind of shriek she cried,
> 'Oh Christ! you're like your mother!'

And the latter, unfortunately, is typical of the bulk of his work. Slogging through the *Collected Poems*, the reader's problem is not that Coleridge sometimes nods, but that he ever wakes. The Oxford edition runs to nearly six hundred pages, but Coleridge's reputation as a major poet rests on a mere fifty-five of those pages, on five poems in all: 'The Rime of the Ancient Mariner', 'Christabel', 'Kubla Khan',

'Dejection: an Ode', 'Frost at Midnight'. The rest of the verse is mostly so prolix and indifferent that it casts doubt on the five great poems. It would be understandable if the five were merely good; any poet can produce a handful of good poems in the course of a lifetime's effort. Coleridge's masterpieces, however, are unique – like nothing else in English literature – and in the context of his other verse, they seem almost out of place.

Coleridge knew this better than anyone; it was one of the abiding torments of his life and the subject of 'Dejection', the finest of all his poems. Dejection, he claims, has destroyed his spontaneity, his liveliness, his 'shaping spirit of Imagination'; it has deprived him of his youthful vulnerability, that blessed condition in which, like the Aeolian harp at his window, he was blown on by every emotion and made music of it. Yet when the storm breaks and the harp is finally inspired with the poems the poet himself can no longer write, they turn out to be conventional Romantic high dramas – a florid battle scene and a pathetic abandoned child à la Otway – much inferior to his own subtle masterpieces. In other words, Coleridge was deceiving himself. He always had access to the triter sources of Romantic inspiration – that is why he wrote so many bad poems – but the sources unique to him were more elusive and harder to handle.

'There is in genius itself an unconscious activity,' he wrote; 'nay, that is the genius in the man of genius'. A large part of Coleridge's genius was his ability to use his dreams or, as John Livingstone Lowes brilliantly demonstrated in *The Road to Xanadu*, to recycle his vast reading in dream form. He was pre-eminently a night poet and, in their different ways, his five great poems are all night pieces: 'Dejection' and 'Frost at

Midnight' are, among other things, about being awake while the rest of the world sleeps; 'Kubla Khan' is pure dream; 'The Ancient Mariner' and 'Christabel' are steeped in dreams, which Coleridge himself called, after the fashion of the time, 'the supernatural'. Their framework may be Romantic Gothick – a nautical ballad and a tale of knights and ladies – but it is Gothick transformed by dream imagery and sudden dream-shifts of focus.

When Geraldine lays her spell on Christabel, she does so at night, in bed, in a kind of nightmare revelation – an ancient, freezing witch's body beneath the beautiful damsel's clothes – and Christabel submits as though to a nightmare – unable to move, asleep, yet with eyes wide open. The following morning, the bard Bracey tells a terrible dream he has had about Christabel, which her father misinterprets. When the girl tries to protest, Geraldine turns on her and undergoes another dream transformation – 'Each [eye] shrunk up to a serpent's eye' – as swift and secret and chilling as, in a nightmare, a friendly face changes into a monster.

*The Rime of the Ancient Mariner*, too, is full of images Coleridge had read in travel books and then transmuted, not just into poetry, but in ways that would fit them comfortably into Allan Hobson's elaborately scientific scale of 'dream bizarreness':[66] the eerie Antarctic landscape and rotting equatorial sea, the phantom ship, with Death and Life-in-Death playing dice for the soul of the Mariner, the ghost crew and the ghostly, abbreviated journey home.

Even more dream-like in *The Rime of the Ancient Mariner* is the pervasive, sustaining sense of guilt and the terrible inevitability of its plot: a casual crime, casually reported – 'With my cross-bow/ I shot the Albatross' – which locks the criminal into a series of torments until he – unwittingly – repents. This is the same logic that Kafka exploited: bewildered innocence – 'Who? Me? What have I done?' – hand-in-hand with an utter conviction of guilt. It is also the logic of the compulsive, repetitive nightmare, which is exactly how Coleridge describes it in the poem:

> Since then, at an uncertain hour,
> That agony returns:
> And till my ghastly tale is bold,
> This heart within me burns.

'If a man could pass thro' Paradise in a Dream', Coleridge wrote in his notebooks in 1815, '& have a flower presented to him as a pledge that his Soul had really been there, & found that flower in his hand when he awoke – Aye! and what then?'[67] That is what happened to him in his creative youth, when he wrote 'Kubla Khan'. But there were four other flowers, equally beautiful, unique, unexpected and, as it turned out, not to be gathered at will. As he grew older and increasingly overwhelmed by commonplace unhappiness – a bad marriage, drug-addiction, overwork, shortage of money – dreams and the 'almost epileptic night-horrors' of his sleep changed from a source of inspiration into a source of terror, so he turned away, having lost the energy and the will to face them.

# NERVAL

*I am feeding off my own substance, and do not renew myself.*

Gérard de Nerval, letter to George Bell

By the 1830s and 1840s, Romanticism had degenerated into high fashion. Young men cultivated the Byronic look, dark and dangerous and doomed; they dressed in black, collected Gothick bric-à-brac, joined secret societies and held Satanic orgies in the hope of making their perfectly normal youthful bad behaviour seem serious and subversive. Carefully chaperoned young women devoured Gothick novels and tortured themselves to achieve *l'air romantique*: a pale, melancholy face (they drank vinegar and sucked lead pencils), luminous eyes (they dilated the pupils with belladonna), a sylph-like figure (they starved themselves and wore iron corsets), and a brooding, enigmatic manner, three parts suppressed passion, one part languor. In their daydreams, they were châtelaines of turreted castles with all mediaeval conveniences, including a love-lorn page to dog their foot-steps and a love-lorn troubadour to wake them with aubades.

Nightmares and vampires were as much a part of the Romantic baggage as the fancy dress and Gothick yearning. But behind this fantasy world, there was also a cult of dreams. The Romantics believed in dreams in the same feverish, unfocused way as students in the 1960s believed in revolution. Dreams stood for freedom from the social constraints of their fathers – from classical decorum and bourgeois self-satisfaction. Dreams were strange and mysterious and unpredictable, and they fitted the dreamy image of the artist as a vulnerable creature, all soul and sensibility, blown on by the haphazard winds of emotion. Théophile Dondey, who, because Sir Walter Scott was all the fashion, made a Celtic anagram of his name and called himself Philothée O'Neddy, wore spectacles when he went to sleep at night in order see his dreams more clearly. Gérard de Nerval (born Gérard Labrunie) began *Aurélia*, his most famous novel, with a Romantic statement of faith: 'Our dreams are a second life.'

*Aurélia*, in fact, is Nerval's dream-book. Its subtitle, 'Life and the Dream', describes it precisely: an autobiographical framework for a series of lurid dreams:

> Then the monsters changed shape. They cast off their first skins and raised themselves up more powerfully on their enormous paws. The great mass of their bodies crushed the branches and vegetation, and in this chaos of nature they engaged in struggles in which I myself was part, for I had a body as strange as theirs. Suddenly a singular harmony echoed through our solitudes and it seemed as if the confused cries, roarings and hissings of these primitive beings now took on this celestial melody. Infinite variations followed, the planet grew gradually lighter, heavenly shapes appeared among the shrubs and in the depths of the groves and, thus mastered, all the monsters I had seen shed their weird shapes and became men and women; others, in their reincarnations, assumed the bodies of wild animals, fishes and birds.[68]

Maybe Nerval really dreamt like that. Dreams, after all, are unverifiable, beyond proof, beyond argument. (That is one of the many reasons why 'hard' scientists object to psycho-analysis.) What is not beyond argument, however, is that the dreams in *Aurélia* are unusually high-flown. This may be because Nerval was clinically schizophrenic and *Aurélia* is about being mad, about, as he put it, 'the overflowing of the dream into real life'. He spent his life in and out of lunatic asylums, paraded in the gardens of the Palais-Royal with a lobster on a pale blue ribbon – when challenged, he said he preferred lobsters to dogs because they don't bark and they know the secrets of the deep – and finally hanged himself with an old apron-string which he insisted, according to which source you believe, was the Queen of Sheba's garter or the corset-string of either Madame de Maintenon or Marguerite de Valois. *Aurélia*, his friend Gautier said, was '*la folie se racontant elle-même*' (madness speaking itself).

But it is not the strangeness of the dreams in *Aurélia* that makes them seem unreal. No dream could be stranger than 'Kubla Khan', yet part of its power for the reader is the underlying conviction that the poem is not 'just a dream'. Although Coleridge insisted it was merely a fragment, a psychological curiosity, 'Kubla Khan' has a sustaining sense of purpose, an inner, inward logic that imposes both formal and emotional shape on its strangeness. It satisfies Coleridge's own definition of poetry; it 'contains in itself the reason why it is so, and not otherwise'. Nerval's dreams, by contrast, sound like what dreams *should be* if life were lived according to the hysterical principles of high Romanticism. They are not so much dreams as dreams of dreams, dreams reworked not just for their drama, but tenderly, almost nostalgically, as signs of a rich inner life, in the same spirit as *Sylvie*, his earlier auto-biographical novel, reworks his pastoral youth and loves.

Yet all the literary devices in the world could not stop 'the overflowing of the dream into real life'. In his sane moments, *le pauvre Gérard* was a sweet-natured man, a *'tendre fol'* and *'doux rêveur'*, recklessly generous. Heine, who loved him, said he was 'more a soul than a man – an angelic soul, I mean'. But he was also mad, and sweetness was no defence against the nightmares and hallucinations his madness induced. Nerval wrote down his dreams in an attempt to turn them into literature, according to the florid principles of his time. But eventually they began to write him and he ended up hanging from a grating at the bottom of the stone stairs leading to the rue de la Tuerie in Paris.

# STEVENSON AND THE BROWNIES

*The past is all one texture – whether feigned or suffered –*
*whether acted out in three dimensions, or only witnessed*
*in that small theatre of the brain which we keep brightly*
*lighted all night long, after the jets are down, and darkness*
*and sleep reign undisturbed in the remainder of the body.*

Robert Louis Stevenson, 'A Chapter on Dreams'

The Romantics cultivated nightmare as an essential ingredient
of the Romantic agony; a century later, the Surrealists enlisted
it in homage to the new-found land of the unconscious; but in
between, it was assimilated into late Victorian society in the
minor art-form of the ghost story. For masters of the form,
like M. R. James and Bram Stoker, nightmare has a Gothick
face and is spooky not because it is mediaeval and strange – full
of romantic castles and clanking armour and the mumbo-
jumbo of witchcraft – but because it is in some way
domesticated, because it intrudes into the comfortable family
circle. The vampire or the evil curse is brought back to life,
usually by someone with antiquarian interests and psychologically questionable motives, and erupts among the over-
stuffed furniture of decent, middle-class homes where decent,
unsuspecting people lead their ordinary lives. (The same
formula still applies: in contemporary horror stories and films,
Satan and his minions usually appear when nice young

modern couples unwisely move into old houses which, at some distant point in their histories, have been contaminated by evil, or even – a clever variation in the film *Poltergeist* – when they move into shiny new houses built an old cemeteries.)

In other words, the late Victorian passion for ghost stories – even Henry James experimented with the form in his devious way – was a highly specialised variation on the Gothick. It was, literally, Gothick by gaslight. In the centuries before proper street lighting, when people had to make do with burning torches and candles, night was full of danger and peace-loving citizens stayed at home behind locked doors after sunset. Gaslight changed all that, but gaslight was inefficient. The little puddles of illumination it created made the surrounding darkness seem even more dangerous and threatening. Dickens walked the chronically fog-swaddled streets of London by night in much the same risky spirit of exploration as Dr Livingstone travelled Africa, the 'dark continent': to explore it and to colonise it. In Dickens's novels, night and fog are not merely a background against which his characters act out their parts; they are substantial presences with their own roles to play.

Just as the dim, unsteady clearings of light cast by the gaslamps somehow emphasised the darkness beyond, the Victorians were uneasily aware that behind their prosperous, well-regulated lives, their confidence and their propriety, lay a whole world of darkness which they preferred not to notice. The darkness manifested itself in many forms – everything from Tennyson's melancholia and Edward Lear's manic-depression to Jack the Ripper's spectacular sadism. The Victorians disapproved of it, they denied it, but it fascinated them, and, as a tribute to their denial, they turned sordid domestic murder into a form of popular art and immortalised it in the Chamber of Horrors at Madame Tussaud's Waxworks Museum.

This was not solely an image of the dank, echoing cellar of their psyche, it was also part of their Romantic inheritance. Romanticism had turned people back towards their inner lives and the Victorians were beginning to understand how little they knew about the subject. The more light spread physically (gaslamps in the street, gaslight on tap in the houses) and metaphorically (the slow spread of literacy throughout the whole population began in 1880, when Parliament passed the first Education Act, which made schooling compulsory for all children between the ages of five and ten), the more people became aware of the inner darkness we now call the un-conscious. But like the darkness of night or the dark continent, the inner darkness was *terra incognita*, unmapped, uncompre-hended, threatening and ripe for exploration. To put it another way: for all his originality, Freud didn't start from scratch; by the time he was a medical student, psychiatry was already the great new topic for scientific inquiry; he turned to it in much the same spirit as a gifted and ambitious young intern today might decide to specialise in the neurophysiology of the brain – because it was a radical new discipline, because it was where the action was in medical research.

Gothick nightmare and the rediscovered fascination with the dark side of the psyche intersect in the most popular of all Victorian horror stories, *The Strange Case of Dr Jekyll and Mr Hyde*. Stevenson called it 'a gothick gnome . . . but the gnome is interesting, I think', and he wrote it as a 'crawler', a horror story, because 'crawlers' made money and Stevenson was always strapped for cash. On those terms, the book was a vast success. It was published in January 1886, sold forty thousand copies in Britain in the first six months, then swept America in both authorised and pirated editions. According to Graham Balfour, Stevenson's cousin and first biographer, 'Its success was probably due rather to the moral instincts of the public than to any conscious perception of the merits of its art. It was read by those who never read fiction, it was quoted in pulpits, and made the subject of leading articles in religious newspapers.'[69] The 'moral instincts' of Stevenson's audience may have been titillated by the theme – the struggle between good and evil in one man – in the same way as later audiences, curious about Freud and what he had to say about the duplicity of the mind, read Stevenson's book as a plain man's guide to schizophrenia and the behaviour of the Id, but the story's continuing grip on the imagination is another matter entirely.

Although even the title makes it sound like a moral fable or a clinical study, *The Strange Case of Dr Jekyll and Mr Hyde* works in the same way as a dream, which is also the same way as all true art: it takes abstract concepts – good and evil, Ego and Id – and turns them into people with distinctive physical characteristics, appetites and patterns of behaviour; it then makes them act out their metaphysical debate in dramatic terms. The drama, the dream charade, is far more powerful than the implied moral debate or psychological conflict.

This is as it should be since the key scenes of the novel – 'the scene at the window, and a scene afterward split in two, in which Hyde, pursued for some crime, took the powder and underwent the change in the presence of his pursuers' – were given to Stevenson in a dream. I say 'given' because that is exactly how Stevenson makes it sound in his extraordinary essay 'A Chapter on Dreams'.[70] The essay might also be called 'The Strange Case of Robert Louis Stevenson' because, like *Dr Jekyll and Mr Hyde*, it is at once a clinical study – Stevenson tells it in the third person and only reveals that he is talking about himself near the end – and a kind of moral fable about the creative processes. Its subject is a man, like the Marquis Hervey de Saint-Denys, with a dream-life so powerful and absorbing that, in recollection, it blends inextricably with the life he leads when awake: 'There is no distinction on the face of our experiences; one is vivid indeed, and one dull, and one pleasant, and another agonising to remember; but which of them is what we call true, and which a dream, there is not one hair to prove.'

Stevenson was a frail, sickly child, given to fevers – the first stirrings, presumably, of the consumption that finally killed him – and, he says, 'an ardent and uncomfortable dreamer'. But 'uncomfortable', he immediately makes clear, was a gross understatement. As a child, he was so tormented by bad dreams that, despite loving parents and a beloved, attentive nanny, sleep terrified him so much that he 'struggled hard against the approaches of that slumber that was the beginning of sorrow. But his struggles were in vain; sooner or later the night-hag would have him by the throat, and pluck him, strangling and screaming, from his sleep.' His childish nightmares were so overpowering that, late in his life, when he wrote 'A Chapter on Dreams', he could still describe them in frightening detail. And they continued to plague him nightly until some time in his twenties when, 'trembling for his reason', he went to a doctor, 'whereupon with a simple draught he was restored to the common lot of man'.

If that sounds like the scene which came to Stevenson in a

dream, 'in which Hyde, pursued for some crime, took the powder and underwent the change', it is for a good reason. 'A Chapter on Dreams' is not, in fact, just about dreams; it is also about creativity. Stevenson's mother recalled that, when he was six years old, Louis dreamed he heard 'the noise of pens writing', and he himself says that around that age 'he began to read in his dreams – tales, for the most part . . . but so incredibly more vivid and moving than any printed book, that he has ever since been malcontent with literature'.

In a way, he never recovered either from the impact of those first literary dreams or from the consequent belief that dreams were the true source of creativity. Instead, he split his talent in two: on one side were what he called his 'Brownies', 'the little people who manage man's internal theatre' in which dreams are acted out; on the other was himself, the passive spectator of their play, lounging in his box-seat above the stage, watching the drama unfold, then laboriously sifting and cutting and hammering it into shape once he had woken. As evidence of their talent and his own inadequacy, he describes an elaborate plot, full of subtle twists and surprises, with a dénouement so clever and unexpected that,

> with a pang of wonder and mercantile delight, the dreamer awoke . . . To the end [the little people] had kept their secret. I will go bail for the dreamer . . . that he had no guess whatever at the motive of the woman – the hinge of the whole well-invented plot – until the instant of that highly dramatic declaration [of love]. It was not his tale; it was the little people's! And observe: not only was the secret kept, the story was told with really guileful craftsmanship . . . I am awake now, and I know this trade; and yet I cannot better it.

The story the Little People had acted out for him was about a son who murders his father, gets away with it, then continues to share the paternal house with his young step-mother. Slowly, as the two of them grow closer together, he begins to believe she suspects him. Then he watches her unearth incontrovertible proof of his guilt from the scene of the crime. Yet she makes no mention of it, even when he confronts her twice, face to face, with the damning evidence between them. Still he waits for the denunciation and still it does not come. Finally, he can bear the strain no longer:

> all the time of the meal she had tortured him with sly allusions; and no sooner were the servants gone, and these two protagonists alone together, than he leaped to his feet. She too sprang up with a pale face; with a pale face she heard him as he raved out his complaint: Why did she torture him so? she knew all, she knew he was no enemy to her; why did she not denounce him at once? what signified her whole behaviour? why did she torture him? and yet again, why did she torture him? And when he had done, she fell upon her knees, and with outstretched hands: 'Do you not understand?' she cried. 'I love you!'

This is the unexpected dénouement that woke Stevenson with the wonder of it. In these more case-hardened times, it needs no ghost of Freud come from the grave to tell us that the Little People's play is a variation on the story of Oedipus. But that, for Stevenson, was not the point. What astonished him was not the bare bones of the plot, but the artistry with which it was developed, and the fact that he himself did not know what his Brownies were up to.

It is as though his dream-life put his whole artistic talent in doubt:

Who are the Little People? They are near connections of the dreamer's, beyond doubt; they share in his financial worries and have an eye to the bank book; they share plainly in his training; they have plainly learned like him to build the scheme of a considerate story and to arrange emotion in progressive order; only I think they have more talent . . . Who are they, then? . . . What shall I say but they are just my Brownies, God bless them! who do one-half my work for me while I am fast asleep, and in all human likelihood, do the rest for me as well, when I am wide awake and fondly suppose I do it for myself. That part which is done while I am sleeping is the Brownies' part beyond contention; but that which is done when I am up and about is by no means necessarily mine, since all goes to show the Brownies have a hand in it even then. Here is a doubt that much concerns my conscience. For myself – what I call I, my conscious ego, the denizen of the pineal gland unless he has changed his residence since Descartes . . . – I am sometimes tempted to suppose he is no story-teller at all, but a creature as matter of fact as any cheesemonger or any cheese, and a realist bemired up to the ears in actuality; so that, by any account, the whole of my published fiction should be the single-handed product of some Brownie, some Familiar, some unseen collaborator, whom I keep locked in a back garret, while I get all the praise . . . I am an excellent adviser, something like Molière's servant; I pull back and I cut down; and I dress the whole in the best words and sentences that I can find and make; I hold the pen, too; and when all is done, I make up the manuscript and pay for the registration; so that, on the whole, I have some claim to a share, though not so largely as I do, in the profits of our common enterprise.

On one level, Stevenson, in his breezy way, is talking about the occupational hazard of the creative arts: self-doubt. 'We work in the dark – we do what we can – we give what we have,' wrote Henry James. 'Our doubt is our passion and our passion is our task. The rest is the madness of art.' The better the artist, the more keenly he knows that whateever he does falls short of what he might have done or what his chosen medium is capable of. Unsullied confidence in the excellence of one's work is usually a sign of failing powers. 'He used to be a great artist,' Braque said of the ageing Picasso, 'but now he's only a genius.' Although Stevenson lived a wild bohemian life, he had no illusions about genius. The books he had read in his dreams as a child had set a standard he knew he could never equal and left him 'ever since . . . malcontent with literature'. What James called 'the madness of art' Stevenson called his Brownies, and he cast himself self-deprecatingly in the role of their dogsbody, taking down their dictation, cutting and trimming it, sending off the finished manuscript and coping with the publishers – 'a realist bemired up to the ears in actuality' and utterly bereft of imagination. Apart from practical help and the scene-setting, all he could add to the pot was 'morality, worse luck! [for] my Brownies have not a rudiment of what we call conscience'.

The psychiatrist Ernest Hartmann has suggested that people with artistic talent and people who are chronically prone to nightmares have minds with 'thin boundaries': compared, say, to an obsessional neurotic, who tries to tidy his whole life away in neat, watertight compartments, they are more vulnerable to their own feelings and fantasies, more open to the experience of others, less able to distinguish between waking and dreaming.[71] For Stevenson, the boundaries were so thin that they seem scarcely to have existed. So he did what he could to keep his dream-life at bay by projecting it on to his Little People. Compared to what they got up to behind his closed eyes, his footloose, adventurous waking life was a dull and featureless routine.

The tone of 'A Chapter on Dreams' is flippant, but not flippant enough to disguise the fact that Stevenson is deadly serious – not just about the terror and desolation of his childish nightmares, which he vividly recreates, but about something trickier and more hidden. In one way, the lawlessness of his fantasy life was an embarrassment: his Brownies have no conscience, he says, and one of his essential functions as their menial was to keep up the moral tone. The 'pang of wonder and mercantile delight' with which he woke from his Oedipal dream was instantly followed by the realisation 'that in this spirited tale there were unmarketable elements' – in other words, it was too strong for his strait-laced Victorian audience.

But the pang of wonder was real. Stevenson was in awe of his own imagination – that, ultimately, is what 'A Chapter on Dreams' is about – even though modesty forbade him to take credit for it. So he heaped ironic praise on his Little People, his Brownies, and excused himself by saying, '*I think they have more talent.*'

After Freud, it became commonplace to believe that dreams were 'the royal road to the unconscious', but when Stevenson was writing not only was the inner world still green on the map, uncharted and unexplored, but the whole concept of the unconscious did not properly exist. Stevenson knew about the 'conscious ego, the denizen of the pineal gland', but the unconscious was like a black hole in space – a place of force, full of gravity, yet utterly mysterious.

More important, it did not even have a name. Coleridge and Carlyle, being addicts of German metaphysics, had both used 'unconscious' as a noun but, according to the supplement to the *Oxford English Dictionary*, the word was not used in its modern sense until 1885, and then only in an obscure learned publication and as a translation from the German, *Unbewusste*. The *OED*'s next example is from a lecture given in London by Freud himself in 1912, eighteen years after Stevenson's death. When William James used 'unconscious' as an adjective in his *Principles of Psychology*, he considered the term odd or technical enough to put inverted commas around it. That was in 1890, when Stevenson had already settled on the remote South Seas island where he died.

Yet, like all artists, he had experienced the power of the unconscious, he knew how to harness it for his own purposes and, above all, he was in awe of it. All that was missing was a formal concept of this strange force and a word to define it. So he solved the problem the only way he knew how: he turned the unconscious into fiction. He anthropomorphised it, gave it a name (Brownies) and a shape (Little People) and a role (play-acting). In this way, he did for his unconscious precisely what his dreams had always done for his creative imagination. Considering his strange diffidence in the face of his inspiration and his bemused gratitude for what seemed to him its unearned gifts, perhaps he felt he was repaying a debt.

# SURREALISM

Genius is a kind of madness in our midst, but
madness is not genius.

Geoffrey Wagner on Nerval

Surrealism was the last swoon of Romanticism and its patron
saint was Gérard de Nerval. André Breton invoked him in the
*First Surrealist Manifesto* of 1924, Eluard collected his manu-
scripts, and all of the French Surrealists admired him, in a
mildly patronising way, as a '*fol délicieux*', the outcast genius
who brought madness to art.

In Surrealism, however, Romanticism was given new
impetus and dignity through the writings of Freud – or rather,
through a hazy, inflated version of what Freud was said to be
about. None of the Surrealists was particularly interested in
how the psyche functions, which is the true subject of
psychoanalysis, but the best of the painters – Ernst, Arp, de
Chirico, Magritte – were fascinated by its mystery, deviousness and wit. They used dreams, when they used them at all,
not as a reflection of their unconscious fantasies, but as just
another visual language, a way of transforming apprehension,
pleasure, desolation, memory and desire into images. In other
words, they did not make pictures of their dreams, but the
pictures they made sometimes worked in the same way as
dreams and with the same authority.

Further down the scale, Surrealism, like Dada, shaded into frivolity and Grand Guignol. When Breton announced 'Surrealism will introduce you to death, which is a secret society', he was invoking dreamland in much the same way as the Romantics invoked the Gothick – as a political gesture, as a way of cocking a snook at the bourgeoisie who, it was assumed, were remorselessly out of touch with their own unconscious.

Breton also defined Surrealism as 'pure psychic automatism'. He believed in automatic writing and the willed inducement of dream-states. Like Dali, he was a literalist of dreams, who cherished them less because they were a mysterious form of thinking and feeling than because they were outlandish. For Dali himself, dreams were just part of his showmanship; he used them to create a kind of landscape art, beautifully painted, but artistically no more radical than the landscapes of any Academician or commercial artist. Like Nerval, whom Norman Cohn called 'Dali in words', he mistook daydream for inspiration, 'psychic automatism' for art, or, in Coleridge's terms, 'Fancy [which] is indeed no other than a mode of memory emancipated from the order of time and space' for genuine 'Imagination [which] dissolves, diffuses, dissipates, in order to re-create.'

The distinctions between good art and bad art, imagination and whimsy, dreams and daydreams are, however, beside the point. New art starts as a minority interest, for connoisseurs only, but its effects spread gradually outwards into the cultural environment and become a common language. Just as Mondrian's gridirons, his chaste blocks of white and grey and discrete patches of colour, were eventually writ large in Mies van der Rohe's skyscrapers, so Magritte's odd and witty images – oddly calm and oddly memorable – were hijacked by the advertising industry and became part of the iconography of our time:

> [They] have been used to sell books, records, insurance, credit cards, televisions, typewriters, calculators, cars, cosmetics, wallpaper, chocolates and clothes, starting even before a major American television company [CBS] appropriated *Le faux miroir* as its logo. Pressed into the service of politics and bureaucracy, they have even been called on to sell ideals, win votes and uphold the law.[72]

For the Surrealists, Freud was merely an excuse. They were not much interested in mental life as it shows itself in dreams, but they were fascinated by the mannerisms of the dreaming brain, by its uncanny and disjointed juxtapositions, its bizarreness, its visual rather than its intellectual processes. Although Surrealist polemics and theories were consistently more extreme than its often decorative practice, Surrealism nevertheless changed the way the world is perceived. By creating a universal hieroglyphics for the unconscious, it helped to obscure the dividing line between waking and dreaming.

Surrealist literature was never as persuasive as the painting, but the Surrealist perspective – the belief that experience is both multi-layered and permeable, and that dreams and the unconscious soak through – became a basic premise of modern art. 'World is crazier and more of it than we think./ Incorrigibly plural', wrote Louis MacNeice. In their different ways, Borges, Márquez, Ionesco and Calvino are surreal; so is the humour of the Marx Brothers, S. J. Perelman and Zero Mostel, the films of Buñuel, the soap operas of David Lynch, the stories and pictures of Maurice Sendak; so too, in retrospect, are *Alice in Wonderland*, Gogol's 'The Nose' and Kafka's meticulously factual narratives. We now take for granted that reality is not what it seems and, at any moment and in any place, a trapdoor may swing open without warning and drop us into our unconscious.

The achievement, of course, is largely Freud's, and Freud, who was intellectually adventurous but profoundly conservative in his aesthetic tastes, never had much time for Surrealism. On the one occasion he met Salvador Dali, he is alleged to have said to him: 'It is not your unconscious that interests me, but your conscious.' Even so, the Surrealists were, in every sense, his facilitators: they created a visual language in which it seems right and proper that waking and dreaming should coexist easily and in comfort; they produced images that were haunting, strange, yet instantly recognisable – recognisable, in fact, because their strangeness itself was strangely familiar, like a dream-face or a dream-landscape reassembled from half-remembered fragments. And because, as Freud himself remarked, visual language is closer to the unconscious processes than thinking in words, so images are easier to comprehend than abstract ideas. Freud may not have cared much for Surrealism, but Surrealism helped him become what Auden called 'a whole climate of opinion'.

---

The fallacy of Surrealism is that all dreams are interesting. The truth is, other people's dreams are generally as boring to the listener as they are fascinating to the dreamer. (There are many aspects of Freud's life that his admirers have called heroic – his self-analysis, his originality, his persistence in the teeth of opposition, scandal and malice – but nobody mentions his valour in the face of boredom, his endless patience and attentiveness to his patients' dreams.) Dreams may be 'a kind of involuntary poetry' – just as poetry, as I have tried to show, is a kind of involuntary dreaming – but, to the outsider, dreams communicate like poems only when they are subjected to the disciplines of art which, as it happens, are not much different from the strategems of Freud's dream censor: condensation, displacement, symbolisation and disguise.

Without that kind of concentration and control, even the wildest dreams lose their appeal. By the middle of Freud's century, the artist had lost his status as an exotic endangered species. He was no longer the cloaked, doomed, dangerous outsider – Lord Byron, Count Dracula – or the sensitive plant or the unacknowledged legislator or the holy fool. He wasn't even a connoisseur of the landscape of psychosis, like the Surrealists. He was just another loser on the margins of society – alienated, neurotic and poorly paid. Bad dreams he took for granted; they went with the job. What really troubled him was insomnia. 'I haven't been to sleep for over a year,' says a character in Evelyn Waugh's *Decline and Fall*. 'That's why I go to bed early. One needs a good night's rest if one doesn't sleep.' John Berryman wrote a 'Dream Song' about his nocturnal habits (sleep wasn't one of them), Kafka devoted pages of his diary to scrupulous observation of his chronic inability to sleep, and Ogden Nash wrote a plangent ode to marital insomnia, 'The Stilly Night', which ends:

Oh, sleep it is a blessed thing, but not to those wakeful ones who
watch their mates luxuriating in it when they feel that their own
is sorely in arrears.

I am certain that the first words of the Sleeping Beauty to her
prince were, 'You *would* have to kiss me just when I had
dropped off after tossing and turning for a hundred years.'

Modernist artists didn't discover insomnia – Pushkin and
Kipling were martyrs to it, and W. S. Gilbert immortalised a
bad night's sleep in 'The Lord Chancellor's Song' in *Iolanthe* –
but they made the most of its creative possibilities, perhaps
because electric light allowed them to work while the rest of
the world was blissfully asleep.

As for dreams: after Surrealism, the Romantic fascination
with dreamland was belatedly reborn as Magical Realism, a
specialised style of *faux naif*, self-consciously different from
the European and American mainstream, a kind of Third
World *folklorique* artifact, made in South America, Africa,
India, but designed strictly for export.

Elsewhere, we've lost our innocence. When artists use
dreams now, they do so to make a point. At the end of his
memoir *Patrimony*, for example, Philip Roth describes two
moving and intricate dreams – one that came to him just
before his father died, the other soon after. Then, *as a matter of
course*, he produces equally moving and intricate interpretations of the dreams. Maybe this is a habit born of years of
psychoanalysis, though if it is, Roth is certainly not saying.
But it is unquestionably the product of a psychoanalytic habit
of mind. Like most artists of his generation, Roth assumes that
Freud essentially got it right: dreams are a way of speaking;
what is odd about them has nothing to do with their bizarre
juxtapositions and abrupt shifts of time and place: it is, instead,

their ability to express so much thinking and so many mixed feelings simply, richly, in brilliant images and dumb show.

And this, despite his knowingness and sophistication, Roth finds astonishing. When he writes of one of the dreams, 'this is not a picture of my father, at the end of his life, that my wide-awake mind, with its resistance to plaintive metaphor and poeticized analogy, was ever likely to have licenced', he sounds as much in awe of his unconscious, and as faintly disapproving of it, as Stevenson was of the antics of his Brownies. Yeats wrote, 'In dreams begins responsibility', and Roth's determinedly unpoetic, wide-awake mind would have no trouble with that concept. It could, after all, be interpreted as a rationale for psychoanalysis. But the irresponsibility and inexhaustible creative power of the sleeping mind are concepts altogether harder for a realist to accept.

# POSTSCRIPT

Heraclitus was right about sleep. Every night we enter a private world, the world inside the head. It has its own geography, as endlessly and minutely complex as the fractals which physicists have discovered in chaos systems, and very similar to them, both physically and mentally – a fern-like system in which neuron leads to neuron and association to association. It also talks many languages. It uses words, abstract symbols, sensations, but above all – for sound physiological reasons concerning the predominance of neuronal activity in the right hemisphere of the brain – it uses things, actions, visual images. And it thinks with all of them, logically and mathematically, as well as dramatically. In sleep, thinking takes place in bizarre forms because it is taking place in a pure culture, as it were, free from sensory input from the external world. Yet it is almost always drenched with feeling, perhaps because the brain, when it is not constrained by waking reality, can tap into its virtually infinite nexus of associations.

Neurophysiologists and psychoanalysts agree on two things at least: that brain work never ceases, even in sleep, and that the traditional belief that thinking is done only in terms of logic and language no longer holds. The brain works in different ways under different conditions, and dreams are as much a form of thinking as symbolic logic. So, too, are the arts, although that does not mean that dreams themselves are art or that everyone, in his dreams, is an artist. There are some works of art – 'Kubla Khan', Tartini's 'Devil's Trill' sonata – that seem to have emerged fully-fledged from dreams, but only, I suspect, because the artists had been mulling them over unconsciously long before they slept, and then went on thinking in their dreams, like Loewi, Howe, Kekulé or Morton Schatzman's problem-solvers. But the dream is only a beginning. What follows is a process like that of any other difficult professional work – a matter of hard labour, talent and intelligence, as well as the kind of technique that is acquired only by a long apprenticeship. In other words, it depends on the artist's realistic, utterly undreamlike understanding both of the possibilities of his medium and of his relationship to his internal world.

The private world of sleep is connected at almost every point with that of the waking consciousness. The brain goes on working behind the sleeper's closed eyes – its neuronal activity falls off by a mere 5 to 10 per cent even in deepest sleep – even though it works in a different way, with different formal rules of operation. Conversely, behind the busy person's wide-awake eyes and under the perpetual noise reality makes, the waking brain is also dreaming. In that way at least, the brain *is* like a computer: the unconscious is a window working away behind the window on the screen. But unlike a computer, the unconscious continually intrudes: in slips of the tongue that express a meaning altogether different from the one intended (a 'not', for example, where it seems not to be meant), in body language that reveals the aggression or revulsion behind a bland exterior, in a scent or a sound or a taste – Proust's famous madeleine – that suddenly brings back entire, with every detail intact, some long lost person or scene or event. The subject of psychoanalysis is the interplay between these two worlds, the conscious and the unconscious – that is what analysts mean when they talk about 'working in the transference' – and the arts are its expression.

Illumination is one of the few twentieth-century experiments that hasn't failed. One hundred years ago, day and night, waking and sleeping, were separate worlds, and the unconscious was a mystery that did not even have a name. Now we are beginning to understand that they are all intricately and inextricably intermeshed. And when night fell, moonless and occluded, we couldn't see. Now we can.

———

What did E. S. like about dreams?

Their similarity to life and their dissimilarity; their salutary effect on body and soul; their unrestricted choice and arrangement of themes and contents; their bottomless depths and eerie heights; their eroticism; their freedom; their openness to guidance by will and suggestion (a perfumed handkerchief under one's pillow, soft music on the radio or gramophone, etc.); their resemblance to death and their power to confer intimations of eternity; their resemblance to madness without the consequences of madness; their cruelty and their gentleness; their power to pry the deepest secrets out of us; their blissful silence, to which cries are not unknown; their telepathic and spiritist faculty of communication with those dead or far away; their coded language, which we manage to understand and translate; their ability to condense the mythical figures of Icarus, Ahasuerus, Jonah, Noah, etc., into images; their monochrome and polychrome quality; their resemblance to the womb and to the jaws of a shark; their faculty of transforming unknown places, people, and landscapes into known ones, and vice versa; their power to diagnose certain ailments and traumas before it is too late; the difficulty of determining how long they last; the fact that they can be mistaken for reality; their power to preserve images and distant memories; their disrespect for chronology and the classical unities of time and action.

Danilo Kis, *Hourglass*

People who dream when they sleep at night know of a special kind of happiness which the world of the day holds not, a placid ecstasy, and ease of heart, that are like honey on the tongue. They also know that the real glory of dreams lies in their atmosphere of unlimited freedom. It is not the freedom of the dictator, who enforces his own will on the world, but the freedom of the artist, who has no will, who is free of will. The pleasure of the true dreamer does is free of will. The pleasure of the true dreamer does not lie in the substance of the dream, but in this: that there things happen without any interference on his side, and altogether outside his control. Great landscapes create themselves, long splendid views, rich and delicate colours, roads, houses, which he has never seen or heard of. Strangers appear and are friends or enemies, although the person who dreams has never done anything about them. The ideas of flight and pursuit are recurrent in dreams and are equally enrapturing. Excellent witty things are said by everybody. It is true that if remembered in the daytime they will fade and lose their sense, because they belong to a different plane, but as soon as the one who dreams lies down at night, the current is again closed and he remembers their excellence. All the time the feeling of immense freedom is surrounding him and running through him like air and light, an unearthly bliss. He is a privileged person, the one who has got nothing to do, but for whose enrichment and pleasure all things are brought together; the Kings of Tarshish shall bring gifts. He takes part in a great battle or ball, and wonders the while that he should be, in the midst of those events, so far privileged as to be lying down. It is when one begins to lose the consciousness of freedom, and when the idea of necessity enters the world at all, when there is any hurry or strain anywhere, a letter to be written or a train to catch, when you have got to work, to make the horses of the dream gallop, or to make the rifles go off, that the dream is declining, and turning into the nightmare, which belongs to the poorest and most vulgar class of dreams.

Karen Blixen, *Out of Africa*

———————

Dreams are what you wake up from.

Raymond Carver

# 5

# KEEPING THE PEACE

*Light thickens,*
*And the crow makes wing to th' rooky wood.*
*Good things of day begin to droop and drowse,*
*While night's black agents to their preys do rouse.*

Shakespeare, *Macbeth*

# I

Americans have always been lavish with electric light –
perhaps because they were the first to benefit on a large scale
from Edison's inventions – and one of the side-effects of their
profligacy has been to create beauty where there is none. By
day, northern New Jersey is an encampment of industrial
nomads: oil refineries, sheds and container parks, wire mesh
fences, mountains of junked cars, breeze-block diners and bars
and gas stations that look as if they were run up yesterday and
will be gone tomorrow. By night, this desolation is strung
with coloured lights and looks like fairyland. By night, the
delicate traceries of lights on iron railway bridges form
imperfect circles with the delicate traceries of lights in the
polluted rivers below. By night, from the air, drab little prairie
towns sparkle like jewels and the emptiness is star-studded and
festive. America, more than any other nation, has taken over
the night and turned it into an event.

The event of all events is the Manhattan skyline, which is
beautiful at any time and in any conditions – day or night, sun
or rain or fog. Glimpsed from the distance, it seems to hang
just above the horizon like a mirage, an image of what the
future might be like if we are lucky and successful. Closer up,
as you cross the Triborough Bridge or take the wide right turn
down towards the Lincoln Tunnel, the great packed sweep of
the city is one of the wonders of the world – delicate,
variegated, dazzling, the future come true – especially at night.

But once you are across the bridge or through the tunnel, the place closes in on you, the crowded buildings become what they were intended to be – expressions of power, monuments to money and success – and what looks from the distance like a vision of the future turns out to be more like Ben Jonson's Bartholomew Fair: bustling, dirty, bursting with life, casually brutal and profoundly dilapidated.

Above all, there is the din. New York makes a noise like no other city I know. In London, it is easy to pick out the different sounds: passing cars, a plane going over, the occasional siren, and sometimes the wind tossing the trees outside or tugging at the window, trying to get in. But wherever you are in New York City what you hear is a steady roar, like a turbine at full throttle, churning out energy and power. The first time I noticed it I thought it was the air-conditioning, yet when I switched off the unit and opened a window the noise became louder. It has nothing to do with car horns; they are merely treble flourishes over its moving bass. It's not the wind either, although the wind, booming around the skyscrapers, is part of it. The New York noise is a steady state, an environment. It is deep and constant, like the sea, and the car horns, sirens and steam-brakes are the spume on its surface. I have been going to New York all my adult life, and every time I arrive I remember that what I have missed most while I've been away is that sound of a great city on the move.

More than most other cities, New York changes according to where you are on the vertical scale. In Mel Brooks's movie *The Producers*, Zero Mostel takes Gene Wilder to the top of the Empire State Building and shows him the city spread out below: 'There it is, Bloom,' he says, 'the most exciting city in the world: thrills, adventure, romance! Everything you ever dreamed of is down there: big black limousines, gold cigarette cases, elegant ladies with long legs! All you need is money, Bloom. Money is honey.' As Satan knew when he tempted Jesus on the mountain top, the view from up high, the penthouse view, promises every worldly fulfilment. When Wilder finally succumbs, he cries, 'I want . . . I want . . . I want everything I've ever seen in the movies!'

Part way down – around, say, the fifteenth floor – the city changes. It becomes Gothick – peaks and canyons, skyscrapers jammed up next to townhouses, conical black water-tanks sprouting like mushrooms on every roof, puffs of steam rising from ventilation shafts – a Gustav Doré landscape of stone, steel, concrete and glass, a hundred different levels whichever way you look, with billowing, sickly, yellowish clouds above.

The noise is constant wherever you are, but to understand it, you need to be at street level. The traffic blasts up the avenues in a kind of rage. (They say the shortest time in the world is between the moment when the light turns green and the man behind you hoots.) The rage increases at night, not because people are impatient to get home – impatience is a permanent condition for New Yorkers; they don't need an excuse for it – but because all you can see are the angry headlights storming towards you. The traffic is probably no worse than in other big cities – it is even more brutal in Mexico City – but in Manhattan the buildings are so tall and tightly packed together that the din has nowhere to go. So it echoes back on itself and never lets up.

Neither does the city. Down the middle of the street roars the buffalo stampede of traffic, on the sidewalks the melting pot is permanently on the boil – all shapes and sizes and colours, business suits and bomber jackets, sweatshirts and cable-knit cashmere, Nikes and McAfees, furs and parkas. New York is not just the richest and poorest city on earth, it is the richest and poorest at the same time and on the same block. Added to that, a significant proportion of both rich and poor behave with the same dedicated aggression, as though it were both their right and their democratic duty to shove their wealth or their poverty right in your face.

Night life, too, is a democratic right, freely available to everyone, regardless of race, colour or creed. New Yorkers have always taken pride in the brilliance and liveliness of their city after dark. Jimmy Walker, who was Mayor of New York in the 1920s, said it was a sin to go to bed the same day you got up, and 'the great white way' is a permanent celebration, a triumph over the natural adversity of darkness.

When municipal authorities installed street lighting, however, what they had in mind was crime, not celebration. In the early 1870s, Gustav Doré made a series of engravings of London by night. By that time, there were gas lamps in almost every street, yet all Doré seemed to see was the darkness of the city, the way people emerged from the night and belonged to it. Dickens had seen London in the same way twenty years earlier, when Inspector Field of Scotland Yard took him on a nocturnal tour of the slums and thieves' kitchens. One of the policemen who went with them had a bull's eye lantern strapped around his waist to light their way, and the scenes revealed by its narrow, unsteady beam appeared to Dickens like visions of hell:

> Wherever the turning lane of light becomes stationary for a moment, some sleeper appears at the end of it, submits himself to be scrutinised, and fades away into the darkness.[1]

Gustav Doré portrayed Bluegate Fields in a similar spirit, as another version of Dante's *Inferno*: the slum dwellers were like the damned in torment, picked out by a single, paltry gas lamp as they lounged in doorways or squatted against the walls with their feet on the edge of the runnel of filth that meandered down the alleyway. In Doré's pictures, darkness was a precondition of urban poverty, teeming with life and menace. By the same logic, street lighting was a precondition of law and order; it was less a public amenity than a way of keeping an eye on the unruly underclass.

In Imperial Rome there were plenty of lamps in the houses, but very few in the streets. To go out to supper without having made your will, said Juvenal, was rank carelessness. Fifteen hundred years later, nothing much had changed. 'Compared to Paris,' Boileau wrote in his sixth satire, 'the darkest and loneliest forest is a safe retreat.'[2] If the thieves didn't mug you, the mire and unpaved streets would break your neck. Yet by the time Boileau wrote his satires, the systematic lighting-up of Paris was already under way, presided over not by a civil servant, but by a certain M. de la Eyrnie, the chief of police. There was nothing unusual about this arrangement since Louis XIV's police were, effectively, in charge of all civil administration, regulating everything from the Bourse, which they founded, to the size of paving stones, the employment of foster mothers, the brewing of beer and the sale of oysters. They also censored posters, read people's mail and had spies everywhere. (The police chief Sartine boasted to Louis XV, 'Sire, whenever three people speak to one another in the street, one of them will be mine.') For Louis and his police, street lighting was just another means of surveillance. Night, which had previously been a time when criminals could go about their business unhindered, now became subjected, like everything else, to the control of a despotic monarch and his servants.

Inevitably, the street lanterns were fiercely resented by the common people. The first gesture of public discontent was to smash them and when the mob finally exploded in 1789 they hanged their victims from these hated symbols of repression. In the first weeks of the Revolution, before the Committee of Public Safety and the guillotine imposed their own terrible order, the hunting cry of the *sansculottes* was '*A la lanterne!*'[3]

Public order and public lighting are two sides of the same coin. In France, the police came first and the lighting followed. In England, the streets were lit by gas two decades before Sir Robert Peel organised the Metropolitan Police in 1829. But the 'Peelers' were not centralised and political; they were a local force whose forbears were town nightwatchmen – Shakespeare's bumbling Dogberry and Verges – who kept the peace ineffectually and whose main function was reassurance. The duties of the nightwatch were nothing more stringent than 'crying the hour after the chimes, taking precautions for the prevention of fire, proclaiming tidings of foul or fair weather, and awakening at daybreak all those who intended to set out on a journey'.[4] But the cry of 'Twelve o'clock and all's well!' was a great deal less reassuring than 'Stop in the name of the law!' Until there were policemen on the beat and lights for them to see by, an orderly night life was impossible.

Dickens was never much impressed by the posturing of high society or the huffing and puffing of the courts of law but, as a connoisseur of night, he was truly impressed by the recently established police force, particularly as personified by Inspector Field of Scotland Yard. During his night out with the Inspector, the deputy keeper of one of the flophouses showed Dickens a stinking, vermin-infested dormitory. Dickens's reaction was part horror and outrage, part gratitude and relief:

There should be strange dreams here, Deputy. They sleep sound enough, says Deputy, taking the candle out of the blacking bottle, snuffing it with his fingers, throwing the snuff into the bottle, and corking it up with the candle; that's all *I* know. What is the inscription, Deputy, on all the discoloured sheets? A precaution against loss of linen. Deputy turns down the rug of an unoccupied bed and discloses it. STOP THIEF!

To lie at night, wrapped in the legend of my slinking life; to take the cry that pursues me, waking, to my breast in sleep; to have it staring at me, and clamouring for me, as soon as consciousness returns; to have it for my first-foot on New-Year's day, my Valentine, my Birthday salute, my Christmas greeting, my parting with the old year. STOP THIEF!

And to know that I *must* be stopped, come what will. To know that I am no match for this individual energy and keenness, or this organised and steady system! Come across the street, here, and, entering by a little shop and yard, examine these intricate passages and doors, contrived for escape, flapping and counter-flapping, like the lids of the conjurer's boxes. But what avail they? Who gets in by a nod, and shows their secret working to us? Inspector Field.[5]

The system is more organised and even steadier now, and the Inspector's successors move around the city as easily by night as by day. Even so, the job is harder and the success rate down.

Shortly before Edison had perfected his invention, the New York authorities were busy erecting arc lights mounted on high poles. It was an expensive procedure and the Chief of

Police justified the cost by declaring, 'every electric light erected means a policeman removed'.[6] In practice, he was wrong, not just because he was reckoning without the twin epidemics of drugs and guns, but because crime has its own version of Parkinson's law and expands to fill the space available to it. It had always flourished under cover of darkness; it flourished even more when brightly lit streets encouraged law-abiding citizens to come out and enjoy themselves. Jane Jacobs has written:

> Today barbarism has taken over many city streets, or people fear it has, which comes to much the same thing in the end. 'I live in a lovely, quiet residential area,' says a friend of mine who is hunting another place to live. 'The only disturbing sound at night is the occasional scream of someone being mugged.'[7]

But lighting, according to Jacobs, is not worth much in itself. It is valuable only because it brings people out onto the streets and so creates a social environment, a crowd of witnesses to keep barbarism at bay:

> The value of bright street lights in dispirited grey areas rises from the reassurance they offer to some people who need to go out on to the sidewalk, or would like to, but lacking the good light would not do so. Thus the lights induce these people to contribute their own eyes to the upkeep of the street. Moreover, as is obvious, good lighting augments every pair of eyes, makes the eyes count for more because their range is greater. Each additional pair of eyes, and every increase in their range, is that much to the good for dull grey areas. But unless eyes are there, and unless in the brains behind those eyes is the almost unconscious reassurance of general street support in upholding civilization, lights can do no good. Horrifying public crimes can, and do, occur in well-

lighted subway stations when no effective eyes are present. They virtually never occur in darkened theaters where many people and eyes are present. Street lights can be like that famous stone that falls in the desert where there are no ears to hear. Does it make a noise? Without effective eyes to see, does a light cast light? Not for practical purposes.[8]

Cops on the beat and patrol cars nosing through the back streets are the organised, institutionalised form of those eyes that help keep the peace, particularly when most ordinary citizens – the ones who are not only law-abiding themselves but help keep the law simply by being around – are home in bed.

## II

Apart from the 'organised and steady system', something else hasn't changed since Dickens went out with the police: the 'individual energy and keenness'. But police take on the character of their territory. In London, the energy and keenness are masked, like the city itself, by a certain reticence; in Manhattan, they come with a New Yorker pace and appetite. When I called Lieutenant Raymond O'Donnell, the head of media liaison at Police Plaza, the NYPD's downtown redbrick fortress, to arrange a couple of nights as a 'ride-along' in the back of a patrol car, I asked to go to precincts where I might see some action.

A gravelly voice at the other end said, 'Whaddya want, drugs or whores?'

'How about both?'

'You got it!'

What I got, in fact, were the 9th and 10th precincts. The 9th Precinct covers the lower East Side, from 14th Street to East Houston, from Broadway to F.D.R. Drive, and includes Alphabet City – Avenues, A, B, C and D – which is where much of New York's drug dealing is done. The 10th Precinct runs from 14th to 34th streets, from 7th Avenue over to the docks, and includes the blocks at the end of the Lincoln Tunnel, where hookers wait for the johns from New Jersey and blow them for the price of a hit of crack. It also includes the blocks around the meat market where the transvestites hang out. (The desk sergeant at the 10th Precinct looked like Walter Matthau and had the same slow-burn delivery. 'The biggest tits in the area', he drawled, 'are on a guy. He's wearing five pounds of silicone minimum; maybe five pounds each side.')

As it happened, the police who took me as a ride-along in London were concerned with the same problems: the Brixton force has a famously druggy area to control and the Kentish Town police patrol King's Cross and the industrial wasteland around it, where the waifs and strays who parade near the station take their tricks. But they order these things differently in Britain – or at least, with less panache.

The night I was out with the Kentish Town police was cold – it was the end of November – and the few girls we saw were bundled up against the weather. They looked more like bedraggled children than hookers and the policemen seemed embarrassed to point them out. There were no customers to be seen near the station, so we drove slowly through a maze of sparsely lit streets behind York Way, past darkened factories and lorries parked behind wire fences, then turned into a narrow dead end between an embankment and a wall topped with razor wire. A shiny new Ford Scorpio was parked at the far end. 'Watch,' said the police driver and flicked the patrol car's headlights on to high beam. Instantly, two heads – one bald, the other tousled – popped up from the front seat and another girl, who had been loitering near the car, scrambled urgently up the muddy bank. We didn't stop and the sight of the desperate child scrabbling up the embankment shut us all up.

There was nothing sad or apologetic about the first whore I saw when I went out in a 10th Precinct patrol car. She was a great black swaggering peahen of a woman, extravagantly dressed, extravagantly built, and as much part of the passing show as the flood-lit Empire State Building which dominated the whole area, looming majestically over the long perspectives of the avenues, disappearing on the cross streets. The hooker, too, appeared and disappeared from her beat, but the first time the patrol car cruised past her, she stuck out her tongue and gave us the finger. Lieutenant Mike Herer, who was in the car with me, waved at her and laughed. 'For that, she has to go to jail,' he said cheerfully.

She did, but – because the police were making a preliminary tour of the area to check out what the action was that evening, and where it was happening – the arrest did not take place until hours later, when she had probably turned enough tricks to earn her keep for the night. There were other hookers working the same block, but they pretended not to notice us. So did the thug who was standing in the shadows of a doorway. He had massive shoulders, a massive belly and two days' stubble on his sullen face. He wore a pair of headphones over the hood of his sweatshirt; a Walkman and a beeper were stuck in his belt. Dean McManus, the police driver, beckoned him over to the car.

'Move your ass out of here,' he said. 'How many times we gotta tell you?'

The big man shrugged and strolled towards the corner.

'Is that their pimp?' I asked.

Lieutenant Herer shook his head. 'Pimps don't come out on cold nights. And they don't dress like that,' he said. 'That's the pimp's little helper. He's keeping an eye on the goods.'

When we cruised back down the block an hour later, the big man was still there, but he turned his back and huddled into the doorway when he saw us.

The bust came at two o'clock. The lieutenant met up with a second police car on 10th Avenue and talked in a low voice to the officers in it. The second car idled towards the cross street the whores were working while we zoomed around the block to its 11th Avenue end. Then the yellow blinking lights of the patrol cars went on in unison and the officers jumped out. Yells, confusion, the sound of scurrying feet and three women's voices shouting abuse, one throaty and powerful, the others higher pitched and full of venom.

Lieutenant Herer, who is a slight man with a pale moustache and thin hair, walked slowly back to the car, shaking his head. 'That's some gal,' he said. 'Her tits are so big her arms don't meet behind her back. We had to use two sets of cuffs.'

There had been three girls on the block. Two were now on their way to the precinct station in the back of the other car. The third had disappeared.

'She's wearing a red skirt,' said Herer. 'Let's go find her.'

McManus swung the car around and we doubled back on 11th Avenue, lights flashing, against the oncoming traffic. But there was no sign of a girl in a red skirt. At that hour, in fact, there was no sign of anyone on the sidewalks this far west. On the cross streets, however, brightly lit garages were crammed with taxis being set right after the day's mayhem. The cops stopped at each, asked questions, searched briefly. The mechanics glanced up without interest, shrugged and went on with their work. We paused outside an unlit garage, its door half open to reveal the great chromed radiator of a truck. New York police cars are equipped with hand-held spotlights that blast out a dazzling blue glare with the force of a water cannon. McManus swivelled the spot into the darkness behind the truck. The hooker was not there. On the next block two homeless giants had built themselves a fire in an oil barrel. But she was not with them.

It took fifteen minutes to catch up with her, scuttling unsteadily across 11th Avenue on her high heels, as we were nosing out of a cross street. Her red skirt was under her arm and, despite the cold, she was wearing only a low-cut red bra and red panties that exposed her buttocks. The lieutenant jumped out of the car, tussled with her briefly, then bundled her into the back with me. She sat rigidly upright, angry, out of breath and obstinately silent. Her wig of curls was stiff as a helmet and reached almost to her shoulders, but her profile was like a child's, smooth and elegant, and she had a childish rosebud mouth. She looked no older than the sad little whores I had seen in London, but when I mentioned this later to Lieutenant Herer he said, 'I've seen her around. She's twenty years old minimum, maybe more.'

Earlier, a cop had told me, 'No way a hooker will talk to you unless you pay her. To them, time is money.' Well, I thought, this one has five minutes to kill while we drive back to the station; it's worth a try. I also felt sorry for her – because she was young, because she was cold, because she was in trouble – and I suspect Herer and McManus, who were both family men, felt the same.

'You've got to be freezing,' I said.

Silence.

The lieutenant tried next. 'Why run?' he asked, quite kindly. 'Give us all a hard time. You knew we'd catch up on you.'

Silence.

Finally, McManus lent back, winked at me and said good-humouredly, 'So why did you rob this guy?'

'That's not funny,' she answered. And that was all she said.

Back at the precinct station, the girl was finger-printed, then lined up with the others while an officer took Polaroid pictures – three of each of them, full-face and in profile. But the atmosphere at the station was charged when we arrived. The hooker with the giant breasts had lashed out when they fingerprinted her, thereby parlaying the minor charge of soliciting into the more serious crime of resisting arrest. She let fly a salvo of 'Fuck-you's, then retreated behind the great ramparts of her bosom into what was intended to be outraged, dignified silence. But dignity is hard to maintain in a blue fake fur boa, rhinestone-studded boots and a skirt that stops short just below the crotch, and the cops seemed embarrassed by the mess she had got herself into. The third hooker stood beside her, glaring at each of the officers in turn; she looked like a wild cat, lithe and feral and dangerous. The youngest hooker stood apart, sunk in her own misery. Then the three of them were hustled out to the holding pen at the back of the station.

When I asked what would happen to them, Lieutenant Herer replied, 'They'll be locked up for a few hours. Maybe their pimp will bail them out; maybe not. Then they come up in court and the judge fines them. Or maybe he decides the time they've done in jail is enough. In short, nothing happens. They don't work for the rest of the night is all.'

'It's a hard way to earn an easy living,' I said.

'You get cops that like working the streets,' McManus answered 'and you get girls that like working the streets. Outdoor girls, that's what I call them.'

Good humour seems to be a universal police procedure when dealing with prostitutes. It gives way to gloom only when the girls are very young and the police have children of their own. For the rest of the time, the oldest profession is one of the easier problems the police face on night duty. They are never going to beat it and they can't exactly join it, so they treat it as a crash course in the vanity of human wishes.

Ten years ago, for example, when Captain Vincent Rosiello was still a young cop working in Bedford-Stuyvesant – 'plain clothes and in an unmarked car, but not undercover. I mean, how could I be undercover in Bed-Stuy?' – he and his partner were called, at two in the morning, to settle a dispute: 'It was on the top floor – it's always on the top floor – and this man was having an argument with a woman in a nightgown. The woman's a prostitute – a call girl, high class, the kind you make an appointment with by telephone – and the guy's complaining that she's taken his money and hasn't performed everything he wanted. So what does he do? He calls the police. I mean, how dumb can you get? We say, "You admit to patronising a prostitute?" He says, "Sure." We say, "Why don't you just pack up and leave?" So he did. A week later, we saw the girl out on the street and she gives us the wave and the wink. She was really an attractive woman."

Rosiello has a narrow face, a forehead battered by recent

surgery, dark hair, dark moustache and dark eyes snapping with life and intelligence. He laughs easily and seems like a man who enjoys himself. He is studying Romance languages and history in his spare time, partly because he wants to find out about his Italian roots, partly because he loves books and would like to teach when he retires. ('All I want to do is sit and read,' he said to me, 'and here's you looking for action. Maybe we should switch jobs.') Meanwhile, he is Captain in charge of the 9th Precinct, which is less of a battle zone than Bed-Stuy, but still one of the toughest areas in Manhattan. Even the precinct station on East 5th Street looks battered beyond repair – crowded and squalid, the dirt ingrained, then covered over with thick black paint. All that survives of its turn-of-the-century glory is a brass rail in front of the duty-desk.

All cities are collections of villages, each with its own character and style. This is literally true of London, which swallowed village after separate village as it grew – Hampstead, Highgate, Wimbledon, Croydon, Kingston, Purley – and goes on growing outwards – Barnet, Mill Hill, Harrow, Orpington, West Wickham – moving north towards St Albans and Watford, south and east towards the coast. As the villages were ingested, each became first a suburb then, as the city grew, just another part of the body of London. But to the native's knowing eye they remain distinct. The squad cars from Kentish Town police station patrol areas that might as well be separate provinces: the brightly lit, bustling high streets of Camden Town and Kentish Town, the prostitute country around King's Cross station, seedy council estates and square miles of sombre middle-class housing; they also patrol the roads off Highgate Hill where grand, shadowy houses look out over the ponds to the mist and darkness of Hampstead Heath and it feels like deepest countryside.

On Manhattan Island, however, there is no room to grow and its villages are harder to define. They come block by block, jumbled together one on top of another, and each is reconstructed by its inhabitants, according to individual taste, as a neighbourhood. Around midnight, for instance, on 8th Avenue and 16th Street, there are bars and restaurants and shops and crowds of well-dressed people going about their business. Two blocks west you might as well be in a besieged and devastated city – raw brick warehouses, debris, boarded-up windows and, on a corner near the meat market, four transvestites gossiping together, who wave derisively as the patrol car passes. A couple of blocks away, a stretch Excalibur limousine, the length of a Greyhound bus, is parked outside the Pure Gold Club, which boasts muscular doormen and a strong line-up of topless dancers. A block or two further is a flophouse called the Terminal Hotel, which has a harshly lit lobby half the size of the Excalibur. And mixed in with all these, lights are blazing in the huge mail-sorting building and the headquarters of various courier services, where trucks come and go and people are getting on with their work as though there were no such thing as night. On the ceiling of the police station hangs a white silk banner saying, 'Welcome to the 10th Precinct', and on the wall, along with photographs of the precinct's famous alumni, is a notice: 'Precinct Problems: 1. Robbery. 2. Narcotics. 3. Prostitution. 4. Clubs. 5. Homelessness.' What it does not say is that all the precinct problems are compressed together like pulped paper.

The 9th Precinct has a similar crazy mix. According to the head of its detective squad, Lieutenant Kevin F. Gilmartin,

'It's a very diverse community, everything from the Hispanic section over in Alphabet City, through the punk rockers, to the poets in St Mark's Place. You get your coffee houses and nice restaurants, and over in Tompkins Square Park you get people who are considered anarchists.' What you don't get is any clear demarcation between one section and another. At one in the morning on East 12th Street, an elderly woman sedately walked her poodle and a yuppie couple unloaded the contents of a U-Haul into a smartly redecorated house, while around the corner on 1st Avenue was a scene that Dickens and Doré would have recognised: an impromptu street market – old clothes and shoes, toys, radios, battered suitcases piled randomly on blankets along the sidewalk and presided over by a bunch of derelicts. 'It's the stuff that's left over from break-ins,' Luis Cabrera, the driver of the squad car, told me. 'The stuff the thieves can't sell.' Neither, apparently, could the pedlars. When Cabrera's companion on patrol, Michael Grullon, swung the car's spotlight on them and shouted. 'OK, break it up!' they stuffed their pathetic wares into plastic sacks and shuffled off despondently, not even bothering to protest. An hour later, they were back again.

The street markets in Alphabet City were different: groups of young men hanging out at every corner or lounging in doorways, beepers in their back pockets, boom-boxes blaring, waiting for customers, for the casual, sidling approach and the quick exchange – bag for dollars – brief as a handshake. When the squad car passed they affected an air of studied indifference. Cabrera and Grullon seemed to recognise most of them and they muttered into the squad car radio as we cruised by. But recognising a drug-dealer is not enough. 'To make a drug collar, you actually have to witness a sale,' said

Lieutenant Gilmartin. 'I can know that an individual is a drug-dealer and the officer that has the beat, he can know it. But unless he actually catches him in the act of selling that drug, there's not much more he can do than make intelligence reports. Most of the big drug collars are done by the narcotics units building a case. They get a tip that there is heavy drug activity in a certain location. What they then have to do is send out people, first to make observations, then to make what they call "buy-and-bust deals". Undercover agents make drug buys, then, when they've got enough, they go in and make an arrest. But these days there's a new breed of drug-dealers and they're heavily armed. They come from outside the US, from deep poverty, and they see drugs as an easy way to make big-time bucks. They've grown up with no respect for the police, so they'll fight us all the way. And when they get the big money, they go into these heavy weapons. It's a nightmare. We keep fighting and maybe someday somewhere there's going to be a success. But it doesn't look too good right now.'

It looked, in fact, like another, more thriving version of the derelicts' street market. Business was being done, but always just out of sight. As we cruised the streets of Alphabet City, every group we passed seemed to be in the middle of a transaction. They paused when the squad car came into sight, then went back to their business before we were even around the next corner.

Luis Cabrera is in his middle-thirties; he has a comfortable, spreading stomach and the placid air of a man who has seen everything. 'They know we can't do nothing,' he said. 'They stare at us to see which officers are in the car. If they don't recognise the faces, they reckon we don't recognise them either, so they just get on with their business.'

Recognition is a key element in the relationship between the police and the criminals, particularly at night when darkness blurs the sharp edges and the details. At one point on the patrol, we were flagged down by another squad car. Sitting in the back was a sharply dressed Hispanic who affected not to speak English. Cabrera translated while the man rattled away indignantly about visiting friends in the neighbourhood and the cops in the front seat looked bored. When he finally ran out of steam, one of them said, 'Tell him, fuck him. He's under arrest.'

'He's a dealer from uptown,' Cabrera said when he climbed back into the car. 'Things got too hot for him in Harlem, so he came down here. He reckons he's got it made because we don't know him, and it's night, and there's a lot of action going down. But he doesn't know us, either. That's why we got him.'

'The people out there are street smart and police smart,' Captain Rosiello told me. 'They see a nice new uniform, a nice clean shirt, a young guy, and they know he's a rookie. They see the new leather belt and holster and they know. It wouldn't come to my mind, but it comes to theirs.'

Keeping up appearances matters in Alphabet City. On nearly every block there are delicatessens and grocery stores, with green plastic canopies and illuminated signs, brightly lit at two in the morning, although hard to see into because their windows are stacked solid with boxes of detergent. But the packages are arranged one-deep and look more like a pop-art painting than part of a store's inventory, and when a door swings open there seems to be nothing much to buy inside. A skinny black youth was coming out of the first store we passed. When he saw us coming he made a show of opening a packet of potato chips.

'What do you know?' said Mike Grullon, who is toothy and talkative and ten years younger than Cabrera. 'All they ever buy is potato chips.' A couple of blocks later, when we passed a hole-in-the-wall advertising 'natural juices', he said, 'The only juice they ever sold was the kind you can shoot up.'

Many of these neat little neighbourhood shops give a new, literal meaning to the term 'drug store'. The police know what they sell and the dealers know they know, but they also know that without a buy-and-bust deal nothing can be done. So the two sides circle each other, night after night, in a Mexican stand-off, looking for an opening, waiting for a false move.

I wondered what would happen to a child or some young housewife who wandered in to buy a bar of candy or a packet of soap. Nothing presumably, since the purpose of a front is to maintain a front, but to the outsider the area seemed full of menace, like a war zone during an uneasy truce. By 3 am, when I arrived back at the precinct station, there had already been one murder – 'On a quiet Wednesday night, for Christ's sake,' Lieutenant Gilmartin said. He sounded exasperated, but not shocked. On the wall of the detectives' room – at the opposite end from the little cage with flat iron bars, painted white, where special prisoners were kept – was a list of the year's homicides. 'Forty so far and that's an improvement,' Gilmartin said. 'It used to be fifty or sixty per annum. But we've still got two months to go and crime always picks up in the holiday season. You get a lot of people out shopping or partying – people with money in their pockets at a time when everyone wants money. Even the bums need cash to do the right thing by their families, and that leads to crime. There are also a lot of assaults in families. Brothers who haven't talked to each other for years get together for the holidays and that turns out to be a wrong move; there's alcohol involved and before you know it there's a major dispute.'

A large proportion of the homicides on the list were committed by kids in their late adolescence. 'Eighteen and nineteen is the age when everyone is invincible, particularly the male,' Gilmartin said. 'They buy themselves a nine millimeter and they have a couple of drinks to get their courage up and you get a lot of shootings, a lot of what we call "dis" crimes. "You dissed me," they say. "You looked at me in the wrong way. Who do you think you're looking at? What are you going to do about it?" Disrespect is what they're talking about, and usually there's a girl involved. Before you know it, the guns come out and there's shooting. They're immature and they're impressionable. They see the big-time hoodlums in their Mercedes and Cadillacs and Jaguars and they want to be tough guys, too. Unfortunately, they don't think of the consequences, so they end up lying in the street with a bullet in them.'

Most of the homicides, however, were what the police call 'drugs-related': an undercover agent blown away in a buy-and-bust deal, a father and son shot in the back of the head in their Jaguar on FDR Drive, a man killed by two masked gunmen in a bar on Avenue C – 'A professional job,' said Rosiello. 'Nine shots in the head. The marksmanship was very accurate. I'm sure retaliation will come.'

'For the month of October, we've had four homicides,' Gilmartin said. 'That's a heavy month for us. In the small area we're in you don't figure to have four people killed in separate incidents in four weeks. We live in a violent world.'

Yet despite the violence, ordinary life, amazingly, goes on. In the small hours of the morning, supermarkets and vegetable stores were open for business and little old ladies trotted along the sidewalks, toting brown bags of groceries, indifferent to the junkies and crack dealers and panhandlers. There were kids on bikes and kids on roller-blades, couples out walking their dogs, a little girl walking hand-in-hand with a shambling, spectral man – 'Her father,' said Grullon. 'The guy's a junkie.' – and down near Cooper Union Square a Paris-style sidewalk café was packed with well-dressed late-night diners. Grullon's pretty young wife was among them, sitting at a window table, waiting for her husband to come off duty. When he shone the squad car's spotlight on her, she gave him a big smile and raised her hands in mock surrender.

In other words, a 'neighbourhood' is a kind of magical safety net for the people who live there. To the outsider, the lower East Side looks impossibly dangerous. To the locals, who patronise certain shops and frequent certain bars and restaurants, who know which faces to greet and which areas to avoid, it is simply the place where they live their lives – shabbier than uptown, perhaps, but, to them, a good deal less intimidating.

Yet the menace is always there, waiting to show itself. At one point, the squad car paused outside a Spanish-American seafood restaurant. Two heavy-set men in leather jackets were sitting at the bar at the front of the restaurant, looking out on to the street, taking in the passing scene. 'Dealers,' said Cabrera and began muttering into the radio. One of the men climbed languidly off his bar stool, came out of the restaurant and strolled towards us. He stopped a couple of yards from the car and stood, bouncing slightly on the balls of his feet, hands in his pocket, stone-faced. His teeth were very white, his moustache was carefully trimmed, he had no forehead to speak of. He seemed like darkness personified – an embodiment of everything that is dangerous and scary about New York at night. He stared into the car and the cops stared back. A statement was being made, although nobody said a word. Then he turned abruptly and sauntered back into the restaurant. 'These guys are *stoopid*!' was all Cabrera said.

Grullon, however, seemed outraged by the man's arrogance. 'FBI agents come down to Alphabet City and what do they know?' he said. 'As far as they're concerned, the bad guys wear Armani suits and have fifty thousand dollars. Ours have a hundred bucks and a gun.'

The dealers are always about in Alphabet City, but night brings them out in force. It is what Lieutenant Gilmartin primly calls 'an opportune time'. 'The cover of darkness always encourages the criminal,' he said, 'particularly the shooter. You'll always have the screeching of wheels late at night, the screaming car and the bang, bang, bang. Shortly after, you'll hear the sirens and see the blue lights coming. Then all the people come out and a crowd builds. Everybody has to see what's going on. They all *know* what's going on, of course, but they still have to come out and look.'

As it happened, on the night I was in the 9th Precinct, the squad car was called to only one emergency – a break-in near St Mark's Place. The apartment was on the second floor: a single filthy room, divided down the middle by a plastic shower-curtain. The floor, which had once been painted white, was scattered with discarded clothing – soiled shirts and socks and sweaters, left where they had been dropped. The sink was piled with dirty dishes. An electric toothbrush stood on the microwave.

The woman who had made the call wore a long, sagging,

blue-grey cable-knit sweater, thick black tights and white Reeboks. Her face was sallow, her chest was flat, her stringy blonde hair was black at the roots. She seemed at once harassed and profoundly depressed. She also seemed embarrassed because, in fact, there had been no break-in; the man she called her husband had simply run off with her wallet.

Cabrera questioned her gently, jotting down the particulars in his notebook: height – six foot one; weight – one sixty pounds; hair – dreadlocks; street name – 'Asky'.

'Anything else we should know?'

The woman ducked her head and shuffled her feet. Her gloom deepened. Finally, she muttered, 'He got himself arrested last night.'

Cabrera closed his notebook. 'Don't you worry none. We'll find him. No problem.'

Back in the car, Grullon said, 'You see her hands? She's a junky.'

'So's he,' Cabrera said. 'I know the guy. He's not her husband. He's using her to hide out.'

Both the officers seeemed subdued, as though the woman's depression had been contagious. And this is the other side of keeping the peace. Finding the junky and the stolen purse was a minor issue. The real job was to cope with the misery that had driven the woman to call the police.

'Whether it's black or Hispanic or white doesn't matter,' said Lieutenant Gilmartin. 'The root cause of crime is poverty.' And poverty, along with drugs and booze and theft and violence, is the night side of urban life, no matter what time it is. Day and night, the police spend their working hours opening windows on shabby lives. But that is the easy part. The hard part is the windows they open on horror and danger.

Although cops live according to a macho code and take toughness and fortitude for granted, the officers I spoke to on both sides of the Atlantic seemed obsessed both with the blackness of the world they had to cope with on a daily basis, and with the outsider's incapacity to understand how upsetting police work can be.

The outsiders who understand least, they tell you, are the lawyers and judges who let criminals walk free. In New York, everyone complained about the difficulty of getting a charge to stick. 'Sometimes a guy gets shot and his family doesn't want the police. They say, "We'll take care of it ourselves",' explained Lieutenant Mike Sneed of the 9th Precinct. 'They don't have any faith in the criminal justice system and I can't really blame them. If a loved one of yours gets killed and we catch the guy that did it and we manage to convict him, what's he going to get? Three or four years max. Most of the homicides don't even make the newspapers.'

The main objection, however, is not the fallibility of the law, but its distance from reality. 'Judges and magistrates only deal with words. They don't see the actual consequences of criminal acts,' Police Constable John Cruttingden told me during a long, eventless night patrolling the back streets and council estates of Brixton. Cruttingden is the son of a policeman and he has been in the police force for eleven years, yet he is still appalled by the scenes he witnesses every day in the line of duty – starved and battered children, tortured animals, old people dead from hypothermia in locked flats, the blood and brain matter and fragments of bone left on the tarmac after a road accident – an unending overdose of horror.

A psychotherapist who works as a counsellor for the

Metropolitan Police once spent Guy Fawkes Night with a group of senior officers. Every time a firework went off they all jumped. 'When you hear a bang,' one of them told her, 'the best you can hope for, if you're a policeman, is that some poor kid's had his face blown off. The worst is an IRA bomb. You never think it's just fireworks.'

These were middle-aged men with years of experience behind them. The young constables have an even harder time dealing with the daily nightmares of their work. 'They are shocked by what they see,' said the psychotherapist, 'and by the feelings churned up in themselves – the excitement, the sadism. So they act out with terrible practical jokes on each other. Or they project their troubles into one of their group; they pick on the awkward ones and turn them into scapegoats – they treat them brutally, they refuse to speak to them for weeks on end – until finally the scapegoat falls ill, goes on sick-leave, then gets moved to another shift. Their only relief is boozing together, but even that has changed since the drink-drive laws came in; if they are caught drunk in charge, they are kicked out of the force.'

They also have no one to talk to. The motto of the NYPD is 'It's a matter of pride', and pride is an ambiguous virtue. According to the psychotherapist, the Metropolitan Police's counselling service was not much used because officers feel that to seek help when they have troubles brands them as inadequate; they are also convinced, wrongly, that it goes on their record. Cruttingden said the same: 'It's like a stigma if you own up to seeking help . . . We have this tough-guy image of ourselves in the police; either you sweep your feelings under the carpet or, if you do try to talk to your colleagues about them, they say, "What's the matter with you?" '

They can't even talk to their wives. Police marriages are notorious for not working, and the brutal hours and shift work are only part of the trouble. The other, major part is the feeling that the wives would never comprehend the violent squalor which is a routine part of police work or, if they did, they would be racked with foreboding every time their husbands left for work. Cruttingden, who had recently remarried after a messy divorce, put it this way: 'When you take off your uniform you're only human underneath. You go into unpleasant situations and you contain your emotions because that's what the public expects of you. Then you go home and take out your upset on your family. I never talked about the job to my first wife, which was probably a mistake. Things get bottled up, then you release them in the worst possible way: you pick a fight, you shout at the kids. The strain was a contributing factor in my divorce. My wife didn't understand the pressures I was under and I didn't understand how difficult it was for her to be a policeman's wife. It was hard even on the simplest level like the hours I worked: for example, when all her friends who were married to men with 9-to-5 jobs were going out with their husbands at weekends and I was on duty; or when we'd plan a night out and I'd have to cancel at the last moment because I had to appear in court . . . Shift work is a strain in itself – it makes you feel you're suffering from permanent jet lag – and there were times when I didn't see my kids for days on end.'

There is also the continual strain of maintaining a stolid, reasonable front in the teeth of all that wretchedness and violence. When the public call in the police they want reassurance, and they want it to come properly dressed up in a uniform they recognise. In New York, that means the armed defender in his warrior gear: the gun and night-stick and walkie-talkie, the ID tag and the gaudy badges, the handcuffs and keys and flashlight hanging from a creaking leather belt strung with mysterious little pouches, the fat notebook stuck in a back pocket. In London, where the police presence is more comforting and avuncular, bobbies on the beat wear the traditional Grecian urn helmets and blue serge jackets with silver buttons and insignia. The jackets look more like armour than clothing, so stiff it seems a miracle that they can move their arms, and the high blue helmets crowned with nipples make all but the tallest constables look top-heavy. The effect is formal and old-fashioned, like a dress uniform, and looks far too uncomfortable for ten hours of pounding the pavements. The gear of the mobile units – navy blue V-neck pullovers, with cloth epaulettes for the insignia, cloth patches for the walkie-talkies, and discreet cloth Metropolitan Police badges – is more relaxed and also more appropriate to their transport – the white cars with the zippy orange flash along each side and the spinning blue light on the roof.

Police uniforms have their own mystique and power: to people in distress they say 'help is at hand'; to the criminals they are a deterrent presence; and to the anarchists of Tompkins Square in New York they represent oppressive government. When a policeman arrives on the scene, it is the uniform that gives him presence and authority and the uniform that stereotypes him – either as Superman or as the enemy. That is why, for the public at large, the moment when policemen begin to look young is always dismaying. It is an omen of mortality, signifying the onset of middle age and full of foreboding, because, before it comes, the person inside the uniform has been virtually faceless. He may be a veteran who has worked the streets for years or a scared twenty-year-old rookie straight out of police school and overwhelmed by a level of casual violence and despair he or she never dreamed of. But the public sees none of that. It responds to the uniform, never to the inexperienced, frightened kid who may be inside it.

For the police, however, the fear does not go away over the years. 'The macho image we have of ourselves means we don't want to show the people we work with that we're scared, so we rely on adrenalin to keep us going,' Cruttingden said. 'But the fact is, when you knock on the door at the scene of a crime you never know what is going to be on the other side. I still get wound up about things, and the day I stop getting wound up I'll probably have to leave the job for my own safety.'

Lieutenant Gilmartin explained what can happen when a police officer drops his guard. The previous week, he said, two detectives had been called out one night to investigate an assault. The assailant was 'a sixty-two-year-old male Hispanic', the victim was his friend and both men were drunk. The old man was easy to find and seemed unfazed when the detectives told him they were taking him in for questioning. He asked politely if he could dump some magazines in the garbage before he left. 'Sure,' they said. The old boy picked up the magazines, turned away, then pulled out a .38 and shot both the detectives. One was hit in the leg, the other in the chest. 'The bullet entered at the top of his vest', said Gilmartin, 'and went right through his body, exiting in the abdomen area. Luckily, it didn't kill him, but it caused a lot of damage and he lost a lot of blood. It looks as if he's going to survive, but it was touch-and-go for a time.' The old man fled, the building was cordoned off, a SWAT team and hostage negotiators were called in. When the man was finally run to ground in another apartment, he came out shooting again and wounded another cop before he himself was gunned down.

'A guy that had survived that long, you'd think he'd have burned out all the violence,' Gilmartin said. 'Maybe something just snapped. But my point is, you never know; you gotta take care. Two veteran detectives going after a sixty-two-year-old man involved in a dispute, they're not thinking he's going to come out shooting, that's for sure.'

All this had happened at night but, for the lieutenant, the point of the story was that the police are always working in the dark, whatever the time of day. Gilmartin again: 'Some people think we're over-cautious, but you gotta live it, I suppose, you gotta be a cop out there to understand. I remember when they first put tinted glass in automobiles so you couldn't see into them. Probably one of the most dangerous things a police officer can do is make a car-stop, whether it be for a traffic violation or for an accident or for a car that's suspicious. The reason is that people are so heavily armed. When you approach a car and you can't see in it, the hairs kind of rise up on your back. It's like going into a dark room from the sunlight. All of a sudden, you're totally blind. You know that there's something in there, but you don't know what it is. And your training and your background and your general sense of what policework is all about make you think, Who's behind the wheel? Who's sitting in that car? It may be a nice little old lady on her way home from a bingo game or it may be some guy that's got a warrant out on him some place in the US of A and isn't going to be taken alive. And you just don't know. That's a general attitude a police officer has to take now. He always has to be ready; he has to be suspicious of everything. It's a constant, constant vision that the officer must have.'

A constant vision, that is, of the heart of darkness. The police are experts in the dark side of society – criminals, whores, accidents, killings and urban disaster – and the public turns to them only when things go wrong. They work with their faces pressed continually in the dirt and, despite their swagger, they need to maintain a permanent state of controlled anxiety in order to survive. In the circumstances, it seems inevitable that they should sometimes behave badly, and a miracle that they manage to behave as well and as patiently as they do.

When I arrived at the 10th Precinct station, for example, a young Hispanic and his even younger girlfriend were standing at the desk. The boy, who had just been released from the holding pen, was collecting his personal belongings from the duty sergeant. He was trembling with rage. As he stuffed each item into his pockets, he kept up a muttered litany of outrage: 'It ain't right. I done nothing. My cash is short. Where's my pocket-knife?' He was a violent incident waiting to happen, but the duty-sergeant never faltered. Finally, he said wearily, 'Don't take it personal. Once it's over, it's over. Your don't take it personal, we don't take it personal.' The girlfriend burst into tears.

'It takes a particular kind of person to go on, year after year, fielding that kind of stuff,' the London psychotherapist said. 'What is needed is a certain kind of highly structured personality – technically, it might be called "paranoid" – who decides who is good and who is bad and then acts accordingly. In an ordinary job, people like that would probably find themselves fighting good and bad at once; they'd be against authority and would get themselves into all kinds of trouble. But in the police force that muddle disappears. They become the ideal bobby, tough on villains, fatherly to their comrades, loved and respected and looked after.'

I suggested to the doctor that if, in the line of duty, you are constantly having to face situations in which someone might turn a gun on you, then paranoia is a perfectly sane reaction.

'But what does it do to you to live in an organisation where paranoia is sane?' she replied.

Yet paranoia is the natural, archaic response to night. It can never be lit brightly enough to dispel the ancient belief that bad things happen when the sun goes down: ghosts walk, criminals go to work, 'chaos is come again', and night people, in general, are up to no good.

On the far west side of the 10th Precinct the squad car tucked in behind another vehicle, followed it for several blocks, then swung away. When I asked why, Lieutenant Grullon shrugged: 'Curiosity. Also, they kept looking back. I mean, so why are they worried?' A little later, we drew level with a teenager strolling along a deserted cross street. The lieutenant stopped the car, swung the spotlight on him and kept it there until the kid reached the avenue. Why? Another shrug. 'It's how they walk and where they walk. Most people stay in the centre of the sidewalk. Him, he was walking on the edge, right up close to the cars. I reckon he was looking to break into one.'

The same rules apply in London. Brixton has acre upon acre of high-rise council estates, relics of the 1960s and 70s, shabby parodies of Le Corbusier's Radiant City, bleak and impersonal and gone to seed. Beneath the high-rise blocks are concrete warrens of garages, each with a wire-mesh door. But most of the doors were smashed and hanging at eccentric angles, and the cars in them were vandalised wrecks. Howard Potter, the driver of the patrol car, seemed to know every back alley and dead end, and we cruised them all slowly, stopping every so often and for no obvious reason, while Cruttingden lowered his window and peered into the shadows. When I asked why, Cruttingden said, 'You get a feel for something not looking right.'

'And if you don't look, you don't see,' Potter said.

Maybe because it was a few days after New Year, and no one had the money or the appetite for partying, or because the night was cold and a fierce wind was blowing – not fierce enough to topple chimney pots, but the kind of wind that turns umbrellas inside-out and keeps people off the streets – whatever the reason, there was no action in Brixton that night on the graveyard shift. The only excitement came when the patrol car had to respond to an emergency call. That was like being plunged, without warning, into deep water. The blue light came on, the siren screamed and the car weaved in and out through the traffic, mostly on the wrong side of the road. The driving was controlled, precise and very fast, and whenever we arrived at our destination the inside of the car smelled pleasantly of hot oil. But that night, all the emergencies turned out to be false alarms.

Because London is a far less violent city than New York, fast driving is sometimes all the excitement the police get on the night shift. Whenever a car chase was reported on the radio, Cruttingden and Potter followed its progress longingly, hoping it would come in our direction. But they all fizzled out.

Working the night shift is 'ninety five per cent boredom, five per cent non-stop', a policeman at the Kentish Town station told me, and probably four parts of that 5 per cent have less to do with cops and robbers than with catastrophe – with terrible sights and bad smells and plain human distress, not with violence on the streets. The rest is what the law, mildly and accurately, calls 'disturbance of the peace'.

The truth is, crime statistics notwithstanding, London is still a peaceful, orderly community. This is not to say it doesn't have a thriving criminal underworld. It simply means that the London underworld is like other British power structures: it prefers not to draw attention to itself. If it has firepower, it takes care not to flaunt it. For the population at large, petty criminals included, guns are hard to come by and the police go unarmed. All the cops I spoke to in New York – at Police Plaza as well as in both precincts – found this hard to comprehend. To a man, they believed that none of them would survive a single night unarmed in a town where anyone might pull a gun on them at any time. For them, the brilliantly lit streets of New York were still charged with the ancient tribal terrors of a night in which violence may erupt without warning, without reason. That ubiquitous sense of menace is the underside of the excitement that comes naturally to New York and, in comparison, London is not an exciting city. Henry James was right when he called the place 'the most possible form of life'. Given the right training and the right gear, Dogberry and Verges might still be able to cope perfectly well.

Yet the policing of both cities is essentially similar: a vigilant, deterrent presence cruising a territory that each officer knows as well as the face he or she sees in the mirror every morning. The shadows are familiar; what they are looking for is a disturbance in the shadows.

'You get a feel for something not looking right.'

'And if you don't look you don't see.'

In a way, darkness makes the job easier. Because there are fewer people around, the scene is less cluttered, the players are in sharper focus, the irregularities stand out. Small breaches in the rules – a car driven imprecisely or too fast or too slow – suddenly become significant: Is the driver drunk? Is he up to something? Is he nervous because the car is stolen? The police are looking for the flickering, almost subliminal signs of tension that poker players call 'tells'.

But the uniformed policemen in their gaudy vehicles and the cops walking the beat are only part of the pattern. The cities are also crisscrossed with plainclothes officers in un-marked cars – regular police, Special Branch, the FBI, the DEA, the Diplomatic Protection Group and all the other metastasising cells of national security. Together, they form an invisible grid that imposes on the night a coherence the rest of us know nothing about. In a totalitarian country, that degree of surveillance would be as oppressive and frightening as impenetrable darkness was to primitive man. In a well-lit and mainly benevolent democracy, it is merely reassuring. Night is not a problem for the police because they themselves are part of its solution.

The nights I spent with the police in New York and London, as a ride-along in their squad cars, were like journeys into unknown countries. Even the streets patrolled by the Kentish Town police, which I had walked and driven countless times, were strange and different. The familiar shops and pubs and restaurants, the crowds on the streets, the flow of traffic were all transformed, through police eyes, into 'potential flash points', 'individuals loitering with intent', stolen cars with phoney licence plates – a confused mass of interlocking detail which the outsider ignores or takes for granted or fails to notice, but which, for the police, forms an arcane nocturnal script which they have been trained to read.

One familiar figure, however, haunted this strange new world. He made his first appearance at 3 am at the top of Highgate Hill. As we drove past St Michael's Church, with its tall spire and graceful façade, one of the policemen said, 'We knicked a burglar there last week. He was after the silver.'

His companion ignored him. 'I'll tell you something about that church,' he said to no one in particular. 'Samuel Taylor Coleridge is buried there. Bloody great stone he's got. Well worth taking a look at.'

The poet's second appearance was on the lower East Side. Lieutenant Kevin Gilmartin, who is pink-cheeked, silver-haired, plump and distinguished, and looks more like an Irish politician than a cop, had been talking about the fascination of his work: 'It's a difficult job. It always has been and always will be. But interesting – absolutely. I've just celebrated my thirtieth year in the NYPD and I'm not ready to quit yet.' Yet nothing is as it seems with the police. Gilmartin had also just completed an external degree in English literature, specialising in Chaucer and the Romantics, and suddenly, in the middle of a graphic description of the intractability of the drug problem in the 10th Precinct, policework and literature collided. 'Coleridge had a drug problem,' he said. 'I guess he was the first famous addict.' He paused and, for the first time

that night, he seemed puzzled. 'Things have sure changed. Coleridge in Alphabet City. Think of it.'

I thought of it: flustered, unhappy, unworldly, loquacious Coleridge, out there on the mean streets with his night terrors and his habit and no gun. It was a long way from Xanadu.

# 6

# NIGHT OWLS

*The night shows stars and women in a better light.*

Byron

*I began in the dark and would no doubt end the same way. But somewhere between the beginning and the end there would have to be an attempt to explain the darkness, if only to myself, no matter how strange a form the explanation would take, and regardless of consequence.*

Don DeLillo, *Americana*

When you live in a big city you forget about night. There are things not to do after nightfall – flash your wallet, leave your car unlocked – and people to avoid – the drunks, the crazies, the predatory – and every city has its wild sides where you don't walk. But much the same rules apply during the day and, in a curious way, cities are more easy-going by night than by day. The dimensions of night – night time, night space – seem larger: the crowds are thinner, the pace is slower, the parking easier. And after a certain point of no return, people even become friendlier, maybe because they are fewer, maybe because insomniacs have a freemasonry of their own and there is a companionship in being up and about while the rest of the world sleeps. Down in the London Underground, trains wait longer between stations to give stragglers a chance to get home, voices are louder, more animated, and occasionally you even hear laughter – something that never happens during the day when everyone is grimly intent on going places and doing what has to be done.

Night in the city is time out – time for leisure and intimacy, family and lovers, hobbies and pastimes, reading and music and television. It is also the time for excitement and celebration: theatres, movies, concerts and party-going, wining, dining, dancing and gambling. For people who hold down boring or unsatisfactory jobs, night is the time when they feel they lead their real lives. A century ago, the pioneers of the

American labour movement defined the decent life as 'eight hours work, eight hours sleep, and eight hours for what you will'. Now the times for sleep and for what-you-will have merged together, day-shift and night-shift are interchangeable, and night has become the continuation of day by other (electrical) means.

Every city has its own nocturnal rhythms, but all of them begin with a rush, with a sudden release of noise – footsteps and chatter and car horns – as the shops and offices close, the buses fill and the home-bound traffic builds up. Dickens talked about 'the restlessness of a great city, and the way in which it tumbles and tosses before it can get to sleep'. But restlessness takes many forms and the pleasurable sense of release never lasts long. After the initial tumult, a kind of surliness takes over in the bus queues and unyielding traffic jams. The rush-hour stampede on the tube, shoulder to shoulder and back to back, is silent except for the din of the trains. Relief turns to fatigue, impatience and plain bad temper, fuelled by an overpowering need to get home, kick off your shoes and collapse mindlessly in front of the television with a drink in your hand.

Then the city tosses and turns again and new traffic jams build bound for the centre, as the evening crowds move in to theatres, cinemas, restaurants. Then a lull while youngsters take over the streets, moving between the pubs and the fast-food joints, hanging out, eyeing the passers-by, waiting for nothing in particular. Around eleven o'clock the places of entertainment begin to empty and a third rush hour starts, homeward bound, more easy-going this time and better fed. The pace builds briefly, then gradually slows for the long, quiet stretch between midnight and dawn.

Like the brain, however, the city only seems to sleep. Scattered across its darkened cortex are bright points of activity. In police stations, hospitals, newspaper offices, television studios and whorehouses, the night-shift is in place. Firemen and ambulance crews wait for a call, disc jockeys jabber away in their sealed cubicles, bakers pound the dough for the morning bread, the food markets are in full swing, the pubs and cafes around them are packed, and the watchers and listeners whose livelihoods depend on computers and satellites are busy at their terminals: air-traffic controllers, the defence establishment, the young tigers and tigresses in the financial district, who monitor figures from the Nikkei and the Hang Seng and talk into two telephones at once.

In the casinos, only the hard cases are left. For the losers, this is when dreamtime begins: one last spin of the roulette wheel, they tell themselves, one last throw of the dice, that's all it takes to break even. At the poker tables, the hustlers drift in casually, full of charm and implacable good humour, just when the amateurs, already frayed by a hard day's work, are running out of steam. I know one hustler who gets up bright and early with the rest of the world, puts in a long morning at his office, eats a late lunch, then goes home to bed and sleeps until 10 pm. Then he showers, shaves and drives down to the casino to work the graveyard shift. Sometimes, to disguise the fact that he is fresh and sharp-eyed when everyone else is wilting, he shaves in the morning so as to appear suitably dishevelled by midnight. But he often forgets and the smell of his aftershave gives him away.

By the time the casinos close at 4 am, the streets are deserted and the city has shrunk. A cross-town journey that would take a sweating hour or more at rush hour becomes a pleasant fifteen-minute cruise. The maintenance armies are on the move – the office cleaners and service engineers – but invisibly, and out on the streets there is only the eerie, unnatural silence of what Sky Masterson, in *Guys and Dolls*, called 'my kind of time – a couple of deals before dawn', when the great echo-chamber of the sleeping city falls quiet and you can hear the small details: a car changing gear in another street, footsteps, a far-off shout, barking dogs and amorous cats, leaves stirring faintly in the night breeze, the first, uneasy notes of a waking bird. Then the dawn chorus begins, the first of the red-eye flights roar over, en route to Heathrow, the early shift workers appear, the mail vans and long distance lorries, and the street lights pale.

But in the shadowy interval between night and day, between sleeping and waking, you seem to be floating free – free of crowds and noise and interruptions, of the pressure, pace, structure and detail that daylight brings. According to Karen Blixen, 'The thing which in the waking world comes nearest to a dream is night in a big town, where nobody knows one, or the African night. There too is infinite freedom; it is there that things are going on, destinies are made round you, there is activity on all sides, and it is none of your concern.' The freedom of the hours before dawn is the same – pure and very lonely, like the loneliness of the long-distance truck-driver.

Even shift-work is freedom of a kind, although sometimes it seems to be not quite sane. People who work nights live out of sync with the normal world, sleeping and waking at the wrong times, alienated from their children, whom they rarely see, resented by their partners, never around when they are needed – neither for the domestic and social rituals nor for the crises – and cut off from the common decencies. This creates havoc for couples who enjoy each other's company, but in bad marriages it is a blessing: no quarrels, no confrontations, no mutual nagging and recriminations. 'Night workers don't have to punch the family time clock,' said a printer who always worked nights.[1] When the sex goes wrong, the night-shift is better – less final, less insulting – than separate bedrooms.

Yet even during the deadest hours life goes on, and not just in places of work. There used to be a time when it seemed as if they rolled up the sidewalks in London after the pubs closed, and the whole town was dead before midnight. Not any more. London still may not be like New York or Los Angeles, where you can eat and shop and amuse yourself at any hour you choose, but it has a scattering of all-night stores and seedy cafes, and their number is slowly growing, even though it is still unreasonably difficult to buy a drink. Even in London, night is no longer a separate, hedged no-go area, an impenetrable jungle outside the stockade. The ancient terrors are gone, banished by the flick of a light switch. Cities like New York or Detroit or Rio de Janeiro are probably more dangerous than London or Paris or Rome have ever been, but that is true by day as well as by night; where you are in town matters more than when. For all practical purposes, city life everywhere goes on much the same, day and night, and when you prefer to live it is a matter of choice. Once that is decided, it's like jet travel: all you need do is reset your biological clock.

Once I had grown out of my childhood fear of the dark, night not only lost its power over me, it lost its separateness, its distinction, and I forgot all about it. At most, it was a minor inconvenience, but only irregularly. I rediscovered it, however, twenty years ago, in an old farmhouse in Italy. The house is in Tuscany, though not in Chiantishire, the expensive rolling countryside south of Florence, with its vineyards and cypresses and swimming pools. It is up in the mountains, on the edge of the wild Garfagnana, Tuscany's northernmost boundary, on a steep hillside covered with chestnut trees, beside a stone mule-track that was once a Roman road. The Appennines rise up behind it, slowly at first and thickly wooded, then bare rock and turf. In front is the valley of the River Serchio, with Barga, a little Renaissance town crowned by a diminutive Romanesque cathedral, poised on its hill just beyond the flank of the next mountain. Across the valley are the Apuan Alps – the Marble Mountains above Carrara, where the stone was quarried for Michelangelo's statues – fold upon fold of them, rising to the bleak cone of the Pania della Croce. It is a place full of history, yet history has left it behind because it is too rough and remote to smoothe down and assimilate.

In summer, life at the farmhouse goes on outside, on the cramped little terrace; people eat there, sunbathe, read, or potter in the terraced garden beyond. But most of the time they simply stare out at the Apuan Alps, hypnotised by the shifting light, by the mist rising from the Serchio in the morning, by the clouds drifting across the peaks in the afternoon.

This being Italy, it is not quite as peaceful as it sounds. The Italians are addicted to noise and they have a genius for making it. They like their motorbikes unsilenced and their car engines rorty, and the road in the valley below is the kind of temptation they can't resist: a sporting series of sharp curves which gives them an excuse to play arias on their car horns and make their car tyres squeal. The sound bounces off the hillsides and rises, mingling with the hiss of the wind in the chestnuts and the dry clatter of the leaves of the walnut tree at the edge of the terrace. The din is just far enough away to be comforting, rather than irritating, a reminder that life goes on, despite indolence and isolation.

Twenty years ago, the house had no electricity and a cable had to be strung up from the valley below to connect it to the grid. Not all the other houses were electrified at that time. There were still *contadini* on the mountain who got by with oil lamps and candles, and regulated their days by the sun: they got up at sunrise, worked until sunset, ate by lamplight, then went to bed. The *contadini* are dying off now, their children have gone up in the world and have mostly emigrated to the big towns – Lucca, Viareggio, Pisa, Florence – and the mountain is gradually emptying. But that primitive diurnal rhythm seems to be part of the place, and when I am there I fall into it without even trying.

In northern cities, night is something you shut out. You switch on the lights, close the doors, draw the curtains and forget about it. But out in the country night is a presence to be reckoned with and its slow approach is a subtle pleasure. Twilight – particularly summer twilight – is always the best time of the day in Italy. In town, people come out on to the streets to enjoy the cool air and watch the *passeggiata*. Up on the mountain, there is no *passeggiata*, so the only thing to do is go out on to the terrace and watch night fall.

The weather begins to break in late August. The days

remain hot and sticky, with a haze over the mountains and, every so often, a faint roll of thunder somewhere far off to the north. But at sunset, the sky usually clears in the hills and the heat relents. The mountains are layers of blue, each layer shading imperceptibly into the next, and the air is full of feeding swifts, dipping and arching. Far above them, a single hawk glides lazily towards the Apuans, riding a thermal, not bothering to stir its wings. Traffic rasps in the valley. The last rays of the sun pick out the white façades and pink roofs of the houses in Barga and the honey-coloured cathedral floating above them. As the light thickens, the nearby trees seem to gather weight and greenness, an extra dimension.

Every evening I wait for the critical moment when the swifts and the bats change guard: a brief stir and confusion, always expected yet always astonishing, a muted flurry of wings and small, high-pitched cries. Then the swifts regroup and vanish towards the Appennines with a rush of wingbeats. With their narrow heads and curved wings, swifts are perfect creatures, taut and precise and aerodynamically flawless, and they fly like acrobats on the trapeze, a sequence of graceful miracles. Compared with them, the flight of the bats is pure anarchy. They erupt from the darkening trees into what is left of the sunset, flickering, stuttering, impossible to predict. They seem to stop dead and go into reverse, dipping towards the house, then off somewhere else entirely. This is a chaos theory of flight, bewildering fractals instead of direction and purpose. Bats seem less like creatures of flesh and blood than emanations of the night, blobs of darkness, soft-edged; if you touched one, your hand might go right through it.

By eight o'clock, the light is rosy mauve, deepening to purple. The moon swings up above the ridge opposite the farmhouse, pink-faced at first, as if vaguely embarrassed to be visible this early. It storms up the sky so fast that the earth seems to be tilting under your feet – five minutes from the first curved sliver of light to the full glowing disk. When it touches the outermost branches of the walnut, the tree seems to grow; its outlines become sharper and deeper; it acquires a new, commanding, nocturnal presence.

Slowly, the lights come on across the valley: a line of four along the houses bordering the road at the foot of the mountain, a rising tangle marking the place where Barga climbs its hill, two strings of pearls slung across villages on a distant Apuan foothill. Cars are points of light on the road below, white or red, coming or going. Night spreads its black skirts and settles slowly, almost formally.

The stars come out, first one by one, then suddenly in their thousands. The Milky Way is a thick smudge of light, trailing back towards the Appennines, so bright that it seems artificial. Every so often, somebody cries. 'Look, a shooting star!' but no two people ever see the same star together. Instead, they watch the satellites, tiny points of light moving unnaturally fast from one horizon to another, and the winking red and green lights of the planes flying south to Rome. Occasionally, an intercontinental flight goes over high up, dragging behind it a grey-white, moon-lit con trail.

By nine o'clock, the valley is studded with scattered lights, Barga Cathedral is floodlit a ghostly green, and even the local village church is illuminated by a yellowish spotlight. Twenty years ago, when not everyone was hooked up to the grid, people around here thought of electricity as an expensive luxury and used it sparingly. The nights were darker then and the valley was a great lake of blackness, its surface broken

intermittently by pinpricks of light that seemed too inconse-
quential to survive. Year by year, the lake has begun to fill.
But there are still broad stretches of darkness out there, night
as it has always been in these parts, and blackest of all is the
ridge opposite the farmhouse. It sweeps straight down from
the high Appennines and has only two buildings on it,
shepherds' houses, both of them far back into the mountains,
high up and out of sight. The rest is untouched forest –
chestnut, scrub oak and fir – too steep and tangled for anyone
to bother with, even in this part of the country, where every
foot of usable earth is terraced and cultivated and has
someone's name on it. By day, the ridge is silent and
forbidding; by night, it is a great slab of darkness, a night
within the night, the real, true thing. It makes all attempts at
illumination seem intrusive as well as pathetic, so in deference
to the ridge and the night and the mosquitoes, when the
household has dinner outside they keep the house lights off
and eat by candlelight.

People go to bed early in the Garfagnana and when the lights
go out the night creatures emerge. One evening someone left
scraps of food on the terrace table; in the morning they were
gone and the white plastic tabletop was smudged by the paw
marks of a fox. All this happened without a sound and there
has been no trace of fox before or since. Yet the night is full of
small noises, faint scrapings and rustlings, a strange unquiet,
punctuated, every quarter of an hour, by the chime of the
village clock. Whenever I am in the house, I have to share the
mountainside with creatures I never see.

Above all, I share it with a screech owl, an *assiolo*. It lives in
the woods behind the house and every night, in the small
hours, it goes hunting for food. Screech owls screech and so

does their prey, repeatedly and with increasing desperation, loud enough to wake me and sometimes, when the mayhem seems to be taking place right outside, to send me stumbling out of bed to the window. But even when the moon is full, there is never anything to be seen: no owl, no prey, just icy light and black shadows, the looming mass of the ridge and, beyond it, the few scattered street lights that stay on in Barga after the cathedral floodlights are switched off. The screech owl might be part of my dream-life, mysterious and insubstantial, except that I am always wide awake when I hear its sinister cry.

There used to be doves at the house, plump, amiable creatures that strutted around the parking lot, made love incessantly, fussed over their chicks, and filled the days with pleasant cooing. Occasionally, they would take off all together and fly in formation over the valley, banking and gliding. With the sun on their white wings, they looked like a flight of angels. But the screech owl got them one by one, however carefully they were shut in at sunset, however often they were replaced. Finally, I gave up trying. I chopped up the dovecotes to use for kindling and left the night to the owl.

I see now that the doves were a kind of wishful thinking, a city-boy's gesture, well meant but essentially absurd, and based on the frivolous conviction that night and its creatures could be eliminated by turning on a light. And it seems right that I have never seen the screech owl. Shakespeare thought it was a bird of ill-omen, a 'shrieking harbinger, Foul precurrer of the fiend'. These days, it is probably just another timid endangered species. But that is not how it sounds when it goes about its business and I am glad I have never seen it. The screech owl is secret and predatory and it belongs to the other darkness, the darkness of death, the night that gets us all in the end, the night that no amount of electric light will ever illuminate.

Past midnight. Never knew such silence. The earth might be uninhabited . . . Perhaps my best years are gone . . . But I wouldn't want them back. Not with the fire in me now. No, I wouldn't want them back.

Samuel Beckett, *Krapp's Last Tape*

# NOTES

1 William T. O'Dea, *The Social History of Lighting*, London, 1958, p. 223. Many of the scholarly details in this chapter are taken from this classic study.

2 James Hamilton-Paterson, *Seven-Tenths*, London, 1992, p. 174.

3 O'Dea, op. cit., p. 220.

4 Boswell's *London Journey, 1762–3*, ed. Frank A. Pottle, London, 1950. Quoted by O'Dea, op. cit., p. 4.

5 Witold Rybczynski, *Home*, Harmondsworth, 1987, p. 142.

6 Rayner Banham, *The Architecture of the Well-Tempered Environment*, London, 1969, p. 55.

7 Quoted by O'Dea, op. cit., p. 94.

8 See Wolfgang Schivelbusch, *Disenchanted Night*, Oxford, 1988, pp. 81–2.

9 This happened in the newly built Holborn Viaduct area in London, where an Edison-designed combined street-lighting and domestic-mains system was installed. The first public supply areas in the USA were established a few months later, in August and September 1882. In England, however, the gas industry's parliamentary lobby blocked enabling legislation for the supply of electricity through cables laid in trenches in the public streets – the Holborn Viaduct was a legal anomaly – until 1887, when a domestic supply was established in Kensington. See Rayner Banham, op. cit., p. 64.

10 Later, when electricity was commonplace and the colonisation of night was in full swing, a less wondering, more dismissive mood took hold. The Futurists caught the spirit with their battlecry, 'Let's slay the moonlight!' Like other early Modernists, though more belligerently, the Futurists were on the side of the new century's new technology and were reacting against the

penumbra of late Romanticism, its vagueness, its shadowy wash of emotions.

11 Murray Melbin, *Night As Frontier*, New York, 1987.
12 See Witold Rybczynski, op. cit., pp. 138, 142.

### 2 THE DARK AT THE TOP OF THE STAIRS

1 W. R. Bion, *Learning from Experience*, London, 1962, p. 99.
2 A. A. Mason, 'The Suffocating Super-Ego: Psychotic Break and Claustrophobia', in *Do I Dare Disturb the Universe?*, ed. James S. Grotstein, Beverly Hills, 1981, p. 143.
3 Melanie Klein, 'Early development of conscience in the child', *Contributions to Psychoanalysis*, London, 1933, pp. 267–77.
4 Susan Isaacs, 'The Nature and Function of Phantasy', *Developments in Psycho-Analysis*, ed. Joan Riviere, London, 1952, pp. 90–1.
5 John Cheever, *The Journals*, London, 1991, pp. 106–7.
6 Frederick Snyder, 'Towards an Evolutionary Theory of Dreaming', *American Journal of Psychiatry*, August, 1966; quoted by Hilary Rubinstein, *The Complete Insomniac*, London, 1976, pp. 24–5.

### 3 THE SLEEP LABORATORY

1 J. Allan Hobson, *The Dreaming Brain*, New York, 1988, p. 289.
2 According to William C. Dement, people who keep dream diaries at home will record only one dream when interviewed the next morning, while subjects in a laboratory, when awakened during REM periods, will remember four out of five dreams and forget only 20 per cent. See William C. Dement, *Some Must Watch While Some Must Dream*, New York, 1976.

### 4 DREAMING

1 Charles Sherrington, *Man on His Nature*, New York, 1955, p. 183; quoted by J. Allan Hobson, *The Dreaming Brain*, New York, 1988, p. 159.
2 Trans. C. Scott, *Theatre of Sleep*, ed. Guido Almansi and Claude Béguin, London, 1986, p. 42.
3 Hobson, *The Dreaming Brain*, New York, 1988, p. 160.

4 Gerald M. Edelman, *Bright Air, Brilliant Fire*, London, 1992, p. 17.

5 Hobson, op. cit., pp. 132–3.

6 Ibid., p. 131.

7 Gerald D. Fischbach, 'Mind and Brain', *Scientific American*, Vol. 267, No. 3, September, 1992, pp. 24–5.

8 R. R. Llinás and D. Paré, 'Of Dreaming and Wakefulness', *Neuroscience*, Vol. 44, No. 3, 1991, pp. 521–35.

9 Edelman, op. cit., p. 114.

10 Ibid., p. 66

11 'In the organized mind of every human being there is formed a "virtual other" (Braten, 1987), who is prepared to take part in a set of "virtual engagements" with the "self". This dual constitution of the human mind, "virtual other" and "self", is essential and innate. It becomes actual and develops when an actual other meets the self.' (Colwyn Trevarthen and Katerina Logotheti, 'Child and culture: genesis of cooperative knowing', in *Cognition and Social Worlds*, ed. Angus Gellaty, Don Rogers and John A. Sloboda, Oxford, 1989, p. 40.)

12 Hobson, op. cit., p. 9. Lianás and Paré make the same point in a more technical way: op. cit., section 6, p. 531.

13 Charles Dickens, 'Night Walks', *The Uncommercial Traveller*, Charles Dickens Library, VIII, London, n.d., p. 127.

14 Sigmund Freud, *The Interpretation of Dreams*, The Standard Edition, 1964, Vol. IV, p. 34.

15 Liam Hudson, *Night Life*, London, 1985, p. 6.

16 Quoted in Guido Almansi and Claude Beguin (eds), *Theatre of Sleep*, London, 1986, pp. 244–5.

17 Suetonius, *The Twelve Caesars*, quoted in *The Oxford Book of Dreams*, ed. Stephen Brook, Oxford, 1983, p. 157.

18 Freud, op. cit., IV, p. 98, fn.

19 Ibid, V, pp. 682–4.

20 Ibid., pp. 359–60.

21 *Jung: Selected Writings*, selected and introduced by Anthony Storr, London, 1983, p. 184.

22 Morton Schatzman, 'The Meaning of Dreaming', *New Scientist*, 25 December 1986, p. 36.

23 C. G. Jung, *Memories, Dreams, Reflections*, London, 1983, p. 182.

Liam Hudson quotes this dream and analyses it, and the fall-out from it, with great subtlety, op. cit., p. 36.

24 Freud, op. cit., IV, p. 169.

25 Erich Fromm, *The Forgotten Language*, London, 1952, pp. 86–7.

26 Freud, op. cit., V, pp. 546 and 567.

27 Charles Rycroft, *The Innocence of Dreams*, London, 1979, p. 4.

28 Hobson believes that 'one function of REM sleep [is] actively to maintain basic circuits of the brain . . . REM sleep allows us to rev our cerebral motor and actively to test all our circuits in a reliably patterned way.' Another researcher, Howard Roffwarg, suggests that the disproportionate amount of time the baby in the womb spends in REM sleep may be because 'REM sleep plays an active role in the structural development of the brain' (op. cit., pp. 291–2).

29 The most thoroughgoing analysis of the *Project* is in Richard Wollheim's *Freud*, London, 1971, pp. 31–58.

30 Lionel Trilling, 'Freud and Literature', *The Liberal Imagination*, New York, 1950, p. 44.

31 Freud, op. cit. II, p. 160. This conflict between Freud the writer and Freud the scientist is discussed by Janet Malcolm in 'Dora', *The Purloined Clinic*, New York, 1992, pp. 21–2.

32 Freud, op. cit., IV, pp. 311–12.

33 R. D. Lewin, *Dreams and the Uses of Regression*, New York, 1958, p. 11. Cited by Rycroft in op. cit., p. 2.

34 Freud, op. cit., Vol. X, pp. 207–8.

35 William McGrath, 'How Jewish Was Freud?', *New York Review of Books*, Vol. XXXVIII, No. 20, 5 Dec 1991, p. 29.

36 Freud, op. cit., Vol. XI, p. 41.

37 Donald Meltzer, *Dream-Life*, Reading, 1984, pp. 38 and 88.

38 Freud, op. cit., V., p. 467.

39 Michael G. Moran, 'Chaos Theory and Psychoanalysis', *International Review of Psycho-Analysis*, Vol. 18, Pt. 2, 1991, pp. 211–21.

40 Scientists, of course, put it differently: 'The pattern in . . . [a strange] attractor is bounded, but after a certain number of repetitions within the system, it becomes very irregular. This irregularity results in unpredictability, despite the fact that it derives from a completely deterministic system. This unpredict-

ability is associated with a property of chaotic systems known as *sensitive dependence on initial conditions*. This means that if two sets of initial conditions differ by any arbitrarily small amount at the outset, their specific solutions will diverge dramatically from one another over the long range . . . Given that no measurement system is without some error, it becomes clear that if a system is chaotic, general patterns of future behavior may be predictable but specific behaviors over the long range will not.' Scott Barton, 'Chaos, Self-Organization, and Psychology', *American Psychologist*, Vol. 29, No. 1, January 1994, p. 6.

41 Claude Bonnefoy, *Conversations with Ionesco*, New York, 1971, p. 10.

42 Hobson, op. cit., p. 297.

43 Don DeLillo, *Americana*, London, 1990, p. 220.

44 Hervey de Saint-Denys, *Dreams and How to Guide Them*, trans. Nicholas Fry, edited with an introduction by Morton Schatzman, London, 1982, p. 19.

45 Ibid., p. 72.

46 Ibid., pp. 158–9.

47 Ibid., pp. 140–1.

48 Ibid., p. 45.

49 Ibid., p. 63.

50 See, for instance, Harry T. Hunt, *The Multiplicity of Dreams*, Yale, 1989, pp. 180–8.

51 Freud, op. cit., V, p. 534.

52 'Clearly there is a difference in the consciousness of REM sleep, and this difference is related to the relative predominance of the right hemisphere, especially during the earlier parts of the night . . . Thus, analogue coding tends to predominate over digital, the symbolic re-presentation of these in dream consciousness tends toward the spatial and imagistic rather than the verbal and numerical, and the process tends to be passively experienced rather than actively controlled in consciousness. In addition, self consciousness is largely absent in dreaming. However, lucid dreaming . . . tends to occur later in the night, and this is in accord with evidence that (a) self-consciousness and controlled imagery is more the product of the left hemisphere, and (b) there is a tendency for relatively greater influence of the left

hemisphere later . . . in the night.' David B. Cohen, *Sleep and Dreaming: Origins, Nature and Functions*, Oxford, 1979, pp. 133–4.

53 Stephen Brook (ed.), op. cit., p. 139.

54 Schatzman, op. cit., pp. 37–8.

55 Quoted by Roger Penrose, *The Emperor's New Mind*, London, 1990, p. 548.

56 Morton Schatzman, 'Hypermnesic Dreams', unpublished paper presented at the ninth annual international conference of the Association for the Study of Dreams, University of California at Santa Cruz, 24 June 1992.

57 Isaac Bashevis Singer, 'The Letter Writer', *The Collected Stories*, London, 1988, p. 265.

58 Penrose, op. cit., p. 544.

59 Christopher Frayling, *Vampyres*, London, 1991, pp. 3–4.

60 *The Notebooks of Samuel Taylor Coleridge*, 3 vols, ed. Kathleen Coburn, London, 1957–73 [January, 1805].

61 *Collected Letters*, 6 vols, ed. E. L. Griggs, 1956–71, II, p. 986.

62 Kathleen Coburn (ed.), op.cit. [May, 1819].

63 *The Poems of Samuel Taylor Coleridge*, ed. E. H. Coleridge, Oxford, 1912, 1957, p. 296. His italics.

64 See John Livingstone Lowes, *The Road to Xanadu*, Boston, 1927.

65 *Biographia Literaria*, Chapter 15, London, 1952, p. 157.

66 See Hobson, op. cit., Chapter 13, pp. 257–69.

67 Kathleen Coburn (ed.), op. cit. [1815].

68 Gérard de Nerval, *Selected Writings*, translated with a critical introduction by Geoffrey Wagner, London, 1968, p. 138.

69 Quoted by David Daiches in *Robert Louis Stevenson and his World*, London, 1973, p. 68.

70 Robert Louis Stevenson, *The Lantern-Bearers and Other Essays*, selected with an introduction by Jeremy Treglown, London, 1988, pp. 216–25.

71 Ernest Hartmann, *The Nightmare*, New York, 1984. See especially Chapters 5 and 6, pp. 110–70.

72 Sarah Whitfield, *Magritte* (catalogue), Hayward Gallery, The South Bank Centre, London, 1992, p. 11.

## 5 KEEPING THE PEACE

1 Charles Dickens, *Reprinted Pieces*, The Charles Dickens Library, London, n.d., Vol. XIV, p. 140

2 'Le bois le plus funeste et le moins frequenté/Est, au prix de Paris, un lieu de sureté.' Quoted by Wolfgang Schivelbusch, *Disenchanted Night*, Oxford, 1988, p. 84.

3 Shivelbusch, op. cit., pp. 83–5 and 98–104.

4 William C. Sidney, *England and the English in the 18th Century*, Vol. 1, London, 1892, p. 17. Quoted by Shivelbusch, op. cit., p. 88.

5 Dickens, op. cit., pp. 146–7.

6 William T. O'Dea, *The Social History of Lighting*, London, 1958, p. 100.

7 Jane Jacobs, *The Death and Life of Great American Cities*, London, 1962, p. 30

8 Ibid., p. 42.

## 6 NIGHT OWLS

1 Murray Melbin, *Night As Frontier*, New York, 1987, p. 60.

# INDEX